3

45.00
75u

George Herbert's
Christian Narrative

George Herbert's
Christian Narrative

Harold Toliver

The Pennsylvania State University
University Park, Pennsylvania

Library of Congress Cataloging-in-Publication Data

Toliver, Harold E.
    George Herbert's Christian narrative / Harold Toliver.
        p.   cm.
    Includes bibliographical references and index.
    ISBN 0-271-00915-2
    1. Herbert, George, 1593–1633—Criticism and interpretation.
2. Christian poetry, English—History and criticism.   3. Narration
(Rhetoric)   4. Rhetoric—1500–1800.   I. Title.
PR3508.T65   1993
821'.3—dc20   92-33651
                                                                   CIP

Published by The Pennsylvania State University Press,
Barbara Building, Suite C, University Park, PA 16802-1003

It is the policy of The Pennsylvania State University Press to use acid-free paper for
the first printing of all clothbound books. Publications on uncoated stock satisfy the
minimum requirements of American National Standard for Information Sciences—
Permanence of Paper for Printed Library Materials, ANSI Z39.48–1984.

To M. E. Toliver
20 April 1899 to 24 December 1990

CONTENTS

ACKNOWLEDGMENTS

I wish to thank Kevin McNamara and Marc Geisler for research assistance. Each spent an industrious summer gathering and checking seventeenth-century biblical commentary. I am grateful also to Ilona Bell, whose commentary, together with that of the equally insightful Herbert scholar, Claude Summers, helped me reshape the loose and the badly said. Andrew B. Lewis also read the whole with a keen eye. A number of librarians at the UCI microfilm holdings and interlibrary loan office offered timely assistance, as have the always-expert librarians of the Huntington.

INTRODUCTION

History of Times is either Universal or Particular; whereof the latter contains
the deeds of some kingdom, commonwealth, or people; the former those of
the whole world. For there have been those who have affected to write the
history of the world from its very beginning; exhibiting by way of history a
medley of things and abridgments of narratives. Others have attempted to
comprise, as in a perfect history, the memorable events of their own age all
over the world; with noble enterprise, and no small result. For the affairs of
men are not so far separated by the divisions of empires or countries, but
they have a connexion in many things; and therefore it is certainly of use to
have the fates, acts, and destinies of one age described and contained as it
were on one tablet. . . . But if due attention be paid to the subject, it will be
found that the laws of regular history are so strict, that they can scarce be
observed in such a wide field of matter; so that the dignity of history is rather
diminished than increased by the greatness of the mass of it. . . . [F]or as
Universal History preserves some narrations which would perhaps otherwise
perish, so on the other hand it destroys many that are profitable enough in
themselves and would otherwise live, for the sake of that compendious brevity
of which men are so fond.

—Francis Bacon, *De Augmentis*

There can be no doubt that the Renaissance did something to encourage the
compendious brevity that Francis Bacon distrusts in his contrast of local to
global history (*Works* 4.308–9). Equally important in the Christian version of
global history, the scale of such a compendium is matched by a schematic
movement that equates periods with spiritual states and overlaps theological
and historical vocabularies. William Perkins in *A Golden Chaine, or the
Description of Theologie, Containing the Order of the Causes of Salvation and
Damnation*, for instance, hangs categories of moral and spiritual behavior
from the top of a diagram as though simultaneously from a hierarchical apex

and from a storied origin. One thing follows both logically from and sequentially after another. The story culminates in God's glory, which ends history and climaxes a one-directional logic. Being absolute, that glory is not itself subject to growth or detraction, but between the Fall and its correction everything human is subject to contingencies. Perkins opposes the language of decree and election to the only thing that can make sense of the interim chaos, reprobation, which, by supplying a rationale for chance and misfortune, makes the system work. As though enlarging on a section of Perkins's cosmic system in detail, Joseph Mede's *Key of Revelation* offers a breakdown of the last phase, and his scheme too supposes a war of opposites, this one falling under the grand symbolism of Revelation and ending in the resurrection of the dead. Each scheme generates a vocabulary and a set of figures and tropes of no small pretension. They are magnificently aloof from events, and as Oscar Wilde says about Sir Walter Raleigh, it is possible to write "a whole history of the world, without knowing anything whatsoever about the past." It is implicit in Bacon's account of the two kinds of history as well that the motive behind the compendiums is to crowd everything into the index of one book.

That appeal of brief comprehensiveness is not yet dead: Kenneth Burke capitalizes upon it in *The Rhetoric of Religion* when he converts charts of "truth" into rhetorical schemata and a "tautological cycle of terms for order" (184). But I am not interested in the differences among global charts, merely in the fact of their existence and the story-telling method of laying out their comprehensive terminologies and sequences of events, each incomplete until linked to all others. The implications of the whole for lining up lyric moments are inescapable for seventeenth-century poetry. The background presence of such a composite scheme makes epitomizing tropes possible and creates a metonymic and synecdochical lever by which the world can be hoisted at any moment. As temporal maps the charts create crises and transitions and make it difficult to prevent ruptures in progress as the historian attempts to spring from mere incidents to revelatory acts. The art of part-whole relations where the whole is this encompassing one is an art all its own. Several seventeenth-century poets devote themselves to it, Herbert perhaps foremost, or second only to Milton.

Most seventeenth-century interpreters of compendium history use more or less the same sequence that Michael lays before Adam in *Paradise Lost* and that Adam and Eve proceed to enact outside Eden. The long trek through confusion to Revelation and apocalypse follows a trail familiar to everyone, and no one disputes its main stages. Bacon himself renders the briefest possible account of it in a "Confession of Faith," giving the historical vocabulary precedence over the schematic or theological one. He devotes a few sentences each to the Maker, the Mediator who enables the Father to behold his inferior creatures, the communication of goodness to humanity united in "the person of the eternal Son," the first estate under the law of nature, the Fall, the dispensation of the several epochs, the fullness of time that comes with the historical Savior, the work of the Spirit once the Savior has departed, the period of the universal or catholic church (which brings into the mapping the *geographical* whole, space being as important as dialectical order and time), and the dissolution of the world—all compressed into some six pages (*Works* 7.219–26). Raleigh, with the leisure of years in the Tower, took a little longer for his world history. Joseph Mede is downright voluminous on the latter days, as most commentators on Revelation tend to be, given the need to expound on the many smaller wheels turning within the larger one.

These were not eccentrics; they were joined in the world history enterprise by a good many intellectuals, poets, and scientists who did not doubt that such a comprehensive story could be told and even foretold. They used it to categorize people and to interpret local incidents. They were no more subject to a single-explanation scheme than are quantum physicists who believe that a very few governing laws explain the universe from a millionth of a second after the big bang. Then as now, systematic thinking required a unified, global discourse. The difference in the seventeenth century was that places and events across the historical and geographical span were arranged into a panorama with a foreground and a background, a center and a periphery; thought supposed itself fastened securely to reality, each part of which bore a given name; each analogous relation was reflected in a set of tropes.

Or so it seems with the advantage of hindsight. If we narrow the focus, compendious brevity and local history become not merely alternative historiographies but competing frameworks. As interpreters of Revelation discovered when thinking to match veils and trumpets to the actual reigns of princes, particular moments resisted the application of the global vocabulary. Bacon himself favored the more minute examination of evidence that goes with local history and was surely right that "if due attention be paid" to any subject, it will be found to creep along at ground level, at a living pace. Nothing observed closely really wants to be forced into a theoretical scheme. That resistance does not let up when the focus shifts to the interior monitoring of the psyche and human spirit. The discrepancy in scale then becomes a trial of a self that knows where it is supposed to be pointed in the grand scheme of things, yet covets closer goals. That discrepancy can never be adequately patched over, and Renaissance narratives of the ambitious sort that Spenser, Donne, Herbert, Raleigh, and Milton wrote tend to recoil from pole to pole, sometimes without fully realizing it. The ground-level commentary is concrete and incorporates first-person experience; the mountain-top speculation reduces incidents to types, looks forward or backward to phases of the story centered in the antitype, and tends to philosophize, as Michael does about the virtues that Adam and Eve will require in various overgrown places.

To avoid more elaborate paraphrases where they are not needed, I will call the overall scheme simply the "fable," by which I mean both the connecting linearity that gives direction to history and accompanying ideas and tropes. That fable provides the semantic field for George Herbert's poetry, whether the span of a given poem is local or extended. By his time, the details had long been sedimented by the dominant tradition of both Anglicanism and Dissent. Within certain Arminian and Calvinist variants, it belongs as much to Milton as it does to Bacon, Richard Hooker, Lancelot Andrewes, John Donne, Thomas Browne, John Cosin, and a host of Caroline divines.

But Herbert is also capable of troping precedents and returning them to the drama of the lyric "I." No careful reader of *The Temple* can doubt that virtually the entire *mythos* from Adam to doomsday becomes extraordinarily vivid in his mind's eye and a torment to the spirit engaged in the conflicts that arise from trying to reconcile social and natural life with it. It is *not* particularly alive in Bacon, whose attention is largely elsewhere, and this difference goes some way toward explaining Herbert's evident distrust of Baconian science. One gets the impression that Bacon sets the fable forth in confession mainly to fix it in the most efficient abstraction, which is basically what it becomes on the occasions he appends it to the main scientific and philosophic project in hand. Despite its universality, the fable differs in details and force in each of its proponents. Almost every article in Bacon's confession could be challenged on contemporary theological grounds if he were arguing for or dramatizing it rather than merely framing it. Points on Perkins's diagram too represent choices among debated doctrinal alternatives.

For instance, both Roman Catholicism and modern accounts tend to handle the key theological points, especially the issue of individual guilt, differently from the Reformation under Calvin and Luther. In the Protestant emphasis upon individual spiritual condition, the Fall becomes singularly saturated with personal guilt. Milton charges Michael with driving that point home to Adam, although he leaves an opening for Adam himself by making all sin after Eden "inductive mainly to the sin of *Eve*" (*Paradise Lost* 11.519). Herbert too plunges into the individual registering of guilt as a principle moving factor of poetic confession and imprecation, second in importance only to the rendering of praise. He does not question the shape or logic of the fable as a whole—its beginning, middle, and ultimate closure—but relives its crucial movements under sin's forceful intrusion. A second story of individual growth and backsliding unfolds in his meditations, confessions, dramas, subnarratives, and impassioned appeals. He reminds us that at the center of both the life and the fable is the "king of grief" and his lifting of guilt through the sacrifice. Although it does not show very boldly on a diagram that submerges narrative movement in polarized terms, the Crucifixion is the key to the fable. It begins the thrust toward the eschatology that governs Perkins's completion, the human share in which is granted by sanctification.

Thanks to the contamination of all human activity, afterlife to Herbert is defined as escaping normal experience. Indeed, Herbert's tendency to eclipse normal experience is the source of many of his "category abuses" or misuses of language—of tropes that turn the language of the ground level into the sedimented language of the schemata. The small circles at the top and bottom of Perkins's diagram, as the beginning and end of the eventful chain, are equally misrepresentations of the dimensionless "circle" of eternity. Breaks in the chain should logically separate both top and bottom from the middle, but Perkins joins them by foreknowledge, decrees, and predestination at the top and by the passage of temporality into a fixed state under justice and mercy at the bottom. The strain on language and logic generated by such transitions asks to be scrutinized in some detail where it appears in Herbert. It is not uniquely his problem (or exclusively a problem of Reformation theology), but it is crucial to virtually all his poetry. Tropes submitted to the fable are twisted out of local into global history in such figures as catachresis (*abusio*, misuse, misapplication, extravagance), meiosis (belittlement, which Herbert applies mainly to the self), metalepsis (*transumptio*, the far-fetched, the "leaping" trope), oxymoron, and aporia (*dubitatio*, a feigned or real incapacity to speak). As these and other tropes illustrate, the mix of terminological levels often results in incongruity. The more tradition binds certain terms and ideas together (by more people over a longer time), the more normal they begin to seem, but that does not prevent new turns that reawaken us to the violence inherent in the fable.

Herbert's linguistic field is saturated with terms of abuse, against which he sets a colloquial idiom and a discourse of personal instance and moment.

Ordinary figures are suspect unless they too are stretched to fit the fable. The bridges that the poet needs between major components of the universal story are sure to collapse unless desire and faith make a powerful alliance against the lesser forces of comparison and similitude. That is true whether the poet borrows them initially from a language of nature, from poet/patron relations, previous love lyrics, or from biblical types—all rich sources of detail for Herbert, but all requiring renovation. Universal history presents an ever-growing accumulation of details, but Scripture answers that accumulation with visionary expectations. Thus whatever new materials history provides are adapted to the model concentrated in Hebrews and other Pauline Epistles, which Christian hermeneutic uses to transform Hebrew law, biographical stories, prophecy, wisdom literature, and local chronicle. Any new-covenant attempt to foresee the end (prolepsis or foreshadowing being another common figure generated by the scheme) must work with the substance of the visible world—the seasons and their flowering in "The Flower" and "Vertue," the chronicle of the church in "The Church Militant," the biographical record of the affliction and unemployment poems, the state of the sciences in "Vanity 1," the ceremonies and rites of the church and its devotional calendar in *The Church*.

Herbert applies the hermeneutic principle of the Epistle to the Hebrews to these and other sources of conventional metaphor as a first step in their conversion into meaningful stages of the fable. Figures and tropes work with the coat given to Joseph, a bunch of grapes plucked from the story of the Exodus, a posie in the hand, an orange tree. Since such items are of human manufacture or natural growth, they are as far from paradise initially as flowers that glide are from the final garden. When love and grace take glory by the hand in "The World," they make a recognizable human gesture of kindness; and when they "build," they act as stone masons and carpenters. Animated and empowered by human likeness, they are almost as far from the other world of Michael's vision and Bacon's last confessional phase as the houses governed by fortune, pleasure, sin, and death. As "The Flower" suggests, a poet whose spiritual rebirth is expressed in flower language ("now in age I bud again," "I once more smell the dew and rain, / And relish versing") must draw back from such figures, which he knows say amiss. The anchoring ends of the fable and the top of the hierarchy force the poet to concede that "thy word is all," where "all" refers to an "eternity" that does not reflect, but rather discredits the world.

But still worse than making an inadequate representation of the "eternal" is not approaching paradise at all. As the poet laments in "Employment 1":

> All things are busie; onely I
> Neither bring hony with the bees,
> Nor flowres to make that, nor the husbandrie
> To water these.

Or again in "Employment 2":

> Oh that I were an Orenge-tree
> That busie plant!
> Then should I ever laden be,
> And never want
> Some fruit for him that dressed me.
>
> But we are still too young or old;
> The Man is gone,
> Before we do our wares unfold:
> So we freeze on,
> Untill the grave increase our cold.

The fruits are from the common semantic reserve, again theologically defined and rooted in New Testament parables, here threatened by God's apparent refusal to assign duties and help write poems. And so the grave, a common type for transition to the end, makes the gap between typical human stories and their fulfillment seem absolute. In another mood, Herbert will reinterpret the grave and make it into the opening it promises to be in the oxymoronic phase of the fable (where weakness becomes strength and death life). But here, caught in one of the byways of an absent Providence, the speaker produces no fruit.

If in *The Church* incidents and metaphors proliferate without drawing nearer the marriage of temporal desire and otherworldly object, it is because, whatever the fable says about the end, heaven and God's glory are beyond compare and thus beyond narrative transition. That is one of the implications of Herbert's recurrent concern with apocalypse. Often where he does not explicitly name it, he is haunted by it, and as a poet is overwhelmed by its breaking of tropic bridges. Yet the meaning and purpose of the fable must derive from *something* proceeding from and going beyond human cognizance—not from anything exclusively within the processions of the middle or attempts at allegorical forecasting. Otherwise history merely goes through phases. That is perhaps why Milton exceeds Michael's vision and his biblical sources in extending the plot of *Paradise Lost* beyond the beginning and the ending of the world. The chronological narrative of *Paradise Lost* begins with the equivalent of Bacon's first event, the establishing of the mediator-Son, who raises Satan's envy and triggers the first fall. The critical junctures come at the human fall and again at Judgment, which bracket the period of guilt and force the poet-historian to speculate about the change and the carryover (or lack of it) from eternity to time and back again.

Connecting both ends to the historical middle is one problem of the fable; linking contemporary institutions and ideologies to it is another, of greater interest to recent criticism. That Herbert ordinarily resists saying outright what we should think about politics, poetics, and matters of church doctrine makes his version of the fable somewhat less available than Spenser's and Milton's to the prominent critical approaches of recent years. Thanks to the doctrine that articulates and rationalizes the fable, a place in Reformation history has been easier to manage. But even in the matter of works, election, grace, rites, and sacraments, all foundation words in the schemata, or what we might call Christian philosophemes—the minimal units of an articulated philosophy—nothing like unanimity prevails, and Herbert was disturbed by the wrangling of the Dissenters. In the earlier 1620s, he was actively involved in the politics of the church, increasingly prominent in the parliamentary debates of that decade. It is not self-evident just what social and political implications go with what Reformation positions on liturgy and doctrine. John N. Wall links Herbert with Edmund Spenser and Henry Vaughan as poets who promote the "social agenda of the Church of England" but neglects to spell out what that agenda is or how it differs in the 1620s from what it was in Spenser or becomes in Vaughan (Wall 2–3, 166). Certainly, church service and social service are in some way analogous for Herbert, and he never wavers in his disapproval of Nonconformist disruptions of the former. Whatever social or political commentary one extracts from Herbert is likely to be only implicit, but recent criticism cautions us against assuming that a focus on church issues necessarily implies indifference to social and political issues.

Linking social to ecclesiastical matters is difficult, however, and here again the gap between local and universal history comes into play. Perhaps because of that difficulty, the most common function of Herbert criticism since its modern inception in Rosemond Tuve, Louis Martz, and Joseph Summers has been to equate poems mostly to doctrinal rather than to ideological or political positions, and of course to devotional practice, which as the chief ground of dissent stands halfway between. Even that more limited task in intellectual history runs risks, however. The debate over whether Herbert is Genevan or Roman tends to neglect his spiritual struggles. The Herbert that Christopher Harvey and Izaak Walton appropriated in the midst of the civil wars was more decidedly Laudian than the poems warrant, just as the Herbert of late seventeenth-century hymnody and of Calvinist or Lutheran readings would not have written the liturgical poems, devotional sequences, church-calendar and church-furniture poems, and defenses of the British church. One consolation that specifically the literary critic can entertain in this confusion is that many of Herbert's better poems have little to do with specific issues, and it is usually those very poems that tell us most about the relations of personal experience to the global story. For this reason I emphasize them rather than poems more directly relevant to sacramental matters.

On the whole, I find Terry G. Sherwood wise to stress the *various* ways that the poems as a whole imagine God dwelling in man (Sherwood 94)—in the nature that the intellect puzzles over, in Scriptures that must be interpreted verse by verse, in the church and its sacraments, and in artifacts. Equally important to the theme of God's indwelling is the frequent sense of a tormenting and delaying Lord whose absence undermines the artifacts of religion and even the approaches of suppliants to sacraments. The question in this context is whether poetry can be successfully treated as an affair of ideologies and doctrines, or should it be regarded as a symbolic and aesthetic fiction—or perhaps a mixture that makes it difficult to formulate rules for applicable scholarship? If we fit the right modules together from the fable—a view of the Eucharist, or election, or a view of Bible reading—can we come up with applicable labels such as "Lutheran," "Arminian," or "Calvinist"? And if so, do these, as Gene Veith suggests, make up pieces of a jigsaw puzzle that Genevan-minded and Roman-minded critics can use to settle their differences? Are such bits of truth really out there awaiting identification?

The assumption that they are would be in keeping with the seventeenth century's confidence in the availability of truth, but modern criticism is unlikely to accept that assumption, another reason to conceive of the Christian metanarrative as a *mythos*. It is better to concede at the outset that doctrinal matters are more likely to provoke ongoing debates than collaboration, whether among Herbert critics or in the new-historicist readings of the social agendas that accompany doctrine. The original disputants, Calvin, Luther, Arminius, fought in all earnestness, as did most of their seventeenth-century followers; interpreters of Herbert might now do better to convert "truth" into the materials of rhetoric and poetry. Such is my aim, admittedly at the cost of making Herbert seem more disengaged from social, ecclesiastical, and political controversies than in fact he was. Luckily, it is not always necessary to decide once and for all on a given poem's implicit position, or even the poet's habitual one. Are "Genevan" and "Roman" categories that literary history can recognize in such poems as "The Flower," "The Pearl," "Love 3," "Vertue," "Temper 1," "Prayer 1," "Death," "The Forerunners," "Life," "Easter-wings," "Church-monuments," "Redemption," and perhaps a dozen others among Herbert's best? The longer we refrain from even the more justifiable search for evidence of such tendencies in them, the less likely we are to overdetermine what Herbert simply called his spiritual conflicts. Besides being a poet, he was a complex self-assessor living in the opening phase of a national crisis. It is sometimes less clear what path one should take in such a period than it may later seem. In any case, I am less interested in labeling Herbert's poetry than I am in exploring the figures he used to bridge the abyss between ground-level experience and the fable.

Concentration on Herbert's negotiations between the lyric "now" and the key moments of the fable does not mean that the alternative to assigning him agendas is an aestheticism that obscures the choices he made. I do focus on formal problems and their implications for poetry's capacity to work with visionary abstraction, but I mean that formalism to serve an investigation of the interplay between lyric moments and the global story, not aesthetics. Nor need we forget the local occasions of his poetry in concentrating on either its systematic tropes and devices or their transcendence in the apocalyptic conclusion. Herbert's sense of the moment includes personal biography and affairs of church, state, and science, as well as the matters of lineation, stanza, voice, refrain, and number that he applies to it. Where his version of occasions seems opaque, criticism has the right to translate them into its preferred language, but it should do so without obscuring the fact that many of the poems present the ordeal of living in a salvation story that seemed to have stalled. The poems do not often suggest either a settled policy or a polemical edge and are often more aware of their status as poetry than they are of their status as argument or commentary. They are part of a history of biblical materials and Renaissance lyric genres before they are part of the history of parliaments and churches. Whatever biography suggests about other facets of Herbert's life as a country parson, university orator, or applicant for courtly office, his chief (and problematic) vocation was poetry. He may well mean it when he remarks in "The Quidditie" that a verse is that which "while I use / I am with thee, and *most take all*," and if he does, he is substituting poetry for other kinds of mediation. Likewise, when "The

Dedication" offers its "first fruits," it means not first in time, but first in importance—the first fruits of the altar-making heart.

In any case, given the achievement of *The Church* as a whole, it is unwise to reduce those fruits to self-canceling statements. If the loss of confidence in works were as inclusive as Herbert sometimes makes it seem, he could scarcely have written so carefully crafted and extended a record of his spiritual conflicts. Poems are works in a special sense, and in that respect Herbert's Christian poetics is roughly equivalent to Wallace Stevens's modern poetics— among the most interesting and far-reaching that we have. Since several years of dedication went into *The Temple*, one concludes that he was not wholly decided about the issue of works. That too would be in keeping with the tension between local and universal levels. His wavering did not bring confusion about the alternatives, but a fully resolved poet might well have either destroyed or published the poems rather than leaving the decision to a friend. If the following chapters zigzag through this thorny question of works to its resolution in "Love 3," it is because through a series of personas Herbert explored different sides of it. I can't claim to have followed all the permutations, but I doubt that, on one hand, he ever felt that works meant nothing, or on the other hand that poetry was crucial to reclaiming a fallen human nature. When "Love 3" replaces the offering of poems with "My deare, then I will serve," it sets up a final rejection of the would-be servant and suggests that justification comes only from the sacrifice of the one who bore the blame. It is left for us to explore what function that leaves for poetry.

Herbert criticism will no doubt be debating this matter until it grows tired of it, not until it has found a definitive answer. It is obviously not a question to inspire confidence in our capacity to resolve issues of such historical flavor, issues entangled in definitions of Calvinism, the Eucharist, grace, and divine accommodations. But about two things we can be a little more confident: even as a young man Herbert had no desire to write poetry of any other kind; and at a certain point he set aside other potential careers to concentrate on the priesthood and on a poetry that he considered in various ways, with various degrees of enthusiasm and self-doubt, part of his calling. As to other careers and interests, the university, court service, and Baconian science presented the three most attractive ones. He used dramatized parables and lyric moments in *The Church* to cross-examine his rejections of them. In providing an intellectual matrix for the poems, I have stressed the last of these three, because it bears directly on the bridging problem and opposed views of the interim world. Departures from Bacon are crucial to the unfolding seventeenth-century panorama of relations between the sacred and the secular. In that larger picture, Herbert deserves a prominent place among the conservative forces that countered secularism, which he resisted as forcefully as he did "wranglers." If an appropriate place has never been afforded him, it is partly I think because readers tend to accept his limitations without attempting to see how he came to them. Just what that place may be we can best determine in the context of modern biblical scholarship and adjacent figures such as his chief tutors and older friends, Donne and Bacon.

In contrast to Baconian science, the civil realm held no great appeal for Herbert beyond a certain point, whatever claims it may have made on him at one time. As Diana Benet ("Herbert's Experience") argues, he could not have failed to learn certain hard lessons about patronage by 1624. The deaths of King James in 1625, Bacon in 1626, and the dukes of Richmond and Lennox in 1623 and 1624 would almost certainly have driven those lessons home to him personally, as the earlier disgrace of Bacon (1621) may have also. Although his view of science is limited to a few statements, these have a decided bearing on the course he takes in *The Temple*, as does his defense of the British church. Indeed, many of the poems dramatize misleading desires before their speakers find how to settle their issues or how to praise God. Perhaps equally important, speakers who have committed themselves to divine service must fight an urge to get to the end before their allotted time, to shorten the way. That is a natural impulse once secular alternatives have been discarded and with them the stronger defense of works. End orientation commands all moments. Inherent in the devotional life, the tendency to rise as quickly as possible is quite different from the temptation to take up secular pursuits or to dwell on the rewards (or lack of them) of divine service. But as "A Wreath" suggests, the human way must be roundabout even when one is determined to pursue a high cause straightway. Being free of doubts concerning vocation and doctrine does not mean that one can avoid detours or progress without slacking off, since life itself can prove long and uneven. A poetry keyed to spiritual trials has to deal with the experience of time and place as panoramic history does not. In taking a wayward course through matters of personal moment, *The Church* sometimes wins through to comparative assurance, but none of its lyrics comes to a real conclusion until "Love 3," which upon reflection makes the preceding moments appear even less settled. Its immediate predecessors feature end events as the framework of what in it becomes an amiable courtship joining the individual soul to a model of the forgiven soul.

Although *The Church* features liturgy and sacrament, its main body consists not of their reenactments but of the troubled spirit's tentative approaches to them. Herbert's later personas do and do not maintain the early mood of willing sacrifice. In "The Dedication" a speaker very close to Herbert himself expects to "strive" and to "make a gain" but also concedes that God is the true source of poems: "for from thee they came / And must return." The recipient of love at the far end of *The Church* persists in offering further service but agrees not to when he is given no choice. He receives; he does not administer or negotiate any further. That is a sign of the encroachment of the end upon the middle and breaking of the causal chain generated by human actions. Up to that point, poetry has plunged into experience while gathering its defining types from church and Scripture. But to get to this conclusion it can be said to have used Scripture without being precisely like it; in the conclusion itself, it is churchly but not merely an extension of the church. It is a highly resonant, dramatic, parabolic lyric in a book of such. The Bible provides the destination and the central figure that Herbert calls "love," but it does not map out every path to that encounter or test the limited perspectives that the minidrama enacts. Some paths the poet must chart for himself as part of his vocation, which, as Northrop Frye suggests, begins with the "blocking off of normal activity" in "something a poet has to write poetry about instead of carrying on with ordinary experience" ("Approaching the Lyric" 32).

Herbert is as aware as Frye that such a block "has traditionally been frustrated love" and that it has "much to do with creating the sense of an individualized speaker" (32). The break with continuous life and its language ideally leads to the poet's attaining a greater continuity, but no definable position—theological, ecclesiastical, or political—can tell us everything that lyric moments take in hand to connect the speaker to the fable's semantic field. Whatever personal recollections those moments carry toward a final encounter with doomsday and Judgment must be erased when he gets there, as more tentative cancellations have all along accompanied timely applications of the fable to its parts.

1
SECULAR LABYRINTHS AND THE SILK TWIST

Such are thy secrets, which my life makes good,
    And comments on thee: for in ev'ry thing
    Thy words do fine me out, & parallels bring,
And in another make me understood.
        —George Herbert, "H. Scriptures 2"

Renaming Glory and Gay Weeds

It needn't be argued that Herbert sets comparatively narrow boundaries for his poetry. In this chapter I shall define those boundaries by their deliberate exclusions of secular lyric tradition, Baconian science, the zeal of Dissenters, and alternative biblical readings that modern readers can perhaps see more clearly in recent biblical studies than Herbert could in midrash and other, diverse hermeneutic approaches. Some of these exclusions need little more than passing mention, especially his "baptizing" of what he picks out of secular lyric traditions; I will return to them when I discuss the sonnets and love poetry. More pertinent for now are his decisions of the mid to late 1620s to drop all pursuit of a courtly career and to reject those aspects of the university curriculum that are best represented in Baconian experimental science. Wrangling had already drawn his attention. These exclusions all represent distractions from the proper conduct of spiritual affairs, which he tends to define from within sacramental Anglican catechism.

Herbert's personas in *The Church* go through this sorting out more than once, even though Herbert himself may have done so more or less decisively. The reasons that the Jordan never remains crossed are built into the demands of Christian eschatology, the same demands that cause spiritual diaries and conversion stories to backtrack and that cause John Bunyan in both *Grace Abounding* and *Pilgrim's Progress* to go through more dream iterations than progresses. The decision to reject alternatives to love of God, by its very nature, has to be reaffirmed. And so Herbert's personas are tempted by secular pursuits and spiritual rebellion again and again, just as they doubt the value of works but continue to seek to serve and relish versing only to find themselves rebuked. In the polyphonic structure of *The Church*, which is full of recurrent types and paradigms, repetends and refrains, the simulated spiritual autobiography circles back and repeats rather than advancing in any straightforward way.

The Temple inhabits a landscape marked by enduring Hebrew and Christian emblems and symbols: Egypt, Sinai, the wilderness, the oasis, the garden, paradise, the Red Sea, Sion, the Temple, Jerusalem. These could be adopted to new uses, as Bacon's title *Instauratic Magna* (*The Great Instauration*) and the temple in *New Atlantis* illustrate, but in Herbert they remain much as Protestant readings had rendered them. In coming to an understanding of the proper terrain of the religious lyric, he avoids autumnal memory and its refrains and reduces regret to the self-condemnation that comes with the overall *mythos*. Thus, rather than a poetry of remembered seasons, he directs desire forward to its consummation, as in "Vertue," for instance, after sounding a romantic note, he reverses the nostalgia of its refrain in the final stanza. When he does think in seasonal metaphors, spring is a naturally critical time for considering the return of God and awakening of the poetic vocation.

It is not merely the constraining of lyric impulses that marks Herbert's limitations. In making the transition from the university to divine service, the future country parson of Bemerton purposely put behind him the secular interests that Izaak Walton believed were developing at Cambridge. Whereas Donne, Fulke Greville, Philip Sidney, and Ben Jonson work on both sides of the secular/sacred divide, once Herbert seriously set foot into divinity (Herbert, *Complete Works* 3.484), he never retreated despite backward glances. Secular matters never inform the verse of *The Temple* as they do his Latin orations and letters. As Sidney Gottlieb points out ("The Social and Political Backgrounds"), we do not see the endorsements and addresses to patrons in *The Temple* that mark other collections. What serve as the preliminary steps are instructional stages for entrance into the church itself. That turn away from what he once had in hand makes plausible Coleridge's view that an apt reader of Herbert must be an "affectionate and dutiful child of the church," both "a devout and a *devotional* Christian" (Herbert, *Complete Works* 2.cxxxviii). Recent contextualizings of *The Temple*, the Latin poems, and the prose have broadened our view of what a devotional poet is, and certainly Herbert is not devoid of historical interest as Michael Schoenfeldt, Sidney Gottlieb, Diana Benet, Jonathan Goldberg, and others conceive of it. But the topical concern that survives in the poems and in *The Country Parson* he uses primarily as a foil against which the character of holiness, as Cristina Malcolmson calls it (249), is asserted. He dissociates not only the parson but the poet from what "The Pearl" (a relatively early poem) calls the ways of learning and honor. He did not inherit a title or property; he needed a vocation, and the one he chose substituted parish for family. Like *The Country Parson*, the poems find their model in the Son who divests himself of glory to tend to the sheep.

Herbert thus not only accepts but purposely creates his limits on several fronts. He uses the repertory of Renaissance lyric primarily to map departures from it. Turning away from not only immediate predecessors but classical poetry, Petrarchan verse, and even the more anecdotal parts of the Hebrew Bible, *The Temple* makes its antecedents mainly into object lessons, reserving a privileged place for what can be brought into the turn of the epochs, where with the Incarnation the whole fable enters history. That he imposes such constraints somewhat reluctantly can be gathered from *The Church* and from the message to Nicholas Ferrar that he sent through a mutual friend. I emphasize that reluctance, because it is the struggle to exclude rather than the accomplishment that enlivens the better poems. A secular post was still conceivable up to about 1624. His pursuit of the orator's post (an elected position) and subsequent absences from Cambridge in the company of James I presumed the application of "sweet phrases" to affairs of state and to what Alexander Grosart calls the vocation of "shouldering it with rivals" (Herbert, *Complete Works* 2.xxxvi).

His willingness and even eagerness in 1619 to take the necessary steps for preferment show clearly in a letter to his father-in-law, Sir John Danvers:

> I have sent you here inclosed a Letter from our Master in my behalf,
> which if you can send to Sir *Francis* before his departure, it will do
> well, for it expresseth the Universities inclination to me; yet if you
> cannot send it with much convenience, it is no matter, for the
> Gentleman needs no incitation to love me.
>
> The Orators place (that you may understand what it is) is the finest
> place in the University, though not the gainfullest; yet that will be
> about 30 *l. per an.* but the commodiousness is beyond the Revenue;
> for the Orator writes all the University Letters, makes all the Orations,
> be it to King, Prince, or whatever comes to the University; to requite
> these pains, he takes place next the Doctors, is at all their Assembles
> and Meetings, and sits above the Proctors, is Regent or Non-regent at
> his pleasure, and such like Gaynesses, which will please a young man
> well. (Herbert, *The Works* 369–70)

Despite the self-deprecatory lightness of "gaynesses" and "young man,"
we've no reason to doubt the seriousness of the conflict that arose when, with
more experience, he discovered the draining and compromising effects of a
political career. How prolonged his interest in such a career might have been
is not at issue, since at any point in the writing of *The Temple* he was capable
of restaging it.

As Walton reconstructed it, Herbert's deathbed message to Ferrar (as
conveyed by Edmund Duncon) describes *The Temple* as either a retrospective
account or a running record "of many spiritual Conflicts that have past
betwixt God and my Soul, before I could subject mine to the will of Jesus my
Master; in whose service I have now found perfect freedom" (Walton 314).
Perfect freedom, but only *now* found, as Grosart emphasizes (Herbert,
Complete Works 2.xxxi). That message does not suggest that we read the
poems as though they were composed by someone seeing the conflicts in a
distant retrospect (Seelig 7; *Complete Works* 2.xxxvi) or having no interest in
the personal except as it is also the doctrinal. Both the poems and the message
point to inner weather and not the interaction of doctrine with souls in
general, as Janis Lull suggests (*Poem in Time* 70, 142). What we know of
Herbert's ideas about a career during the writing of what came to be called
The Temple (which both Amy Charles and F. E. Hutchinson think originated
in his university days) should not be submerged in the vocation.

In this much the recent, new-historicist version of Herbert is surely
justified in keeping contact with the student, the teacher of rhetoric, the
member of Parliament, and the would-be courtier and singling out the

troubled personas of *The Church*, the love of poetry's "enchanting language," the enemy of wranglers, the defender of the British church, and the militant satirist of *Musae Responsoriae ad Andreae Melvini*. These are not all equally characterized presences in *The Temple*, and few actual biographical episodes can be identified with any certainty; but the kinds of struggle they precipitate in one who would be holy are by no means incidental, especially in "The British Church," "Aaron," "The Familie," and "Church-rents and schisms."

With respect to Baconian projects, a parallel concern in Herbert's setting of boundaries, it is one thing to teach that the "silk twist" of "The Pearl" (which I will take up in a moment) is all one needs; it is another to live with having chosen it. Rebellious, witty, uncertain throwbacks to the man of the world are scattered throughout *The Church*. They are no more prominent in the earlier Williams manuscript than in the final Bodleian manuscript. That alone is reason to question readings that assume an overly consistent rejection of works, which would logically have to include poems. We can be thankful that Herbert did not take the narrower way too decisively, and that he did not accept the plain-style reductions he sometimes champions. It is not consistency that is most distinctive about his poetry but inventiveness, technical skill, the dramatic voices of the speakers, and estimates of the cost and repercussions of the main choice. The poems put in personal terms the struggle to match the sacrifice, juxtaposing what the combatant knows a Christian must strive to be with what his attachment to works and the vanities of self tempt him to be. *The Church*'s patterns of spiritual struggle may be more idealized than autobiographical (Stewart, *George Herbert* 83), but their not-fully-disciplined speakers are nonetheless enterprising, ambitious, and reluctant to shut out the natural and social worlds. If their end is simultaneously submission and perfect freedom, the process by which they get to that goal combines struggle with conviction.

Ultimately, the self for Herbert must be defined by the biblical precedents that find it out. Reformation practice in reading scripture bends interpretation to the salvation story and what can be made to prefigure or support it. The diversity of the Hebrew and Christian Bibles that readers such as John Goldingay, Joel Rosenberg, Harold Fisch, and Meir Sternberg reconstruct was less evident to Herbert, who would not have recognized the Bible's borrowings from and likenesses to ancient Near Eastern texts that interest Frank Cross and Mosche Weinfeld. Such things do not of course figure in Herbert's reading.[1] He would have found strange, for instance, the proposi-

1. Since Samuel Reimarus in the eighteenth century and Julius Wellhausen in the late

tion that the Hebrew Bible is an account of a developing nation governed by
intricate codes and laws similar in ideology to other mesopotamian countries.
Even stranger to him would be Frank Cross's observation that "the Yahwistic
work is best described . . . as a propaganda work of the empire" (28).
Instead, he stakes his reading, both of Scripture and of the lyric personas in
it, on the Pauline movement from Old to New Testaments, which is a
movement from cultural specificity to hellenic abstraction. Together with
Calvinist and Lutheran readings, that movement sets Herbert apart from the
Hebraicism of some of his contemporaries and represents still another limit
to the conduct of spiritual conflict.

What the speaker of "The Pearl" attempts to do is govern his view of
things primarily by the parables, which in Herbert sometimes seem in
competition with the psalms. He cannot allow himself to be diverted by the
ways of learning, honor, and pleasure any more than he can by the multiplicity of nationalist details and special choral pleading of the psalms and the
preceding deuteronomic history. Together with typological forecasts, the
translation of specific incidents into a new covenant creates a single book.
Christian hermeneutic does not actually gather a people, take a direction
through an actual wilderness, and arrive in Canaan; instead it collects

---

nineteenth, Herbert's chief source text has been read less exclusively as a guide to eschatology
than the seventeenth century and the Reformation in general took it. The approach to biblical
settings that Reimarus developed has been applied by Albert Schweitzer, Rudolf Bultmann,
S.G.F. Brandon, Walter Schmithals, Hans W. Frei, and Stephen Neill among many others. The
difference between these historically minded critics and the biblical hermeneutic of Herbert's
contemporaries lies basically in the cultural embedding of the reading. Reimarus, for instance,
finds John the Baptist's "repent, for the kingdom of God is at hand" to be a preparation not for
a Savior who will end time but for a Davidic kingdom and believes that no one thought that "at
hand" meant hundreds of year later and in another place. Satan has difficulty believing that too
in *Paradise Regained*, which Milton devotes to the transition from the judaic prophets to Christ's
new understanding of a spiritual kingdom, not to be located historically at all. The Christ of
Matthew, Mark, and Luke also sometimes reverts to immediate locality as Daniel, Isaiah, and
Ezekiel understood it (Matthew 23.34, Mark 13.30, Luke 21.32).

The pressure to shift from a political to a denationalized savior increases sufficiently by the
writing of the synoptic Gospels and the Epistles that a political arm of redemption in the old
sense is no longer feasible. Realizing that, the Pauline Epistles complete the break with the
Davidic idea of theocracy. Augustine subsequently counters the renewed historicism of contemporary millennialists with an apocalypse at the end of time that concentrates on the separation
of the two cities, man's and God's (Tuveson 17), and the requirement that the Christian spirit
seek only the latter. It is primarily this tradition that Herbert inherits and that the militant
reformers of the 1630s attempt to replace with a new Hebraicism and concept of a new kingdom
again both social and spiritual. (This would seem to be Milton's kingdom of industrious
reforming Englishmen in *Areopagitica* but not the kingdom that emerges from the wilderness
contest between Christ and Satan.)

incidents for insertion into a typological and instructional system. What then happens to the historical mission of a cultic church whose Lord is no longer a Lord of hosts, agriculture, architecture, city planning, animal husbandry, law, ethics, marriage customs, and diet? Once the Pauline Messiah is removed from the world and the Church has entered its diasporic phase, the individual Christian is defined by adherence to the text and a reformed heart. The "way" can only go vertically, as the silk twist of "The Pearl" does, not horizontally through the combined sacred and secular entanglements that make politics and empire central to evidence of Providence in Hebrew historicism. For Herbert, who did not expect a millennial return to that historicism, the "way" goes through death rather than the reforming of institutions under an active Messiah or an army of saints. For Herbert, no interim advent or intermediate rule to usher in a new earthly kingdom is likely or desirable.

Baconian enterprise is rejected in *The Church*, whose project is to eliminate whatever impedes the singular commitment shown in the pearl parable. The inventory of things to be set aside is often rather elaborate, and the speaker is sufficiently attracted to them to give them staying power. The three main stanzas of "The Pearl" are elaborately devoted to these temptations before the speaker comes to the four syllables that banish them, "Yet I love thee." Similarly, the complaints of "The Crosse" occupy thirty-four lines to the three that bend to the Lord's will. Both poems are devoted to the lingering and to the prepared turns and thus to the balancing of submission against enticement. Nor do the choices, once they have been made, pass clean out of mind; subsequent speakers remember them.

This persistence of the excluded is further reason to keep in mind the choices Herbert made in pursuing a strictly sacred poetry and in rejecting the reopening of nature's book in contemporary science and even the integrated kingdom of courtly and sacred alliances united under a Christian prince. The difficulty of making and standing by the first of these rejections we can judge from Herbert's linking of the university oratorship to "Sir Francis," the prime example in his university days of the combination of science and civil power.

Bacon and the University Orator

Among the secular alternatives that *The Church* considers, "The Pearl" lists learning foremost and science prominently within it:

> I know the wayes of Learning; both the head
> And pipes that feed the presse, and make it runne;
> What reason hath from nature borrowed,
> Or of it self, like a good huswife, spunne
> In laws and policie; what the starres conspire,
> What willing nature speaks, what forc'd by fire;
> Both th' old discoveries, and the new-found seas,
> The stock and surplus, cause and historie:
> All these stand open, or I have the keyes:
>   Yet I love thee.

Herbert's four Latin poems to and on Bacon suggest that the choice between the empiricism he acknowledges there and the love "The Pearl" reiterates might have been even more difficult for Herbert personally than the speaker here acknowledges. As the prudent life of Bensalem in Bacon's *New Atlantis* indicates, the empirical method need not be limited to experimental science. Its technology can be fashioned into a way of life and a social structure that Bacon makes compatible with the revealed wisdom that once floated to Bensalem.

Herbert's distrust of that "way" is based on a contrast between the scientific method and the biblical hermeneutic implicit in the pearl parable. Even in the midst of his praise of Bacon in a university letter of thanks for the gift of the *Instauratio Magna*, he cannot resist tucking in a caution: "God grant that the same advances which thou has made in the sphere of nature, thou mayest also make in that of grace, and that in due time thou mayest complete the things which thou has embraced in mind to his Glory" (*Complete Works* 3.438). The phrase that saves this from being outright criticism is "in due time," which allows for the indefinite postponement of any bridging of natural history and divinity. The difference is basically one of focal interest. Whatever willing nature speaks and explorers discover depends on particulars and their classification, and on the entire industry of Merchants of Light, Compilers, and Interpreters, as *New Atlantis* names them. In contrast, the parable (the silk twist that conducts its readers to heaven) brings vocation into conflict with traffic in ordinary pearls. It translates surfaces into allegories and ordinary treasure into divine. Bacon's utopian interpreters also read those parables, having watched both testaments arrive, heralded by a pillar of light (Moses's sign) topped by the cross. Bacon himself makes several eloquent defenses of poetic fables and of religion that "delights in . . . veils and shadows." To take them away "would be almost to interdict all communion between divinity and humanity" (*Works* 6.696). His tracking of Pan in *De Augmentis* (*Works* 4.318–27) is an impressive deciphering of ancient myth, under a principle of allegory that he has no trouble building into his scientific and philosophical project. Turning from his explication of myths and addressing James I, he is well aware of both the shifting of gears and the nexus. He remarks, "All History, excellent King, walks upon the earth, and performs the office rather of a guide than of a light; whereas Poesy is as a dream of learning; a thing sweet and varied, and that would be thought to have in it something divine; a character which dreams likewise affect. But now it is time for me to awake, and rising above the earth, to wing my way through the clear air of Philosophy and the Sciences" (*Works* 4.336). Those sciences he distinguishes from "Inspired Divinity" in method while reserving a place for the latter as "the haven and sabbath of all human contemplations" (*Works* 4.336).

But divinity for Bensalemites requires little further interpretive effort, since in the testaments that they have been given, unlike the myths of the ancients, truth is rendered if not transparent in all respects quite certain in the main principles. It is not expected to produce further knowledge, whereas nature's book is still largely unexplored. In *The Advancement of Learning*, which Herbert helped translate, Bacon makes the distinction clear:

> For if any man shall think by view and inquiry into these sensible and material things to attain that light whereby he may reveal unto himself the nature or will of God, then indeed is he spoiled by vain philosophy, for the contemplation of God's creatures and works produceth (having regard to the works and creatures themselves) knowledge, but having regard to God, no perfect knowledge, but wonder, which is broken knowledge. . . . And hence . . . divers great learned men have been heretical, whilst they have sought to fly up to the secrets of the Deity by the waxen things of the senses. (*Works* 3.267)

This in no way lessens the dignity of secular learning or suggests that it too is futile. The wise man of Salomon's house consents to being interviewed by the narrator so that the latter can begin sending the information from the cavern experiments and mountaintop stations of New Atlantis to the European intellectual community. Biblical wisdom has traveled the other way and stopped; secular learning requires a constant exchange.

That Herbert should associate the ways of learning with the ways of honor in "The Pearl" is not surprising. Civil honors not only in Bensalem but in

Cambridge go to the scientist. In the poems on Bacon and in the letter to Sir John Danvers cited earlier, he is well aware of the prestige of the country's premiere scientific apologist. But the speaker of "The Pearl" is also aware of the cost in the intertwining of "vies of favours" and the weight of the world when one has tied a "true-love-knot" around it. Bacon's several prefaces and parenthetical addresses to James I, especially in *De Augmentis*, make James almost a collaborator in the augmentation of learning. The word "dignity" in his first title for *The Advancement of Learning* and his concern to build into the enterprise a parallel with world conquest and glory, despite his own cautions against doing so, show how much learning and honor go hand in hand. After 1621 and what Samuel Gardiner considers in detail in "The Fall of Lord Chancellor Bacon," Herbert must have been doubly aware of the compromises and "drams of spirit" anyone in public life must pay. Under the barrage of charges brought against him by Christopher Aubrey, Edward Egerton, and Lady Wharton, Bacon found the defenses of Buckingham and James melting away rather quickly, perhaps in the face of a hopeless case (Gardiner 56–107) or perhaps for merely expedient reasons.

The silk twist of the parables replaces such narratives of advancement and precipitous fall with pyramidal analogy and an eschatology hinted in the tropes of pearls and treasure. Like Matthew, the speaker of "The Pearl" leaves comparison between the secular and the sacred unargued, but the similitudes that science uses in putting its empirical observations together have nothing in common with those that set the types of the parables and point toward a savior who both tells the stories and is their chief subject. Whenever classification and observation descend to detail in the sciences, they sacrifice the whole, and Bacon insists that they do so rigorously. Whatever the whole may turn out to be in the long run, as Herbert could see in both *The Advancement of Learning* and the *Novum Organum*, a detailed anatomy disintegrates its objects into endlessly subdividable parts. Despite the parallel tracks that Bacon gives natural and divine knowledge, he cannot relieve anxiety on that score merely by asserting their eventual reunion. He stresses instead the obvious first repercussion of his method—detailed observation will not produce instant midlevel axioms and philosophy. Practically all his cautions go against flying too soon to the magisterial style and its overconfident generalizations.

That Herbert might actually go the Baconian way himself in balancing natural history and divinity was probably never a possibility, but judging by the respect that "In honor of the Illustrious Baron Verulam" lavishes on its subject and by the vocational wavering of "Affliction 1" (which seems to be his most autobiographical poem), exclusive commitment to ministerial service was questionable for some time. The encomium to Bacon calls him (no doubt with some playful exaggeration) the "archpriest / Of truth, lord of the inductive method," nature's cosmographer, savior of science ("long an orphan now"), minister of light, the living bedevilment of idols, colleague of the sun, and sophistry's whip. Both in the encomium and in fact, archpriests, lords, and learned men came naturally together in the ambience of the court and the university. And as I suggested, that alliance of learning, social prestige, and pleasure captures more attention in "The Pearl" than the parable does, which we locate explicitly only in the title. It takes a powerful refrain to hold the bulky stanzas captive until the silk twist can assert itself.

The turn in Herbert's "*Yet* I love thee" is implicitly a correction of Bacon's "*And* I serve thee," which is the promise of his arguments for the ultimate collaboration between science and divinity. In a better world where chancellors do not accept bribes, *New Atlantis* honors the emissary from the laboratories as though he were the high priest of society. He arrives in a splendor reminiscent of Elizabethan progresses. Whereas the priests of Bensalem blend into the population, the wise potentate of science sits in state; his wisdom, which embraces the entire material world, is accelerating and will be carried abroad almost evangelically. The Baconian text itself purports to be its emissary.

In contrast, the narrative that Herbert juxtaposes with science in "The Pearl" directs everything to the fable's end from within the lives that begin each story. As Matthew arranges the pearl sequence, a parallel illustration precedes the parable of the merchant, which is then followed by a supplement and an exposition of the several allegories altogether. The sequence provides a model for both the discarding and the interpreting of rival interests. It concludes:

> Again, the kingdom of heaven is like unto a net, that was cast into the sea, and gathered of every kind: Which, when it was full, they drew to shore, and sat down, and gathered the good into vessels, but cast the bad away.
>
> So shall it be at the end of the world: the angels shall come forth, and sever the wicked from among the just, and shall cast them into the furnace of fire: there shall be wailing and gnashing of teeth. Jesus saith unto them, Have ye understood all these things? They say unto him, Yea, Lord. (Matthew 13.47–51)

The parables slide from one kind of choice to another, with some potential for confusion. The repeated "again" indicates an intended parallelism, but the first two figures, the treasure and the pearl, set up models for human election based on conviction and individual life-changing discoveries; the last Figure separates the wicked from the saved at an altogether different level. The parables thus pass from choices embedded in the human economy to the hour of judgment, which is well beyond human agency. It is allegorical language and prolepsis that the teller casts across the gulf between the things that Perkins charts temporally and the circle that "contains" God's glory.

Some preparation for that break is implied by the unnaturalness of the tropes. Treasure does not inherently come with fields, which are there to be tilled and harvested, not abandoned. The great pearl, which is not a pearl after all, puts an end to the merchant's merchandizing. Similarly in the third example, angels are obviously not ordinary fishermen. Matthew leaves open the question of whether what makes one species of fish valuable and another of no use comes before or after the choices of the preceding examples. The arrangement suggests after, but the illustrative nature of parables tends to subordinate sequence to paradigm. In any case, if the first two narratives underscore the folly of anyone who accepts a lesser thing, the third stresses the threat of judgment. Although the categories may be predetermined and the individual parties predestined, the consequences of a choice that may not have seemed particularly dire become so if salvation hangs upon it.

Reasons for such a broadly categorical denial of all things worldly are suggested by the positive answer of the disciples when Jesus asks them if they understand these parables. Coming after an account of wailing and gnashing teeth, his question, "Have ye understood all these things," is a challenge that they cannot ignore. Any return to business as usual, which includes divided loyalty to realm, family, occupation, and secular learning, would be made at great peril. The parables compress into the figures nothing less than the entire master narrative of salvation, and that narrative can have only one conclusion to go with its multitude of exclusions. It demands that old customs, devotional practices, and loyalties be discarded for belief under the covenant of grace. What the Pauline Epistles spell out is what that means for reading the Hebrew Bible and interpreting the life of Israelites, Egyptians, Canaanites, and so forth. What "The Pearl" too proposes is beyond question in its main thrust and eschatological in its verticality:

> not sealed, but with open eyes
> I flie to thee, and fully understand

> Both the main sale, and the commodities;
> And at what rate and price I have thy love;
> With all the circumstances that may move:
> Yet through these labyrinths, not my groveling wit,
> But thy silk twist let down from heav'n to me,
> Did both conduct and teach me, how by it
> To climbe to thee.

The doubleness of "conduct and teach" points to Scripture's forceful lessons. The speaker is evidently not thinking of service in an evangelical church or a mission to perform in the historical world—a "calling"—but of himself as a parallel to the merchant. The concern is personal, not social or apparently even churchly.

What Herbert may have understood science to be is not absolutely certain, despite his elaboration of it in the first stanza, but in this final statement he points up important aspects of Bacon's method in the terms "circumstances" and "labyrinths," both prominent in the preface to the *Instauratio Magna*. There Bacon describes the unwillingness of the material world to yield clear principles. If circumstances in the parables are few but allegorically telling, the circumstances that human wit contends with in the material world are quite otherwise, both in volume and in complexity. When Bacon considers method, he is under no illusion that putting the houses of science and philosophy in order will be easy; it only seems to be in the utopian progress of *New Atlantis*, where the intellectual energy of the state has long since been focused on the scientific project. At what he considers the virtual outset of that project in his own times (which are by no means dedicated to it), the prospect is less encouraging:

> The universe to the eye of the human understanding is framed like a labyrinth, presenting as it does on every side so many ambiguities of way, such deceitful resemblances of objects and signs, natures so irregular in their lines and so knotted and entangled. And then the way is still to be made by the uncertain light of the sense, sometimes shining out, sometimes clouded over, through the woods of experience and particulars; while those who offer themselves for guides . . . themselves also puzzled, and increase the number of errors and wanderers. In circumstances so difficult neither the natural force of man's judgment nor even any accidental felicity offers any chance of success. No excellence of wit, no repetition of chance experiments,

can overcome such difficulties as these. Our steps must be guided by a clue, and the whole way from the very first perception of the senses must be laid out upon a sure plan. (*Works* 4.18)

Resemblance, classification, and the concordances of things are especially perplexing, because analogy, the main principle of analysis even here, causes us to jump to irrational conclusions if we allow ourselves to move vertically at all.

In connecting errors, wanderers, and "woods of experience and particulars" with the labyrinth image, which he does frequently, Bacon evokes a common Medieval and Renaissance figure featured, for instance, in the Red Cross Knight's journey through the woods to the cave of Error in Spenser's *Faerie Queene* and in a critique of secular learning that is at least as ancient as Augustine. Although he is not concerned with any identification of error with Roman heresy, Bacon collects into the image of the maze an inevitable multiplicity and confusion, which he associates with unaided reason. As John M. Steadman points out (167), the maze is frequently associated with rhetoric as well, where the contrast is with the goal-oriented wisdom of Scripture. If interpretations of nature are endlessly problematic, it is because phenomena themselves are. Herbert might add, interpretations of Scripture too, if they are not collected under the guidance of the parables. Left to midrashic ingenuity, the permutations of any several passages combined can approach the countless by incorporating too much of tribal and national life and its circumstances.

An institutional difference reinforces the philosophical one between Herbert and Bacon in their senses of the Temple. Although a temple serves as a center of wisdom for each, Bacon uses the House of Salomon as a model for the most advanced social system. Salomon's wisdom is applied: it assumes an integration of religious observance and national well-being. The difference between this and Christian teleology (in Robert Jan van Pelt's terms) is basically the difference between a one-way journey through the forecourt to the sanctuary and on to heaven (Herbert's method), and a turning back from the inner temple to the utopian forecourt (Bacon's method). The latter does not go on to another world but keeps within the meeting places of the human and the divine where YHWH can be petitioned to descend and resume his works (van Pelt 409). Neither David nor Solomon expected to abandon the world, nor do their immediate predecessors and successors. Bacon feels that within the circumscribed area of inductive philosophy he can establish a "true and lawful marriage between the empirical and the rational faculty, the unkind and ill-starred divorce and separation of which has thrown into confusion all the affairs of the human family" (*Works* 4.19). But not the affairs of science alone, we notice. They are not all that narrowly constrained—those uncharted searches through the secular labyrinth. Affairs various and sundry are included in them, as though despite disclaimers, learning and technology were actually shouldering their way between church and state and preparing to dominate Bensalem, *his* new Jerusalem. What does fall outside the scientist's province? The main thing is the tracing of final causes and the closed narrative that extends to judgment. In nature, God works strictly through secondary causes and finite sequences, and within that realm the proliferation of disciplines and nomenclatures carries so far into the division of parts that it requires the postponement of any pursuit of origins.

Thinking of Bacon in 1620 when *Novum Organum* was published and probably before the concerns of "The Pearl" began to interfere, Herbert stresses much more the successes of the Baconian enterprise than his misgivings about it, nor would he have been unduly nervous about Bacon's breaking of the correspondences between humanly devised icons and divine ideas. But he would surely have balked at the equation of truth and utility that justifies the venture into the secular labyrinth. His view of nature in "Man" is much closer to Paracelsian correspondence than to Baconian pragmatism. The "End of our Foundation," the sage instructor of Bensalem says, "is the knowledge of Causes and secret motions of things, and the enlarging of the bounds of Human Empire to the effecting of all things possible" (Bacon, *A Selection* 447). In contrast, what matters to the astrological system that Herbert reflects in "Man" is an almost mystical tie of bodies:

> Man is all symmetrie,
> Full of proportions, one limbe to another,
> And all to all the world besides:
> Each part may call the furthest, brother:
> For head with foot hath private amitie,
> And both with moons and tides.
>
> Nothing hath got so farre,
> But Man hath caught and kept it, as his prey.
> His eyes dismount the highest starre:
> He is in little all the sphere.
> Herbs gladly cure our flesh; because that they
> Finde their acquaintance there.

This has the look of an early poem (it is in the Williams manuscript) and may predate Herbert's main interest in Bacon, but nothing in *The Church* contradicts it. It places on men the same obligation to serve the Creator that Herbert places on Bacon in the university letter to him. That this is not a passing fancy but part of Herbert's persistent worry is suggested by several other poems, for instance, "Providence," "Praise 3," and "Vanity 1." The first of these also emphasizes the harmony of all creatures and makes nature a great storehouse of provisions and man its chief beneficiary:

> The sea, which seems to stop the traveller,
> Is by a ship the speedier passage made.
> The windes, who think they rule the mariner,
> Are rul'd by him, and taught to serve his trade.
>
> And as thy house is full, so I adore
> Thy curious art in marshalling thy goods.
> The hills with health abound; the vales with store;
> The South with marble; North with furres & woods.
>
> Hard things are glorious; easie things good cheap.
> The common all men have; that which is rare
> Men therefore seek to have, and care to keep.
> The healthy frosts with summer-fruits compare.
>
> Light without winde is glasse: warm without weight
> Is Wooll and furre: cool without closenesse, shade:
> Speed without pains, a horse: tall without height,
> A servile hawk: low without losse, a spade.

Nothing in Herbert's extensive list of blessings depends on occult resemblance or identity, but neither is nature's use obscure enough to require science. "Praise 3" makes a providential god almost beleaguered in fulfilling its many obligations on the run:

> Thousands of things do thee employ
> In ruling all
> This spacious globe: Angels must have their joy,
> Devils their rod, the sea his shore,
> The windes their stint: and yet when I did call,
> Thou heardst my call, and more.

If the world is a well-oiled machine runs smoothly, it is because none of its parts goes neglected. This is decidedly not yet the clockwork universe of eighteenth-century rationalism, which Bacon's spacious globe sometimes seems. And above all for the poet speaking personally is the miracle of God's listening to him, so closely that God hears more than the suppliant intends to say. Herbert is not inquisitive about concealed laws; his concern is unforced usefulness and the sort of ready blessings that generate songs of praise.

Perhaps more important to his rejection of Baconian projects is the depth and kind of human error. For Herbert the Fall is a matter not merely of erect reason but of a hardened heart; head and heart together collaborate in poisoning the very nature of secular learning. The vanity of learning that Bacon finds curable in *The Advancement* he finds inherent in the pride of knowledge in "Vanity 1," which moves closer to the traditional view of secular learning as a mazy wood. Bacon assures his readers that the original fall came from trying to dislodge a specific commandment, not from seeking to know too much. But for Herbert, whatever the forbidden knowledge of Genesis might mean, the fleet astronomer, nimble diver, and subtle chemist undergo adventures of dubious spiritual value. Whereas Bacon seeks to avoid these questions by preaching charity, Herbert throws in his lot entirely with the study of divinity:

> The fleet Astronomer can bore,
> And thred the spheres with his quick-piercing minde:
> He views their stations, walks from doore to doore,
>   Surveys, as if he had design'd
> To make a purchase there: he sees their dances,
>   And knoweth long before
> Both their full-ey'd aspects, and secret glances.
>
> The nimble Diver with his side
> Cuts through the working waves, that he may fetch
> His dearely-earned pearl, which God did hide
>   On purpose from the ventrous wretch;
> That he might save his life, and also hers,
>   Who with excessive pride
> Her own destruction and his danger wears.
>
> The subtil Chymick can devest
> And strip the creature naked, till he finde

> The callow principles within their nest:
>> There he imparts to them his minde,
> Admitted to their bed-chamber, before
>> They appeare trim and drest
> To ordinarie suitours at the doore.
>
>> What hath not man sought out and found,
> But his deare God? who yet his glorious law
> Embosomes in us, mellowing the ground
>> With showres and frost, with love & aw,
> So that we need not say, Where's this command?
>> Poore man, thou searchest round
> To finde out *death*, but missest *life* at hand.

What lies at hand is the Bible, and it is especially accessible in the parables— accessible to the heart as well as the head. Herbert has assembled for display a few workmen of the House of Salomon, and what he sees in them is an overwrought combination of curiosity and ambition that makes each strive to be the first in his field. The stars, ocean depths, and molecules are as much their love as the wearer of the pearl and the acclaim are. Quite grandly at first they force their way with experiments and equipment, when if they had only waited a due period anything they needed to know would have revealed itself.

Whether these acts of pride go beyond those that Bacon himself admits and seeks to cure in *The Advancement of Learning* may be debatable, but the priority of the question "Where's this command?" is not. In the light of the final contrast between death and life, it is difficult for Herbert to think of any reason for the restless attempt to master nature beyond the sly ones hinted by the sexual language of "full-ey'd aspects," "secret glances," the recipient of the lesser pearl, and the bedchamber raid on molecules. If the deep mines and mountains of *New Atlantis* are not populated by similar venturous wretches, it is not for lack of honors that the state is willing to heap upon them for ferreting out "callow principles within their nest." Perhaps equally telling in both "Vanity 1" and "The Pearl" is Herbert's expenditure of wit against the world of wit. Both poems are knowing rejections by speakers who could succeed in such a world of learned reference and sly innuendo if they chose to. They speak the language of the university and court and like the pearl merchant could turn a profit there. In that much they support Walton's confidence in Herbert's own potential for a secular career and thus his saintliness in choosing to forgo it. Whether or not his hopes remained realistic much beyond 1624, in the poems they provide a countermovement, an important road not taken—still another reason that his speakers must cross and recross the Jordan and recurrently reaffirm their priorities.

Another side to that confidence is less visible in "The Pearl." While teaching merchants how to fly to God, the silk twist never actually lets the speaker do so. The choice of the pearl is only preparatory, and at times it seems, if not perilous, curiously unproductive of spiritual assurance. The parable commands world denial, but its apocalyptic level concludes that another world is only to be found at the far end of the history. Meanwhile, one must synchronize an ever-renewed personal narrative with scriptural "constellations." Herbert does not place much confidence in gradual improvement or spiritual staging. (Bacon would find another way to try the climb, seeing "the dependence of causes and the works of Providence" and believing "that the highest link of nature's chain must needs to be tied to the foot of Jupiter's chair" [*Works* 3.267].) In thinking that man can search too far, Herbert may be remembering the conclusion of Solomon's reign more closely than Bacon does; but in denying as well the way through works, he seems skeptical not only of Baconian enthusiasm but of other, plainer pathways. A Christian poetry must be designed to hold in balance the certainty of biblical teachings and the delays of the historical record, which offer none of the enticements and active consolations available to the enterprising astronomer, chemist, tradesman, or university orator.

Schism and Millennialism

For the sake of convenience, I have been assuming that Herbert himself had to choose between science and faith, court and church. It seems likely that he did so, even though secular and sacred alternatives were not ordinarily mutually exclusive in the earlier seventeenth century, and it was not self-evident that they would ever become seriously at odds. Bacon's insistence that they are compatible assumes a suspicion of overly curious learning, and that suspicion is clearly in Herbert's mind in "Vanity 1" and elsewhere. It was possible to blur the distinctions between kinds of knowledge, and also between court and church. Not only Herbert's early preparation for a courtly career but his concern with the Virginia colony suggests that joint enterprises seemed feasible up to a certain point. "The Church Militant" (*The Works* 190–98) follows a threefold division in God's governance, the first applied to "the smallest ant or atom" in nature, the business of science; the second to the counsels and policies of the state, the province of the magistrate; and the third to the church as "spouse," the domain of ecclesiastical structures. The priority among these Herbert compresses into two brief phrases—the "much more" that the state acknowledges and the "above all" of the church ("The Church Militant" 5, 9). Anything well governed must be godly, and anything godly must be well governed. As Bacon insists, the natural and sacred realms are both derived from the same source, and the pursuit of knowledge in either realm must eventually reach that source. It is after all for the footprints of Pan, or universality, that the critical eye of science searches in the mazy wood.

I expect that the key matters for Herbert are not the eventual accountability of science or the possibility of a devout Christian prince but the immediate demands of a vocation and the personal spiritual conflict that *The Church* imitates. More unavoidable in the later 1620s was the matter of church reform and dissent, troubling enough to ruffle the surface of *The Church* in "Church-rents and Schisms" and "The British Church." In the earlier satiric reply to Andrew Melville's *Anti-Tami-Cami-Categoria*, Herbert finds the prospect of a divided church appalling. Schism receives more extended attention and the benefit of a broad perspective in "The Church Militant," where the peace of mind that concludes *The Church* fails to extend to the nation and the visible church. For all that, however expressly polemical issues are not a major concern of *The Temple*, however much we can infer them from its love of church architecture and ritual. Hence, although no necessary connection exists between Herbert's departure from secular concerns and his opposition to activist reform, his attitude toward both depends on the preeminence of individual spiritual welfare, which he pursues not in isolation from the visible church, but not in expectation of its completion there either. Most of the essential communiques go directly from God to the individual heart. Even in the approach to communion in "Love 3," Love negotiates personally with the sinner, and it alone serves the meal, without the help of an ordained priesthood. In "The Church-Porch" it is the poet who lectures and prepares for the lessons of *The Church*, not a country parson, and without the spiritual conflicts themselves, the altar that matters is the heart. The poet's occupation carries him inward much more often than it directs his attention to church floors and stained-glass windows.

Given the contemporary resurgence of millenarian and Hebraic thought, I expect that Herbert's emphasis on the individual represents a deliberate choice not to be overly polemical. An Old Testament style historicism that applies Providence to national events is less evident in his finishing of the global narrative than it is, for instance, in Hugh Broughton, Thomas Brightman, or Joseph Mede. For any party seeking to accommodate universal to local history, providential historicism still meant answering the age-old question of Hebrew and Christian texts "how long?" but except in "The Church Militant" Herbert tends to ask it on an individual rather than a broadly national or international level. By concentrating on individual preparedness in *Alarum to the Last Judgment* (1615), Thomas Draxe, like Herbert, addresses that question in a way that forestalls the idea that the end should be hurried by the sword. It is being delayed in order to fulfill the prophecies of Revelation, to leave the unrepentant without excuse, to guarantee that none of the elect shall perish, and to exercise the patience, hope, and charity of the faithful—the latter to be fully tried among the atheistical, the scandalous, the venomous, and the superstitious (20). No purified church militant is to be expected before the advent of the church triumphant. Concerning the saving of the unfaithful and the need to convert heathens, again like Herbert, Draxe thinks of the Americas and West Indies and hopes for the conversion of Popish and Turkish idolaters (27), but that is not a program-generating, militant hope.

Herbert thinks along similar lines in explaining the ambiguity of fortune. The problem he confronts in "Affliction 1," "Temper 1," and "The Flower" is what to think of apparent randomness, when every event, national or personal, should theoretically reveal an interpretable pattern. He turns to the international aspects of Providence in "The Church Militant" but again denies the hopefulness of a messianic narrative, which keeps schismatic programs out of the spiritual way. What counts consistently is the private heart. In his sonnets on Scripture, he assumes a similar priority. To integrate every phase of life and all chapters of the book one must subordinate the Hebrew Bible to the central fable and focus the act of reading on finding oneself in the text. For an individual thus to place himself, he must be absorbed into a single reigning pattern. Similarly, an Antioch or a Corinth, in becoming linked to the history of Jerusalem through the evangelical movement, must subordinate its other alliances to that one. Making a good many histories into one history requires the subjection of Hebrew law to grace and of the patriarchal proponents of complex law to a spirit that governs without an accompanying politics or even a thriving visible church.

Behind Herbert's intermittent concern for schism and the historical struggle of church militant is a long history of debate over how collective the church needs to be. Herbert's focus on inner and individual matters again probably represents a conscious choice and thus a deliberate setting of boundaries for *The Church*, boundaries that get extended in "The Church Militant." The Spirit's power to overcome splintering is the subject of the Peter-Paul-Barnabas dispute in Luke, the account of which Luther and Calvin make crucial to the doctrine of sufficient grace, which clearly contributes to Herbert's focus on problems of individual merit and reception of the sacraments. Together with other epistles, especially the Epistle to the Hebrews, Luke's text sets the model for the single universal church and its control of sacramental administration. One of the passages from Acts that Luther and Calvin also work with presents that dispute in a relatively straightforward manner. As the cornerstone of the historical church it requires the subjugation of far-flung regions and the Law to the Spirit, which must govern that church:

> And when there had been much disputing, Peter rose up, and said unto them, men and brethren, ye know how that a good while ago God made choice among us, that the Gentiles by my mouth should hear the word of the gospel, and believe. And God, which knoweth the hearts, bare them witness, giving them the Holy Ghost, even as he did unto us; and put no difference between us and them, purifying their hearts by faith. Now therefore why tempt ye God, to put a yoke upon the neck of the disciples, which neither our fathers nor we were able to bear? But we believe that through the grace of the Lord Jesus Christ we shall be saved, even as they.
>
> Then all the multitude kept silence, and gave audience to Barnabas and Paul, declaring what miracles and wonders God had wrought among the Gentiles by them. (Acts 15.7–12)

Calvin stresses both the gravity of the moment and the stilling of the uproar. He imagines Peter assuring the divided group that

> even if the servitude of the Law had been imposed on the fathers, as far as the outward form was concerned, yet their consciences were unfettered and free. . . . For since the covenant of life which God made with His servants from the beginning right to the end of the world, is eternal and the same, it would be absurd and intolerable for there to be taught today another and different way of obtaining salvation than the one the fathers had long ago. Therefore Peter affirms that we are completely at one with the fathers, because they,

no less than we, placed the hope of salvation on the grace of Christ. And so, making the Law and the Gospel one . . . he removes from the Jews the stumbling-block, which they were imagining for themselves. (*Calvin's Commentaries* 42).

Thinking that this will soon become evident to Jews fueled the renewed hope in seventeenth-century England that the final conversion was not far off, an expectation that, as Perez Zagorin shows, gave way to a devastating pogrom when no Jewish conversion ushered in the messianic age (Zagorin 79). The result was to place Christ at the spiritual center of history in the manner of the Epistle to the Hebrews. He or his spirit must be present in any right worship to quell potential sects. Otherwise Corinth would not be defined by its relation to the fable but would be loosely aggregated around its trade routes, cultural history, agriculture, arts, literature, and so on. Incidents of the Hebrew Bible would remain rooted in their cultural circumstance.

If those who remain so seated in cultural differences must be explained, the Pauline way (which is also Calvin's way and Herbert's way) is to attribute their rebellion to Satan and his false prophets, who imitate the Spirit so convincingly that even well-intentioned believers may be deceived. Crises in church history become confrontations between the true spirit and its anti-christian subversions. The "sin" that suggests apostasy among the Israelites and that follows Herbert's church militant wherever it goes is from one point of view merely rooted local history. As a deviation from the single story, it becomes the countermovement of a defined plot. Hans Frei's point in *The Eclipse of Biblical Narrative*, that the biblical story requires all historiography to conform to it, is well illustrated by the concept of sin. No other comprehensive system of explanation exists for Herbert or the earlier seventeenth century, not even for Bacon.

That point really needs no demonstration, but if we wish to see how plot and counterplot work in a single narrative system, we have only to think of *Paradise Lost*. Strictly speaking, neither the first information Milton's muse delivers ("Th' infernal Serpent; hee it was") nor the wealth of embellishments that follows require unusual enlightenment, but Milton asks for the full participation of the Spirit and needs Satan's cooperation if he is to explain not only the durability of God's word but its going unheeded in the messy chronicles that history leaves us. He uses the roll call of the fallen angels in book 1 as a way to gather virtually all known cultures into a single apostasy: the Ammonites in Rabba, Argob, and Basan (like Solomon, worshipers of a disguised Moloch); the Israelites before Josiah's unifying reform in Peor; the

Egyptians in Baalim and in Ashtaroth; the Phoenicians in Astarte (also worshiped by Solomon, thanks to his foreign wives); the Greeks in Thammuz and Adonis; the Gathites in Dagon; and *"Osiris, Isis, Orus* and thir Train / With monstrous shapes and sorceries abus'd" (*Paradise Lost* 1.478–79)—all these fill an extensive roster of regions and nations whose differences are created not by their material or geographical circumstances but by their reception of one or more of the fallen host. And so on into English territories. What fills Milton's world encyclopedia is the dispersal of craven images by which various spirits have infiltrated every nook and cranny through "falsities and lies." Only a battery of counter spirits or some third force (such as chaos) could explain the apparent disunity of the world's nations. The prevalence of an antichristian spirit in this account is paradoxically a demonstration of the presence of the Holy Spirit as well, since it is the expectation of that spirit that opens the way for its false representations. The rhetoric of Peter's rewritten Hebrew history and of Calvin's assurance that Peter makes the Law and the Gospel one presupposes the opposition, as does the very word "militant." The antitype does not encourage deviations; the "antichrist" principle does not allow unity.

Together these binaries make a contested historical drama of the quest for a teleological fable, and it is within precisely that contested quest that Herbert situates both the militant church and the wayward course of his spiritual conflicts. The battle unfolds as myth, catching chronicle historiography of its crossfire. In "The Church Militant" a traveling "Sin" enters history early and matches the migrations of the Church step by step. It infiltrates even the reformed church and will as surely throw England into sectarian splintering as it has Italy and France, until Rome's "calendar of sins" is entirely fulfilled. Power and art may have ushered in religion everywhere, but they also preside over its deterioration. Since "Religion alwaies sides with povertie," colonizers ironically prepare the Americas for the Gospel by carting their pillaged wealth off to Europe:

> We think we rob them, but we think amisse:
> We are more poore, and they more rich by this.
> Thou wilt revenge their quarrell, making grace
> To pay our debts, and leave her ancient place
> To go to them, while that which now their nation
> But lends to us, shall be our desolation.

> (253–58)

As the sad chronicle of an intertwined church and civil hierarchy testifies, "gold and grace did never yet agree." Herbert is obviously not numbering himself among those who preface the apocalypse with emperor worship and use Revelation to support a militant conservatism. As Kenneth Hovey points out (" 'Wheel'd about' " 81), the entire historical world will go the way of Satan's empire "till such a darknesse do the world invade / As Christ's last coming, as his first did finde" (230–31). Neither the Reformation nor all the powers of all churches put together can save Christendom from the universal darkness that precedes the end.

Hence all the more must each soul prepare itself. In any given church it will have to do so in the company of many who would not be allowed past the church porch if Robert Browne or Henry Barrow stood at the threshold. And all the more does the center of gravity in *The Temple* become a spiritual conflict in which reform begins at home. The function of the more public and collective poems is in part to show the dangers and limits of the soul's institutional alliances. Outside the sacraments and the celebration of church calendar events, the militant church is not a powerful influence in the daily issues that *The Church* cross-examines (a matter I will return to later). In "clearing the deck" for those inner conflicts, Herbert makes a deliberate attempt to limit not only the rival interests of learning, honor, and pleasure but the distractions of Nonconformity, militant activism, and a diverse, historical Hebrew Bible.

Constellations of the Story

The practice of making that Bible into the "Old Testament" not only guides Herbert's reading of current moments but says something about the function of a book of poems modeled on a gathering of scattered verses. Outside of the one extensive treatment of the greater story in "The Church Militant," Herbert limits his concern for the gathered church to a handful of poems whose interest lies partly in the discrepancy between the institution and the poet who must move toward it. The church is a collective protagonist in a preparatory way in "The Church-porch" as well as in the concluding narrative. In between, the spiritual odyssey seeks parallels with specific parts of the source text, where episodes and accounts of lives are allocated to chapters and verses. The history of humanity can thus be put under an arm and transported with convenient reference. Its unification is fostered by both internal and external commentaries. Earlier verses converge on later ones that build into their incorporation of new events the reinterpretation of old ones. Assisted by allegory, Augustine, for instance, is able to see in Samson's fiery foxes a clergy that scorches sinners. He makes Solomon's sensuous lover into a soul for the Bridegroom. The more remote the connection between the tenor and vehicle, the more he professes to like it. Where the Canticle of Canticles says, "Thy teeth are as flocks of sheep, that are shorn," he imagines the teeth of the church cutting men off from their errors "and transferring them to her body after their hardness has been softened as if by being bitten and chewed" (Augustine 37). That model governs the reading of subsequent history as well, the expectation being that under the guidance of the Spirit, very little before or after Christ remains unyielding. "Hardly anything may be found in . . . obscure places which is not found plainly said elsewhere," Augustine remarks (38), meaning by "plainly said elsewhere" no doubt mainly the verses that expound the teachings of Jesus in parable or epistle and by "obscure" a stubbornly diversified, historical life such as fills Genesis and the histories and legends.

Even so, the work of interpretation is never finished. As "H. Scriptures 2" recognizes, the reader finds it difficult to make the one design fit all occasions:

> Oh that I knew how all thy lights combine,
>> And the configurations of their glorie!
>> Seeing not onely how each verse doth shine,
> But all the constellations of the storie.
>> This verse marks that, and both do make a motion
>> Unto a third, that ten leaves off doth lie:
>> Then as dispersed herbs do watch a potion,
> These three make up some Christians destinie:
> Such are thy secrets, which my life makes good,
>> And comments on thee: for in ev'ry thing
>> Thy words do finde me out, & parallels bring,
> And in another make me understood.
>> Starres are poore books, & oftentimes do misse:
>> This book of starres lights to eternall blisse.

Since scriptural verses tell of Egyptians and Canaanites as well as Christians and Hebrews, one paraphrase of that opening wish—not Herbert's para- phrase of course, but a modern supplement in the tradition of Hermann Gunkel and Julius Wellhausen—might well be "Oh that I understood how quarreling and warring peoples could combine in a single church," or "how so many writers from different eras could have produced one book." With or without an explanation of the regional differences that shine in each verse of deuteronomic history, an extension of the scriptural principle of unity would be required as well by the post-testament expansion of the visible church to the nations, as realized in "The Church Militant." Coleridge's instinct is appropriate in seeing Herbert's drive toward unification equivalent to what he considers organicism: " 'This verse marks that,' & c. The spiritual unity of the Bible = the order and connexion of organic forms, in which the unity of life is shown, though as widely dispersed in the world of the mere sight . . . as the text" (*Complete Works* 2.cxxxviii–ix). The promise behind the equation of text to life is the same as the one that underlies Coleridge's comment (in his essay on Milton) that "the poet is an historian upon the condition of moral power being the only force in the universe." It is a moral power that abhors both a vacuum and a confusion and requires any Christian historiography to collaborate with Scripture in gathering local history into the universal.

Yet being plural like the cultures they contend with, scriptural configurations and constellations leave open the possibility that an interpreter could be very astute and still end up with unrelated clusters. J (the Yahwist) and E (who calls God Elohim) may contradict P (the priestly legalist) or D (the deuteronomic historian), who may in turn codify, edit, or overwrite—while adapting—his predecessors. Doubtfulness in the face of expected cross-reference is a concern in "H. Scriptures 2" even without higher criticism's variety of scriptural authors and conditions of writing. Yet the possibility of disunity is not easily reconciled with the advice of "Divinitie," which begins and ends more confidently, first with faith's superiority over reason (ever the instrument of dissection) and then with the reductive operation of reason itself, at work now on the biblical equivalent to Bacon's labyrinth of empirical circumstances:

> As men, for fear the starres should sleep and nod,
>   And trip at night, have spheres suppli'd;
> As if a starre were duller then a clod,
>   Which knows his way without a guide:
>
> Just so the other heav'n they also serve,
>   Divinities transcendent skie:
> Which with the edge of wit they cut and carve.
>   Reason triumphs, and faith lies by.

> Could not that Wisdome, which first broacht the wine,
>   Have thicken'd it with definitions?
> And jagg'd his seamlesse coat, had that been fine,
>   With curious questions and divisions?
>
> But all the doctrine, which he taught and gave,
>   Was cleare as heav'n, from whence it came.
> At least those beams of truth, which onely save,
>   Surpasse in brightnesse any flame.
>
>   . . . .
>
> Then burn thy Epicycles, foolish man;
>   Break all thy spheres, and save thy head.
> Faith needs no staffe of flesh, but stoutly can
>   To heav'n alone both go, and leade.

This is the equivalent in divinity studies to the removal of everything but parables from the curriculum in "The Pearl," and it constitutes still another covert reply to Baconian empiricism. Unfortunately, if one assumes that complete knowledge of the text is as desirable as "H. Scriptures 2" suggests, one assumption contradicts the other: one cannot settle for a bold doctrine on one occasion and pursue all the ramifications of all the verses to their ultimate disunity on another. In "Divinitie" Herbert points to the minimum that is necessary for good behavior and salvation—love God, love your neighbor, watch and pray, do as you would be done unto. That is quite another matter from relating Deuteronomy to 1 Kings, and Exodus to Matthew. "Faith" in this context is exasperated with reason and has as its target not a foolishly questioning astronomy or chemistry, which a student of divinity can put aside in good conscience, but a venturesome love of Scripture's own anecdotal diversity. When Herbert talks of "sucking every letter" ("H. Scriptures 1") he is not apparently translating it into something like "reading every chronicle," or if he is he means reading every chronicle allegorically. The "*masse / Of strange* delights" does require emphasis on each component, on its size and oddity, but not necessarily on its quite different enticements to intellectual curiosity and historical scholarship.

The speaker of "H. Scriptures 2" also wishes that he "knew" all corners of the text, which necessarily means many concerns of the Hebrew culture and history that bulk out the story of the Exodus, the monarchies, the Exile, and the ages of the prophets. But he knows that he does not personally have to know everything, and "knowing" undoubtedly means having mastered the art of translating it as Augustine specifies. In that much, "H. Scriptures 2" is more compatible with "Divinitie" than "H. Scriptures 1" seems to be. Reading Scripture is therapeutic because its lessons can be translated, through typological programs, into applicable patterns. The "mass" "makes a full eternity," or will eventually, once the method has finished its work. The Bible is "heaven's ledger" in the sense that anything recorded anywhere is duplicated in a Book of Judgment that misses nothing and in the additional sense that in going beyond the literal story it prefigures heaven itself, being the "handsel" or pledge. "H. Scriptures 2" thereby moves up a notch in interpretive technique from local explication to structural configuration. Even so the word "secret" points up the difficulty of digging out all the applicable principles. Herbert seeks to solve that difficulty by moving from the plenitude of lights and broader questions of curiosity to the speaker's place within the whole, a simpler though by no means problem-free matter. An octave/sestet division of sorts marks the transition from general principle to personal application.

The chief problem that this leaves unsolved we can see in the sliding expectation and the half-concealed dialectic between two reading purposes. The speaker begins by wishing for a key to all verses; the third quatrain then turns the matter of likeness around and uses the familiarity of the speaker's life to interpret certain passages. Those passages then supposedly feed back into the life and interpret it more fully (Bloch 9–12; Stewart, *George Herbert* 67). But such a reading principle, besides being circular, is in some danger of getting snared in a dilemma: in trying to apply the whole to the part, anyone who sees the configurations of glory does not need to read further, having already extrapolated the whole; anyone who does not see the whole cannot know for sure that the text contains one. The dilemma is similar to that of accommodation as A. D. Nuttall puts it: an interpreter who already knows the sacred truths that need figural adjustment doesn't need that adjustment; one who cannot know those truths directly (because they are mysteries) cannot grasp them through accommodation.

The difficulty as Bacon sees it in *The Advancement of Learning* is that the source of revealed wisdom is supposed to be unified but appears not to be. Using the same seamless-coat image that Herbert features in "Divinitie," he remarks that "we see the coat of our Savior was entire without seam, and so is the doctrine of the Scriptures in itself; but the garment of the Church was of divers colours, and yet not divided." Or to change the metaphor, "We see the chaff may and ought to be severed from the corn in the ear, but the tares may not be pulled up from the corn in the field" (*Works* 3.482). Criticism in reading does the separating that life in the field has not managed. But enigmas of the text that recites that life stimulate "curious questions and divisions," and so all the while obscurities pile up faster than they can be made to disappear. Bacon himself parodies the dark parabolic way in his quick tour of sermonizer tropes—chaff, corn, tares: "So, we see, the volumes of the schoolmen are greater much than the first writings of the fathers, whence the Master of the Sentences [Peter Lombard] made his sum or collection" (*Works* 3.483).

Although it is extracted from him not by profound intellectual concern but by a proposed rise in the cost of books, Herbert expresses a similar opinion in remarking to Chancellor Bacon, "Thou seest the multitude of books welling day by day, especially in theology, on which subject if the books were piled one upon another (like the mountains in old time), it is likely that they would climb up to that place to which knowledge itself appertains" (*Complete Works* 3.460). Bacon would apply much the same skepticism to things divine that he does to things natural, but he would also shore up the results and cut down the mountain of commentary by fideism: "And as for perfection or completeness in divinity, it is not to be sought. . . . For he that will reduce a knowledge into an art, will make it round and uniform: but in divinity many things must be left abrupt, and concluded with this: *O altitude sapientiae et scientiae Dei!*" (*Works* 3.484). We do not ordinarily expect Bacon to sound so much like Browne, but he does on this occasion because logic can never catch up to "the mysteries of the kingdom of glory, the perfection of the laws of nature, the secrets of the heart of man, and the future succession of all ages" (*Works* 3.485). Therein lies the secret to the brevity of compendious histories: it is too difficult to allegorize every detail of every local history, even for an Augustine. Sooner or later the industrious interpreter is tempted to turn to the simple truths of a streamlined history. Correspondingly, the churchman may on a given day be tempted to reduce the church basically to its main sacraments:

> But he doth bid us take his bloud for wine.
> Bid what he please; yet I am sure,
> To take and taste what he doth there designe,
> Is all that saves, and not obscure.
> ("Divinitie")

However, searching the same omniscient "inditer" in "H. Scriptures 2," Herbert realizes that finding *some* combinations among *some* verses does not add up to the complete story. Samson and David may resemble one another as liberators and rulers of their people, but that does not bind either of them to the antitype. The important question is how "in another" *can* one be understood when the focus returns to the inner self? Herbert asks the equivalent to that question with some urgency in "The Bunch of Grapes" and implicitly perhaps in "Josephs coat," where he brings the present retrospectively, and Hebrew chronicle by anticipation, into contact with the Crucifixion, always the crux of any compressing of events into the antitype and the invitation to "take his bloud for wine," wine not "thicken'd . . . with definitions." If secrets *were* to be truly "made good"—vouched for and brought from abstract pattern into example—they would no longer be secrets, and history would reveal its divine purpose not only in the end but moment by moment, verse by verse, and not only in sacraments but in the incidents of region upon region.

In questioning the connection of parts to the whole, Herbert leaves the individual reader pretty much on his own, since each begins with his own life and the dictates of personal experience. "H. Scriptures 2," like "The Pearl," mentions no third-party brokerage, although as a kind of teaching poetry, the poem and its companions recurrently coach readers in method. "H. Scriptures 2" sees no special difficulty in that, but to say that secrets are explicable complicates the initial metaphor of the constellations, even as the parallel between scattered scriptural verses and the poems of *The Church* complicates our sense of progress and connection in the collected Herbert. To see how Scriptures work, the poem advises us, observe the stars. By reading zodiacal signs and prophesying individual futures from them, astrology assumes that despite the variability of those born under the same sign we can identify patterns among them. But constellations are also very arbitrary memory charts, and to "make up" can mean not only "to compose" or "to predestinate" but "to invent." In any case, the use of the present tense in these poems stresses the ongoing labor of the reading as much as the underlying plan.

Or to follow Herbert's metaphors further, interpretation gathers this herb and that and then watches their interaction under concocting heat. Since the emphasis throughout is upon the reading of Scripture, presumably it is the reader who supplies the heat or finds the proper formula. The text lies open before us, but because the connected passages are scattered, it is up to us to search out the links. The materials are potentially catalytic, but they come together properly only if one applies the right procedure to them. "H. Scriptures 2" begins intransitively with "combine" and "shine" but is set astir in "marks" and the gathering energy of "make a motion" before it collects into "watch," which suggests "observe" but allows for chemical contriving as well. Altogether, even though Herbert would never concede a reader-*generated* order (as opposed to a reader-discovered one), he expects the interpreter to finish an exploratory task nowhere near as self-evident as it seems to be in "Divinitie." The stirring of these verbs is partly inward, molecular, and secret, and together they suggest something more active and inwardly dynamic than the "seemlesse coat." The words that find us out have to do some seeking also, but even as they come looking for us (carrying their parallels), we are led to wonder what would happen if the reader's eye were to alight on another set of herb-verses or to draw different connecting lines from star to star: would the potion still cure the same disorders, would the new constellations be equally valid? Or would some other self be discovered, and would it too make good the commentary by matching up with it? The Bible is obviously quite wealthy in detail, as not only "H. Scriptures 1" but Herbert's range of biblical allusions throughout *The Temple* testifies: do they all match a given reader's life? Stars may be visible and the action of herbs in some sense predictable, but their intelligibility and their curative powers are limited by specific transfers of given analogies. Or are all these teasing possibilities merely "curious questions and divisions" that, in the light of Hebrew's reduction of David and Saul and Abraham to moral exemplars, the doctrine "clear as heav'n" suppresses?

Finally the poem finds that holy verses are not stars at all. These verse-lights are really conductors along a pathway that directs personal narratives to the end. This suggests that the unfinished nature of the story and unwritten portions of the book are the real source of the interpretive problem. For that matter, how clear *is* heaven? How can its transcendence and ineffability be known? One cannot help thinking here as so often in the poems leading up to the concluding eschatological and sacramental ones of *The Church* that biding one's time in a suspended irresolution shored up by faith, as "Divinitie" and Bacon both counsel (and as Raphael cautions Adam), is an appropriate response to curiosity. This is an extrapolation on my part, not thematized in "H. Scriptures 2," but it is based on the open-ended nature of all apparent solutions to problems in *The Church* that turn out shortly not to have lasted. If problems were not persistent, the personas of *The Church* would make more evident progress and would not have to recross the Jordan so many times. "H. Scriptures 2" leads us back to the business of reading, waiting, and longing, which is as much the business of the deciphering as it is of the biblical teaching. The question boils down to what to do with a historical span that is always in the making and tied to the dispersal of Christocentric doctrine to the four corners of the earth to gather its global components, sent forward and backward to all chronicles and getting tangled in their strange mass.

The simplest lesson is in part that Scriptures are not meant to be applied to trivial incidents. The speaker's confidence in the last statement is the confidence of belief rather than of interpretive achievement. To know the end is to know the foremost thing and thereby achieve priority and subordination. Assuming the same to be true of *The Temple*, Herbert would not have grouped poems into constellations without implying a whole of some sort, but that ideal too many be elusive, despite the constellation of a few parts at a time and what I take to be a decisive ending. Again what it points to is the certainty of bliss and love, both eternal and far off. It is not, after all, the next world that Herbert seeks to bring within view (he offers very few concrete images of it) but the relation of this world to it and the mapping of the way.

Following "H. Scriptures 2" are several highs and lows that in retrospect make even its concluding couplet, qualified as it is, look prematurely confident. Herbert's episodes of parabolic wayfaring come upon very few resting places, none of them very extended. "The Flower" is typical: exchanges of frost and spring are unpredictable, however satisfying the current respite, and the desire for eternal bliss that marks "H. Scriptures 2" becomes so dangerous to one who tries actually to advance along the way (as opposed to merely foreseeing it) that it threatens to cost the speaker paradise. What Louis Martz identifies as sacramental plateaus in *The Church* (309) are no doubt justified, as is the perception of a structure that is "a harmony, flexible, abruptly shifting, and subtle in its composition as those enigmatic last quartets of Beethoven" (295); but we should not mistake plateaus for summits. The struggle continues well past "The Flower," and indeed all the way to the final poems. It continues to be in part a struggle to relate the individual to the biblical text. "Love 3" does so by the means that "Divinitie" predicts— by a reduction to basic teachings and the invitation to "take his bloud for wine." The ritual of the Eucharist temporarily suspends all problems in interpretation.

Where does this struggle in Herbert to read the individual life in the light of the fable leave the potential student of history and science? Are secular concerns also amenable to the fable when they can be made to point in the right direction? It is difficult to find any allowance in *The Church* for such secular supplements. Bacon's empire of learning, his reading of a diversified natural history, is to be put together piece by piece over an indefinite period; Herbert's single story is to be constructed in the present, as an immediate counsel in one's spiritual conflict, out of signs that cannot bring very much with them of the natural world and cultural differences that produced them. Although it would be an exaggeration to say that these two methods divide the seventeenth century, they do offer distinct ways of thought that over time become less and less compatible. The one charts an articulation of material knowledge with an open future; the other closes off time at both ends and subordinates nature to divinity and civil history to church history. Whether Baconian philosophy aims for probative, unsettling effects or for magisterial ones, the reality that the *Instauratio Magna* approaches can be phrased and understood only by those who take the proper precautions and even then not completely. The reality in which *The Temple* trusts is manifest only in a life fulfilled elsewhere whose very existence dictates what "beams of truth" one is to receive. "The Church Militant," which Stanley Fish rightly finds "pessimistic, inconclusive, and anticlimactic," keeps *The Temple* honest with respect to the way of the world in general (*Living Temple* 144); it will not take the lighted way toward "eternall blisse." *The Church* finds the productive spiritual work in preparation for sacraments to be a home industry based on "this book of starres."

In neither Herbert nor Bacon is religion ultimately compatible with that analytical instrument of reason—formal logic. If Bacon's last task in *The Advancement of Learning* is to separate these, almost the first thing Herbert has Christianity do in "The Church Militant" is invade the Greek academies and throw down philosophy:

> Learning was pos'd, Philosophie was set,
> Sophisters taken in a fishers net.
> *Plato* and *Aristotle* were at a losse,
> And wheel'd about again to spell *Christ-Crosse*.
> Prayers chas'd syllogismes into their den,
> And *Ergo* was transform'd into *Amen*.
>
> (51–56)

Bacon is not fond of syllogism either, which is partly why reason has little stake in a theology that must be authorized first and last by the Spirit. "Grounded only upon the word and oracle of God" (*Advancement* 209), divine truth is not available to investigation; "ergo" for him too must become "amen." All the more reason for him to consider divinity a less-enticing field, philosophy arid, and science the promise of the temporal future. Empire and arts are more than harbingers; they are the substance of the improved life that comes of applied learning.

For Herbert the future must squeeze through a different passage to arrive at "Death," "Dooms-day," "Judgment," and "Heaven." More than most, he justifies Kenneth Burke's definition of humankind as goaded by not only hierarchy but "terministic compulsion." It is "rotten with perfection," by which Burke means destiny-compelled, and determined to find entelechial closure (*Language* 19). The prospect of termination rekindles the desire for perfection at every discouraging point of the spiritual conflict in *The Church*. It converts lesser stages and alternatives into negatives, which increases the burden of Herbert's vocabulary. Nearly every ordinary word he takes up serves as a keyhole view of the sublime or gains some contact with it through the tropes I named earlier, chiefly metalepsis, aporia, catachresis, oxymoron, and prolepsis. The linguistic side of self-cancellation, followed by the return of what the "holdfast" keeps secure, is the cancellation of lesser meanings— regional, perhaps more precise, certainly more anecdotal—on behalf of greater, logocentric ones. This is the means by which hints of social situations, politics, learning, and nature are set in place to tempt our historicism, only to be redefined as lesser aspects of the spiritual story at the center. His enterprising scientists in "The Pearl," "Divinitie," and "Vanity 1" are caught in a bind. They are belittled by the futility of the analytic intellect and the bedroom tropes that liken their research to peeping atomism. They are crushed by the profounder research into divinity that Herbert turns against them. Perhaps they should have been parable-hunting all along and discovering the glory that is (and is not) signified by the pearl.

The additional point that "H. Scriptures 2" helps us see is that the selling of all one's lifetime gains to purchase that treasure parallels the reduction of biblical verses to the silk twist: Hebrew texts are to be no less allegorical in that reduction than the parables; they are merely less easily deciphered and applied. Study stars at your peril, "H. Scriptures 2" advises; only one book conducts and teaches and that one by the controlling doctrine of a few passages. How often Herbert says in one way or another, usually with conviction, wit, and metaphoric reach from the now of the saying to the concluding point of the fable,

> Lord, in my silence how do I despise
> What upon trust

Is styled *honour, riches*, or *fair eyes*;
But is *fair dust!*
I surname them *guilded clay*,
Deare earth, fine grasse or *hay*;
In all, I think my foot doth ever tread
Upon their head.

("Frailtie")

This renaming under catachresis and oxymoron ("fair dust," "guilded clay")
reverses the moral values ordinarily applied to these things, the subjects both
of poetry and of career pursuits. But being frail, one sometimes finds the
more customary meanings creeping back in:

But when I view abroad both Regiments;
The worlds, and thine:
Thine clad with simplenesse, and sad events;
The other fine,
Full of glorie and gay weeds,
Brave language, braver deeds:
That which was dust before, doth quickly rise,
And prick mine eyes.

Seeing these things "abroad" is to see them in the world, far enough out to
seem a splendid panorama to the eye, yet part of some local history after all.
It seems a glorious history to the mere eye, compared with the sorrowful
plight of the holy, whose chief event is always the Crucifixion. It is only right
that the glory-struck interpreting eye find these specks of dust assaulting it;
it is the wrong instrument to do the reading. Overcoming that frailty is the
chief goal both of spiritual conflict and of the renaming, under a grammar
and a semantics that are seated in the total fable. The hierarchy of knowledge
that results when faith guides the reading prompts the spiritual quest even as
an unreachable perfection empties it of the interim satisfactions of braver
language and braver deeds.

2

DIFFERENT SCHOOLS FOR HEART AND MIND

One day is with the Lord as a thousand years, and a thousand years as one day. The Lord is not slack concerning his promise, as some men count slackness; but is longsuffering to us-ward, not willing that any should perish, but that all should come to repentance.

—2 Peter 3.3–9

The way is none of mine.
—Herbert, "Dialogue"

Love Unknown and the Long Way

The extended interim between the First and Second Comings inevitably has collective as well as individual implications for anyone who makes a narrative of church militant as Herbert does, but a millenarian forcing of end things is neither his nor generally the Anglican way. Thomas Draxe's *Alarum* and sermonizers such as John Gee (*Hold Fast*, 1624), William Jemmatt (*A Spiritual Trumpet Exciting to the Christian Warfare*, 1623), and John Hull (*Saint Peter's Prophesie of These Last Daies*, 1610), in instructing their listeners in the manner of Peter's connection of "the end of all things" to "be ye sober, and watch," advise a collective wait that trusts more to Providence than to human institutions. Since with watching must come an opening of the individual heart, active spiritual cleansing constitutes the chief interim work. The question for the sacred poet is what falls to his lot that is not already better expressed in Scripture and empowered by the Church.

What is to occupy the suspended world is one issue, how it is to be understood and represented another. Here too Herbert and Bacon come down on opposite sides, Herbert devoting writing to the reform of the heart, Bacon to the advancement of the intellect. Both are narrative-driven in the sense that movement through the interim must be an active work even if the end itself lies beyond human influence. Bacon's account of the reigning story in "A Confession of Faith" (*Works* 7.215–26) puts the investigation of nature within a concession to the study of divinity. Nature itself falls into four ages: the precreation stage of unformed matter; an interim of created perfection and the establishment of natural law; a curse that deprives it of "part of the virtue of the first creation" (221); and still to come, the world after an end "the manner whereof is not yet revealed." God exercises himself in two ways, as a providential will in "all things great and small, singular and general" without violating nature's laws, and the continuous work of redemption, to which are devoted not only grace but also miracles and special signs.

Because nature's order was begun by God, study of it can reach a termination by those who are committed to improving the life of the interim:

> Now in divine operations even the smallest beginnings lead of a certainty to their end. And as it was said of spiritual things, "The kingdom of God cometh not with observation," so is it in all the greater works of Divine Providence; everything glides on smoothly and noiselessly, and the work is fairly going on before men are aware that it has begun. Nor should the prophecy of Daniel be forgotten, touching the last ages of the world:—"Many shall go to and fro, and knowledge shall be increased;" clearly intimating that the thorough passage of the world (which now by so many distant voyages seems to be accomplished, or in the course of accomplishment), and the advancement of the sciences, are destined by fate, that is, by Divine Providence, to meet in the same age. (*Works* 4.91–92)

That this age of completed study is approaching is one of Bacon's (inconsistently) recurrent hopes: "This road has an issue in the open ground and not far off" (*Works* 4.366). Or as he remarks near the end of the preface to the *Instauratio Magna*, one is not "to imagine that this Instauration of mine is a thing infinite and beyond the power of man, when it is in fact the true end and termination of infinite error" (*Works* 4.21).

This hope for termination is reflected in Bacon's recurrent language of endings (in *Valerius Terminus*, for instance), even as he figures the search itself as the finding of a clue to the labyrinth or stages of an upward advancement, in the "just scale of ascent" (*Works* 4.97). It is a work that can be accomplished by the application of intellect despite the Fall, provided that the scientific establishment takes the proper precautions. The gifts of grace pertain mainly to the fourth and final state, "the time of the revelation of the songs of God" (*Works* 7.226). Meanwhile, the study of nature that acts of grace and Providence bracket is a secular enterprise. It has the weight of an apocalyptic ending only insofar as it is to be a completed *world* learning and will renew the instinctive powers of observation that Adam once possessed. As Bacon suggests in *De Augmentis* in assuring James I that he is himself not a combatant but a trumpeter preceding the battle, in this fight men will not cut each other to pieces but join in a united force brought against the "Nature of things," to "storm and occupy her castles and strongholds, and extend the bounds of human empire, as far as God Almighty in his goodness may permit" (*Works* 4.372–73).

Because Bacon frames the secular enterprise within the greater (revealed) matter of divinity and within first and last stages, which transcend natural law, all parts are to be connected to already-received systematic beliefs and laws, and no trope or figure in the rhetoric of the system is to be completely localized. Nor can rhetoric be kept distinct from philosophy. Bacon complains on several occasions that Socrates severed the two, leaving rhetoric empty and philosophy graceless. Clearly the Baconian project aims not only to recapture Adam's capacity to see and name the creatures and their properties but to restore the cooperation of truth and apt language, so that the discoveries of one mind can be communicated to others. Even single-word tropes, though they work with deviations from usage, presuppose the greater semantic field commanded by the great narrative within which natural history is to be fitted. They are not limited to the sentence or the composition but take in the entire scheme. Bacon himself almost endlessly revises and incorporates earlier works into later ones in the gathering of his greater project. No fragment of the opus can safely be excluded from the scheme first outlined in *Valerius Terminus* and later changed to the *Instauratio Magna*. In his idea of collaborative research and habit of sending unfinished works into what he hopes will be the collective stream of the new science, any work by any party may join with the enterprises of the allied sciences. If the hunt for Pan is a hunt for universal wisdom, no footprint-word in any part of the forest (the language is Bacon's) is to be kept to itself.

Bacon takes no step in the labyrinth without thinking about the origins he sketches in "A Confession of Faith" and the twofold destination he reinstates frequently in the always-collecting works—that is, the glorification of God's works and the practical betterment of the human condition. Returns both to adamic clarity and to the ancients are implicit in the move forward, so that natural history and the history of philosophy go hand in hand as we "shake out the folds of the intellect within us, and . . . draw forth the knowledge stored therein." That recovered wisdom also helps us "gain knowledge from without" (*Works* 4.423). The reason is that what the accumulated wisdom of the ancients, lodged in books and memory, gives us—especially in myths— are prenotions that help us cut off the "infinity of search," without which one "seeks and strives and beats about hither and thither as if in infinite space" (*Works* 4.436). Bacon would naturally like to avoid that endless wandering, which would mean coming to the world's end without ever nearing a summary wisdom.

It is on the value of the intellect that Herbert most obviously departs from Bacon, both in "Vanity 1" and in the chastising of "groveling wit" in "The Pearl." Although Herbert and Bacon share the assumption of a coherent fable with a definite beginning and end, and although Herbert too presupposes the interlocking of tropes and figures within that fable, he concentrates on the heart rather than the intellect and is recurrently troubled by the preeminence given to the latter. Indeed, in several poems he characterizes "wit" as one of the dangerous excesses. To Bacon the storming of nature's towers amounts to a second teleology intervening between now and the end, and it is a collective enterprise, albeit outside of Atlantis less a social one than something for a future Royal Society of scientists and philosophers. In contrast, Herbert's local narratives concern individuals laboring as individuals to be included in salvation, not in a collective order with institutional goals.

The strain on a spiritual pilgrimage that has so few social coordinates is evident in poems such as "The Pilgrimage" and "Love unknown," which are useful to illustrate several lyric/narrative principles—the conforming of the individual to the type, the elimination of secondary goals, and the service of local tropes not merely to the sentence or the poem but to the whole scheme entrusted to a unified Scripture. Like the scattered verses of "H. Scriptures 2," single-word tropes are "dispersed herbs" thrown into a recipe that becomes "a potion." "Love unknown" puts the softening of the heart into emblematic equivalents through three life-defining episodes (Clark 88–106; Dickson 118; Bloch 60–64), which it links to certain passages in both testaments and points toward a general pattern of spiritual reclamation. It crosses back and forth between doctrinally defined emblems and first-person experience in a way later taken up by Bunyan, a way which stresses not a one-time conversion but an extended series of assurances and renewed doubts and thus an ongoing spiritual labor:

> Deare Friend, sit down, the tale is long and sad:
> And in my faintings I presume your love
> Will more complie than help. A Lord I had,
> And have, of whom some grounds, which may improve,
> I hold for two lives, and both lives in me.
> To him I brought a dish of fruit one day,
> And in the middle plac'd my heart. But he
>   (I sigh to say)
> Lookt on a servant, who did know his eye
> Better than you know me, or (which is one)
> Then I myself. The servant instantly
> Quitting the fruit, seiz'd on my heart alone,
> And threw it in a font, wherein did fall
> A stream of blood, which issu'd from the side
> Of a great rock: I well remember all,
> And have good cause: there it was dipt and dy'd,
> And washt, and wrung: the very wringing yet
> Enforceth tears. *Your heart was foul, I fear.*
> Indeed, 'tis true. I did and do commit
> Many a fault more than my lease will bear;
> Yet still askt pardon, and was not deni'd.

On the grounds that "Love unknown" is too flatly formalistic to be personal, Rosemary Freeman rejects the suggestion of George Herbert Palmer that the poem's "cordial" fruit is Herbert's own offering of poems or in some way equivalent to the affliction poems. As a parable it is clearly broader than that. But the heart is no more emblematic here than it is in "The Altar," which is obviously meant to seem personal and does equate the heart with the poem-sacrifice it brings forth. Nor is the past-tense detachment of the speaker any greater than that of "Affliction 1," one of Herbert's more autobiographical poems. Clearly the "personal"—however we define it—

must eventually be included in the type without being totally eradicated. The difficulty lies in what "included in" means. One reason for the interpreter friend, who translates the narrator's episodes into moral principles, is to recognize recurrent patterns in what the speaker mistakenly thinks his own story. The technique of the poem is to narrate an episode and then moralize it, and then narrate another and connect the two, and finally to arrive at a spiritual regimen applicable to every day henceforth.

The first-person technique of the narrative causes spiritual education to be a painful experience, especially since for this speaker, as Richard Strier points out (*Love Known* 159–64), lessons are slow to take root and must be repeated. Although not as forward as the speaker of "Redemption," this speaker is still subtly aggressive in his expectations. The replies of his sympathetic friend reverse his initial readings, as the recipient of his offers has broken off the welcome he expects. In those summary replies the three incidents find their connecting logic, which reverses old sacrifices by the new covenant. The recognition of that often constitutes the chief interpretive work in Herbert's deciphering of anecdotal materials. The speaker is learning the way from Hebraic to Christian policies on the heart and the place of the love that intellect tries to make known through readings of its acts. In winding up from the incidental and somewhat puzzling circumstances of his ordeals to the wisdom statements of the friend, the incidents follow a startling pattern of divine-human intersections that convert incidents into sacraments. They reverse initial assumptions and present the mind with riddling emblems. "The Sacrifice" stages a similar progression, as each moment of the passion intensifies the bitterness of Christ's tormentors and winds up his grief "to a mysteriousnesse." The mysteriousness here imitates the painfulness of the Crucifixion but breaks in as corrective therapy rather than as a response to the governing motives of Pharisees and Romans busy about their historical works.

The friend moralizes, but the speaker goes on to other episodes as though nothing has happened. After the first incident—a kind of minimal unit for allegorizing in its beginning, middle, and end—he brings the unreformed impulse into the present telling with "I did and do commit," the present of all malformed hearts. He has been both presumptuous and slack. "One day" in the quotation above sounds as though he came to his decision on a round of visits, and only accidentally does he stumble across the cauldron in the second incident. He does not set out on the sort of urgent search that Vaughan undertakes or that Herbert's own more self-propelled wayfarers do in "Peace" and "The Pilgrimage." Yet his discoveries also seem planted in his way, as though their scheduling and their purposes came if not from him, then from a comprehensive plan for spiritual encounters. Not only are fruits, poetic or otherwise, of no importance in those encounters, but the heart itself is incapable of its own cleansing, or in this case even of realizing the results of cleansing. The speaker can never be free of puzzlement and backsliding as long as he is bound to the law. His dilemma is much like Andrew Marvell's in "The Coronet" in offering flowers ("My fruits are only flowers"): unless he makes the offer, he will find no alternative, but in changing to a devotional phase he only exposes his own presumption. Whereas a penitent Marvell suggests that his flowers be trampled underfoot (humbling the offering without Herbert's sacramental cleansing), the speaker's fruits here are rejected outright.

With the heart on the dish, the skeletal fable passes into an allegory that stresses the speaker's subsequent reflections and guided interpretations. Unlike biblical parables, the telling does not draw upon omniscience; it merely imposes a second perspective on the speaker's, a perspective that weaves the poem into the design of *The Church* but also leaves a residue of questions about the three incidents. How effective is the administration of torments? Who are the several parties? Whoever is responsible for these parabolic materials, they clearly draw upon biblical tropes that assume the cleansing power of the new sacrifice.[1] The speaker gives us the primary episodes, and the poet puts spiritual authority to work to provide parallels and design. It is he of course who controls the release of knowledge, allowing the ignorance of the narrator to play out before the friend turns the incidents around for another view. The technique is a familiar one in Herbert's establishing of links between an eventful personal story and paradigms into which it is incorporated.

Not only here but in poems such as "The Holdfast," "The Collar," "Hope," and "Affliction 1," events and surmises about them are first seen through the limited but expanding perspective of the speakers, then either through a surfacing new awareness or a second voice. Herbert is thus able to adjust the focus and bring a broader spiritual context into view without

---

1. The question of authority applies to biblical texts as well, but Herbert would not of course have raised it seriously. The stature of a Moses or a Daniel is measured by privileged receptions of foreknowledge, but as Robert Polzin remarks in *Moses and the Deuteronomist*, "If the path to God is through Moses, the path to Moses is through the text's narrator" (27). The writer sometimes seems to know even more than the patriarch, yet remains anonymous in many cases. Omniscient narrative is necessary for a number of reasons, not least of which is the imposing of unity on the joining of texts by subsequent redactors undertaking to interpret quite diverse materials and point them toward the present.

foregrounding himself. In "Love unknown" getting to know love depends on the deciphering of emblems he finds in familiar biblical places. The first-person technique is thus more or less a grammatical convenience that veils the recurrent teacher of *The Temple*, whose story-telling method is a homiletic device for the interim work of reforming the heart. The wisdom of the friend's replies is inherited from a considerable line of authorities. The simplicity of "Love unknown" and of other homiletic poems (such as "Divinitie") loosens spiritual life from its individual circumstances while focusing on the overall testamentary location of the private heart. Whatever the final authority, it is often typicality, or the struggle to achieve it from within the personal experience, that interests Herbert. Basic instruction for its reform governs the spiritual vocabulary, and in that respect, "Love unknown" joins "Divinitie" and "The Pearl" in searching out an unmistakable wisdom that does not depend on human capacity. The great teacher "doth bid us take his bloud for wine," which will soften the heart whether the heart is ready or not.

As I suggested, the poet behind the fable becomes merely an assistant in that long-established school. For a heart not sufficiently moved by love, the friend becomes the assistant's assistant, giving instructions for reform, to be acted upon by a devout suppliant whose calendar henceforth, he says, must be filled with constant devotion:

> *The Font did onely, what was old, renew:*
> *The Caldron suppled, what was grown too hard:*
> *The Thorns did quicken, what was grown too dull:*
> *All did but strive to mend, what you had marr'd.*
> *Wherefore be cheer'd, and praise him to the full*
> *Each day, each houre, each moment of the week,*
> *Who fain would have you be new, tender, quick.*

This summary application of the marring/mending fable balances current affairs of heart with a program for renewal that anyone could be advised to follow. It fills the hour with tenderness and the moment with quickness. The adjectives fit the emotions better than the intellect. Shifts in pace mark the discrepancy between the original narrative—sprawly, casual, incidental—and this spiritual revamping, which boils enterprise and time down to a ritualizing residue. It is ruthlessly efficient, as "Divinitie" and "The Pearl" are in voiding the circumstances of the labyrinth. As the final lines change the quatrains to a couplet and as the threefold run makes a quick pass at "all time," other motives are squeezed out. Talk of preferment and leases belongs to the clan of Bunyan's By-ends; a Christian who wants to know the unknown love must understand the Lord's curt behavior and the odd language of font, cauldron, and thorns, all accommodative substitutions supported by parallel figures. The series "New, tender, quick" sweeps aside any lingering self-satisfaction in the manner of the servant throwing the desire-ridden heart into the rinse. The alliterated plainness belies the "long and sad" preliminaries and the attempts at ingratiation, as the quitting, seizing, and throwing have in rescuing the first awkward moment.

This quickened parallelism, which recapitulates scattered tropes and yokes them to the instructional purposes of the whole composition and its sources, is quite unlike such Hebrew doublet constructions as "Ye shall do my judgments, and keep mine ordinances" (Leviticus 18.4), or other reduplicative biblical narratives. The parallels of "Love unknown" are summary and parabolic: each collects a model episode and applies it to a fault. Recuperation has nothing to do with living up to judgments and ordinances that might crystallize out of real historical incidents and be versified in wisdom literature. What remains old, hard, and dull cannot be salvaged. Whereas biblical rewards are sometimes commanded by service and apportioned to it, rewards here come regardless of the length or quality of service. Grace transcends its conditions, and even its celebrational dimension does not really emerge from the incidents themselves. The abruptness of the responses effectively stops whatever momentum the speaker's ledger of complaints has generated.

The speaker remembers everything exactly, not only because the emblems are stark and the precedents familiar but because of the efficiency of pain, "the good cause" of detail in many of Herbert's simulated biographies. The difference in better moments is access to the satisfying explanation that the friend supplies and the implication that the speaker may already be among the elect if the Lord takes such pains with him. That the three phases yield to such exact parallel statements is itself encouraging in suggesting that devotional life can be ordered by the font, cauldron, and thorns. The fourth member of the sequence, *"All did but strive to mend, what you had marr'd,"* puts a seal on the procedure. The diction is lively even for Herbert, and no less so for the placing of "mending" tropes within the large-scale enterprise of redemptive work, initiated by Adam's marring and completed by Christ's mending. Neither the Lord nor the narrative allows any flourishes, despite the exploratory meander of the speaker's erroneous life. The poem names spreading and expatiation only to account for the growing "callous matter" the heart has accumulated. That all scores have been paid says enough without an itemized list or an example of the words that lips spell.

In this much one can seemingly account for Herbert's integration of the three-phased narrative into a devotional pattern without much concern for doctrinal fine points. But two matters suggest that Herbert is also keeping an eye on certain theological disputes and perhaps has chosen a parabolic method because it is less distracting. One is the lack of priestly mediation; the other is communion as a gift of grace. Only the friend's assistance is required to translate the incidents into homilies, and we've no indication that he belongs to what Bacon describes as the ministry either of the "inward anointing" or the "outward calling and ordination of the Church" (*Works* 7.225). The moral preparations of "The Church-porch" and the reserving of the communion feast for the last poem suggest a similar need for purging. The Lord's reactions could point to specific moments in Christ's ministry, but sins do not come forth that sacraments may flow as they do in "The Sacrifice"; they come forth that their motives might be plucked out and the heart scourged. That grace Herbert touches on frequently but unfolds definitively only in "Love 3," the poem that concentrates on the fullest knowing of love through individual instruction and sacrament.

Banishing excess in both temporal life and poetic style binds word tropes to narrative and at times in *The Church* sets the simplifying heart against the ingenious head. The link between plainness and renovation is clearest in the recurrent struggle of Herbert's speakers to subject the one to the other. Whereas the work of the intellect is routed through the book of nature, the corrected heart desires to get to its goal quickly. Any other attachment is a digression. The speaker of "Paradise" is a good deal more positive about that simplifying renovation than the speaker of "Love unknown." I turn to it briefly here for its reduction of personal growth to a vocabulary of spiritual essence that seems pertinent to Herbert's desire for the short way and capacity to summarize it lyrically. Its biographical element is reduced to the pruning that the Lord himself applies in preparation for the quite different fruitfulness to come, in what amounts to another version of the holdfast principle: surrender of the self now will expand its glory later. It is a surrender that Bacon's intellectual progress does not require and in fact precludes. (Although Bacon speaks frequently of offering more "seeds" than actual "fruits," a figure in keeping with his being a trumpeter-herald to the battle proper, that is a postponement of fruits still to ripen, not a policy of self-denial.) Again nothing that looks like an institution intervenes between the speaker and the Christlike friend: their relationship goes through neither formal observances nor phases of realization and nothing like the baptismal phase of "Love unknown." Meter and the regularity of rhyme are all the ritual the poet requires as he makes his own written rite (and visual righting) of what is wrong. The speaker has already decided what he needs, and the poem cooperates by making a visual demonstration of it, ending:

> When thou dost greater judgements SPARE,
> And with thy knife but prune and PARE,
> Ev'n fruitfull trees more fruitfull ARE.
>
> Such sharpness shows the sweetest FREND:
> Such cuttings rather heal then REND:
> And such beginnings touch their END.

In reducing personal reformation to diagrammatic brevity and finding the last rhyme implicit in the first, "Paradise" preserves essential fruit even as it shrinks excess "treeness"—or the growth of living and working. The progress of the individual relies not on any pattern of internal development or on ways to salvage a useful life, merely on what the personal pruner does. If the beginning is comparative luxuriance, the end is a full harvest. Responsibility for salvaging a minimal self lies strictly with the kind gardener. Giving advice to such a friend may be presumptuous, but it allows the speaker some measure of self-maintenance and a semblance of wit to match the art of the knife, which John 15.1–2 applies to all who would produce fruit. A moderate pruning is better than either total rejection or excessive luxuriance. As the poem's words shrink away, they reduce excess lettering to what can render the essence of paradise (where the first parents ate fruit and did their own pruning). As Kathleen Swaim points out, the poem is circular in having the end return to that beginning (26) and thus reflects the cycle of paradise lost and restored that brackets the greater fable. The rhyme words "pare" and "rend" are sandwiched between the comforting ones. The first two lines of each tercet are fully implicated in the world of process and change; only the conclusion reaches timeless being.

Some of the paradoxes of the Jordan poems and Herbert's other declarations on behalf of plainness show in this witty display of cleansing. Words do the showing and illustrate the effects of friendly intervention. As Swaim remarks, "God's lessons are everywhere visible in Herbert's world, and the poet's proper duty is to copy them rather than press the claims of his own ingenuity, to achieve reflection or echo rather than self-imposition upon language, reality, or God himself" (29). But the distinction between explicitly and implicitly pressing claims is a fine one, and to show the wit that is chastised and pared away is one way of making it. Little time elapses between the proud moments of wit and the humble pruning. An earlier line, "Inclose me still for fear I start" asks for protection against upstart motives, against one's own breaking out of control. But emphasis shifts from that initial first-person forwardness ("I Blesse thee, Lord, because I grow") to these concluding hints as to how the Lord might soften a severe judgment.

Avoidance of detail has the advantage in "Paradise" of concealing the authority behind wisdom statements, which here approach proverb through riddle. The speaker says nothing about how often the gardener takes this way; he merely acknowledges in "when" that he sometimes uses other methods, perhaps left for the greater book of deeds and divine miracles to describe. A list of what exactly the friend prunes would give us a better idea whether or not reason would approve, but it would also increase the complaint and proliferate the verbal foliage. Would such a list of sacrifices include, for instance, songs of praise? The ways of learning and honor? Works of charity and the daily duties of the priest to the temple? The desire to serve? Whereas the speaker of "The Pearl" knows the rate and price of the pearl, the speaker of "Paradise" does not regret whatever is necessary. If temporality was never meant for personal accumulation, one should no more lament such losses than a peach tree should lament its pruned limbs. The shearlike clicking into place of the rhymes demonstrates the least painful way. "Fractures well cur'd make us more strong," as "Repentance" says. Eventually getting more into the pruned self is the goal, wherein lies the deft touch of the pruning and the paradox of Christian self-making by self-sacrifice and conformity to the antitype's sacrificial pattern. Such an end, which returns to the luxuriant fruit of paradise, would remove the sting and in retrospect show time to have been full even when it seemed a shrinking to be endured.

Despite the efficiency of the endings of "Love unknown" and "Paradise," we cannot help noticing a contradiction between the ingenious acts of parable-making and the denial of the motives that produce those acts. Questions of authority, intellect, and less-than-omniscient points of view are further clouded by that contradiction. Although the condition of the heart comes foremost, the contributions of wit and artfulness—which theoretically do not assist the heart's reclamation any more than wanton growth or misled offerings do—fill the demonstration. A similar predicament troubles the elaborately witty denunciations of wit in the Jordan poems and "The Fore-runners" and underlies the tension between excursions through biblical verses in "H. Scriptures 2" and the bare story told without elaboration or disguise. This tension shows also in the residual stubbornness of single-word tropes and puns that are never quite subdued, which in some ways parallels the resistance of actual Hebrew anecdotes to the attempt in the Epistle to the Hebrews to reclaim them. The truth is sparingly uniform and moves through well-marked stages, but if simplicity of heart takes one way, ingenuity threatens always to take another and much longer route. The problem is not so much circuitous argument or excessively ingenious metaphor as simply the particularity of instance and vividly grounded trope. Those who cherish these can be chastised, but ground-level language and colloquial idiom keep coming back as part of the unavoidable substance both of experience and of poetry.

Herbert uses several tactics to undermine the cleverness he depends on in poems such as "Paradise," perhaps none of them more deftly than the self-parody of "A true Hymne":

> He who craves all the minde,
> And all the soul, and strength, and time,
> If the words onely ryme,
> Justly complains, that somewhat is behinde
> To make his verse, or write a hymne in kinde.

Awkwardness and brevity do some damage to the reputation of a versifier who requires the word "time" for his rhyme scheme and uses other fillers such as "in kinde" to keep the beat. As Arnold Stein observes, "The amusing incoherence of the stanza parodies the plight of the ambitious poet who starts with high resolution and finds himself hung up, forcing rhyme, splicing syntax, and barely staggering through" (7). Another kind of hymn perhaps lies in the mind's account of what the heart would have done had talent been there from the outset, but this effort hymn is not such an account. It craves all the mind but must settle for a crippled portion forced into a limping gait. Or to phrase it differently, it is a defense of mindlessness carefully staged by an ingenious mind. One part of the trained poet knows what is required; a less ambitious side thinks that it doesn't matter.

The most important countermotive is always love, whose residence is the instructed if not fully reclaimed heart. By some standard, the verse might be better if it were not scant and the wit not absent, but these shortcomings are eclipsed by the final word: "As when th'heart sayes (sighing to be approved) / O, could I love! and stops: God writeth, Loved." From a number of rebuked biographical complaints we recognize the abrupt halt to urgent desire, which carries through certain stages only to be brought up against an event that seems to meet it with a prepared delivery. The intellect quickly arrives at the end of its short tether. Who can say whether the wish triggers divine intervention, or, unable to find its way through to the right word, merely expires? The "as when" casts a hypothetical tentativeness over the writing of final words. Herbert nonetheless imagines a reciprocity between the offering of unripe, ill-shaped first fruits and the perfected final statement, which if it comes will be in response to the moved heart expressing its sincerest wish. While waiting for either that reciprocity or preemptive grace, the willing poet can define what a true hymn would feel like with its according of soul "unto the lines"; but the searching mind, with responsibility for tropes and for craft, remains distinct from the yearning heart, which, before it discovers the right formula, spends much time "mutt'ring up and down," like Astrophel pondering how to begin a sonnet sequence. That leaves the poet an opening to keep trying and yet plagues all efforts that go beyond simple confession. Meanwhile, the instances of "O could I love" continue to pile up in one form or another until a more representative but equally maladroit speaker finds himself beckoned by love itself and over his protests is charmed into receiving it. As in Bacon the end shapes and determines the interim works of intellect and interprets his tropes (the hunt for Pan, the labyrinth, storming of nature's tower), so love's rites consummate and reinterpret the tropes of *The Church*, Herbert's always-being-rewritten work of the heart.

Going Straight and Going Crooked: "Coloss.3.3"

Without necessarily taking up the busyness of wit thematically, Herbert's device poems put it on display and implicitly ask, "Is all good structure in a winding stair?" That question is also implied in passages that challenge the grandeurs of Babylonian splendor, Canaanite myth, and Greek epic. As Harold Fisch remarks, the countergenres of Isaiah, for instance, "seem to be directed against the 'high' poetry of the Canaanite texts," and "urge a reassessment of myth in favor of something more (literally!) down-to-earth" (3). This opposition Fisch finds quite properly parallel to Herbert's bidding farewell to quaint words and trim invention in the Jordan poems. Yet both the countergenres of the Bible and Herbert do so with conventional devices or elevation of their own: "The paradox is that these poems gain their power from the devices that they renounce" (Fisch 4).

The narrative of "Coloss. 3.3" can be viewed as a parallelogram; the bases are the life story and the master story, the ends are opposing head and heart. Where the Jordan poems deny outright the value of clever notions, "Coloss. 3.3" moves obliquely, marking both the graveward decline of all mortal life, and the second or hidden life, which, once extricated, "winds towards Him." But "once extricated" is the catch, because the body of the poem and its metaphoric maneuvering come as one piece with its biblical text. Unstated but implicit in the diagram is the reciprocity of both facets of the poem; one must descend to rise.

Besides simple and devious art, Herbert doubles nearly everything in the poem, words and notion, this life and that life, the title and the Pauline text that it cites, sun and Son, the horizontal lines of the poem and its slanted motto:

> *My* words & thoughts do both expresse this notion,
> That *Life* hath with the sun a double motion.
> The first *Is* straight, and our diurnall friend,
> The other *Hid* and doth obliquely bend.
> One life is wrapt *In* flesh, and tends to earth:
> The other winds towards *Him*, whose happie birth
> Taught me to live here so, *That* still one eye
> Should aim and shoot at that which *Is* on high:
> Quitting with daily labour all *My* pleasure,
> To gain at harvest an eternall *Treasure*.

The pairing of words and thoughts should make words transparent, beginning in a quick notion and becoming clear in the spelling out. Yet a notion is not a certainty but something more like a conceit subject to cleverness, as the prominence of the device confesses this one to be. Flirtation with form, it seems, is inseparable from the teasing thought of paradise, as the delights of artistry play harbinger to a distant magnitude. Death must after all be the chief harvester, and among what it harvests are the figures of the poet's verbal agronomy. Through that dark gateway, the notions, however skillfully manipulated, offer only a foreboding of "him in whom." The chief tropes are thus not metonymic substitutes, such as "sun" for "Son," but combinations of anticipation, leaps, and cancellations that suggest Herbert's frequent difficulty in joining life-as-lived to the paradigmatic story.

Whereas "A Wreath" makes the divine way straight and the poet's way crooked, Herbert proposes something less evident here. The horizontal lines narrate a basic affair of flesh; the slanted poem follows the biblical corollary. Both are to a degree figured or contained in the sun, for the allowing of which Herbert in "The Sonne" blesses the ambiguities of English. That each substantial word of the slanted statement comes later in successive lines makes for a visual climax to go with the acceleration toward the lower end of the poem. The poet issues the horizontal lines more or less on his own; the authority for the slanted extra sentence is Paul. Yet the slanted line does not particularly strain the shared words, which are stressed or unstressed the same in each reading and have basically the same meanings. But when *my* uncouples from *words* and joins *life*, it hooks onto a quite different noun, the first an expressive means, the other the thing itself as offered by the Son and testified to by the apostle. The speaker thus has several tasks—the quitting of the world, the gaining of the hidden life, the deciphering of sacred texts— and all of them come up against the paradox that the more one holds onto the fruits of life the more one denies the eternal harvest.

Unfortunately, that eternal harvest is only partly knowable through familiar images. As the poem has sometimes been read (Wood, "A Reading" 22–24; Miller 116; Bloch 21), the formal statement is reinforced, not reversed, by the conceits. Or perhaps a better way of saying it is that the conceits illustrate one statement while veiling a second. Life does move toward the invisible gradually, within the visual images. The sun's seasonal motion is less visible than its daily one; the latter we can sight minute by minute, the seasonal one only month by month. At one level of logic, the sureness of the sun in both its movements guarantees the heavenly kingdom. But the hidden life cannot be marked finally by either a daily or a seasonal clock, any more than eternity can be gauged by a dial or calendar. The distinction between concrete experience and the intangibles of faith is the source of the difference, which prompts readings that stress the self-sacrifice implied by the "treasure" (Bloch 34–36; Fish, "Letting Go" 203–7). Eternity has a name but no means of disclosure. Hence the second or oblique movement prepares for the sun's yielding to the Son, much as the daily returns of pleasure are denied by Paul's stern message to the Colossians not to touch, taste, or handle the rudiments of the world, since all perish who do so.

These doublings and cancelings reinforce Herbert's general distrust of things temporal even where they yield hieroglyphs and emblems. In addition to them are the less prominent ones that the slanted sentence unfolds. "Life" and "treasure" bracket it and are linked by the repeated *is*. The middle pivots on "in," the "placing" word of *In flesh*. Life is wrapped up *in* the one but winds *toward* the other. It may be accidental that the first *Is* is unstressed and more or less serves *straight*, whereas the second one is stressed and makes its assertion by serving *on high*. In that respect, the second level does not merely circle back but runs up and away while seeming to run down. Although the possessive is repeated (it is *my* life *my* treasure), the second one is less firm, as life passes from the speaker to the holdfast. "Treasure," the final and most critical word and the only two-syllable word in the oblique line, offers us perhaps the best estimate of Herbert's implicit defense of cleverness as a springboard for the leap beyond it. If treasure, the point of the fable, were not so prominent we might suspect anxiety over the canceling of life by this deconstructive slash through the center. But the poem's movement is toward the greater as well as toward the absent "fruit." It carries from ordinary narration (the story of a life leading to death) to celebration.

That movement becomes clear when Herbert assigns the lesser word "pleasure" to the readier rewards of the sun and changes the adjective from "my" to "eternal," a shift that both prevents possession and escalates into high praise. At the same time, like other words situated both horizontally and obliquely, "treasure" is heralded by mortal pleasures and thus by everything that precedes, both horizontal and slanted. It completes meter and rhyme and telescopes all readings into a single trope, at once the poem's vaguest and most promising. It is a metaphor both locally operative as a misnomer and useful to establish links with other end-oriented poems and their chief parent texts. The pressure it applies to the poem's other tropes is designed to prevent them from being merely witty turns of phrase. It honors the sun/Son play, for instance, and yet undoes the likeness, since this "harvest" is beyond diurnal measurement, just as the treasured "pearl" is similar to, and yet radically different from other pearls that merchants buy and sell.

Perhaps the most fundamental question the poem raises is whether the canceling slash includes that final trope or stops with it. Somewhat smuggled into it is the assumption of an earned payoff that challenges Calvinist doctrine (Shaw 73–74). But it is not clear whether the true-sighted speaker garners treasure by self-denial or merely negates his own industrious work, and then the treasure comes regardless; "to gain" doesn't speak to the issue very fully, as "to earn" or "to get" would have. Ordinarily "treasure" would mean a heap of good things, but as an eternal reward, it goes well beyond any imaginable store. It carries both the Pauline authority that promises the treasure to the Colossians and the insubstantiality of faith in its final state, the manner whereof has not yet been revealed. Virtually every earthly thing hangs on it, since if it does not exist, not only does eschatology collapse but along with it all plotting and angling toward it. In "Heaven," Herbert pauses before "Love 3" and the closing of *The Church* to list certain features of that treasure, including joy and leisure. In "Prayer 1" he adds other abstractions, the word "bliss" among them, a word he uses critically in several poems. But these are not very concrete and do not pretend to be turns of phrase. The prospect of treasure unquestionably remains a happy one, but the greater the hope the more it cancels in the downward life, including, in Paul's list of discards, all philosophies and intellectual traditions. Given that blanket denial of secularity in Herbert's source, not only Bacon's kind of interim progress but all civil and perhaps even evangelical projects become relatively insignificant.

Affliction and Answers

Next to his extraordinary command of common idiom, Herbert is perhaps most impressive at realizing the twists and turns of rebellion against the spiritual discipline and costs of denying the motives that make the Baconian and courtly worlds go around. Answers are not usually as programmatic as the friend's counsel in "Love unknown" or as neatly packaged as the two diagram poems "Paradise" and "Coloss. 3.3." The ending is often the turning point of an ordeal whose next stages are left unexplored. The turn may be a chastisement that finishes a complaint without quite placating the questioning mind, whose doubts about Providence are answered not by reason but by command. Anthology readers are usually offered "The Collar" as an example, and it is a good representative of both the folly of petulant self-promotion and Herbert's reluctance to go beyond a timely correction that realigns the individual life and the fable, or at least the heart's portion of it. The heart may find closure; the mind cannot, since the former may host the spirit and love and the latter must always be engaged in searching out the design and its remote purposes.

The voice that interprets the speaker's grievances in this case, however, is the voice not of love but of authority, and it reinstates momentarily forgotten obligations of servant to master, one of the tropes that Herbert uses to link both figures and poems to the ultimate resignation of "Love 3." It does so without asking for the signs that the Lord's servants demand in undertaking service (in Moses, Joshua, and Gideon, for instance):

> as I rav'd and grew more fierce and wilde
> At every word,
> Me thoughts I heard one calling, *Child!*
> And I reply'd, *My Lord.*

What precedes this surrender is typical anguish over the lack of rewards that might signify a worldly providence and apply a cause-and-effect logic to daily life. That Christ received worse treatment in the passion is a telling reproach in some of Herbert's assessments of tribulation, but it is not expressly mentioned here. The poet has had to sacrifice both the recognition and the flourishing—both laurels to crown his effort and garlands to adorn it. An entirely different second self chastises the one who wants such things. In terms of the characters who voice Herbert's narratives and enter at the turns, they are equivalent to the insertion of powerful tropes capable of reversing pleasure or "redemption," or other things mistaken for pay.

Herbert explores several patterns of straightening out and rededication besides these preemptory and paradoxical ones. Turned toward public opinion rather than the Lord's judgment but just as defensive in its awareness of a career choice that produces no cordial fruit is the odd poem "The Answer," which refuses to make a formal turn at all after seeming to promise one. Instead, it skids to a stop before the metaleptic leap we come to expect of Herbert's endings:

> My comforts drop and melt away like snow:
> I shake my head, and all the thoughts and ends,
> Which my fierce youth did bandie, fall and flow
> Like leaves about me: or like summer friends,
> Flyes of estates and sunne-shine. But to all,
> Who think me eager, hot, and undertaking,
> But in my prosecutions slack and small;
> As a young exhalation, newly waking,
> Scorns his first bed of dirt, and means the sky;
> But cooling by the way, grows pursie and slow,
> And setling to a cloud, doth live and die
> In that dark state of tears: to all, that so
> Show me, and set me, I have one reply,
> Which they that know the rest, know more then I.

The comforts that such a one seeks are demeaning, and their pursuit leaves a tarnished reputation. No news in that. The image of the shaken head and thrown-out thoughts is both effective and imprecise with its tree-image and its aging "leaves." It reminds us that one kind of metaphysical imagery crosses emblematic concretion with abstraction and overpowers a minimal imagery with philosophic commentary. The initial goals were not authentic ends, merely the gaining of comforts or their instruments. To bandy thoughts and ends is to rally with them as with tennis balls and to use cleverness against itself. A vigorous head-clearing sends rival activities scattering and makes youthful trophies into a discarded miscellany. A well-oriented career can then be taken up. The poem moves on past what often constitutes the first step in the autobiographical decision-making poems: the career is defined; the pilgrim sets off and after a while begins to ask, what now? To the parabolic mode it does not matter precisely what specific projects he undertakes, whether he chooses the life of a country parson, for instance, or the ways of learning or the ways of honor. Much of the mind's effort once applied to self-making goes into dispersing what is left of illusions and wrestling with paradoxes. In any case, parasite comforts that siphon off one's gains become things of the past.

"The Answer" pursues other matters besides that loss of bounty, but rather than dwelling on the elegiac note of "Repentance" and "The Flower" it turns to the change for the better and to the expectations it raises in onlookers. The speaker's critics have misunderstood what he himself is apparently still trying to understand. He and they alike should after all be heartened by the new dedication and the discarding of trivia and realize that the lack of subsequent prosecution is due to something other than momentary brilliance. The speaker grants some credibility to reports about him in the extended figure of a "young exhalation," a flighty version of the twist of silk. The word "pursie" matches "bandie" in its reduction of living process to folksy wisdom, or apparent wisdom, and it mocks the sagacity of those who wag their heads at the decline of their once up-and-coming friend. What has stopped his progress only seems to be a lack of spirit or failure of nerve. While he bandied he was one of them, as Job is one of the tribesmen as long as he exchanges wisdom with them; in what now seems a dispirited shadow of himself, he seems to have abandoned both his former values and his promise.

The interpretive difficulty is that if he *has* abandoned these, it is for a calling that lies somewhere within the hidden life and apparently has no visible bearing on what he actually does, which leaves his critics free to speculate. That comforts drop away *and* he shakes his head is obviously quite different from specifying a cause. It is certain only that he cannot assign a high priority to the conscious mind and has not come to any reasoned decisions. The loss of comforts may trigger the head-shaking, followed by a deepening realization of fierce youth's illusions, but even to say that and no more is already to imply a self-directed life and to provide a reply that the poem does not endorse. Where "Coloss. 3.3" explicates its own errant horizontal course with the help of the Pauline text, "The Answer" remains closer to genuine riddle. Its affinities are with the psalms and the obscure pronouncements of prophets, except that it drops omniscience and homily on behalf of interim stalling. A good deal of the poem after the ostensible reversal goes to paraphrasing the critics' misguided view, which is stopped for a witty retort that never arrives. That the speaker is still in transition brings on the failure to link his actual life to the works of faith he has endorsed. The mind has not progressed far enough in its analysis to allow the heart to engage its quarry. Clearly some further collaboration between puzzle-solving and desire is in order; one cannot love what one cannot know.

This answer that is no answer issues from within a rhetorical context that begins in plangecy and ends in puzzlement. One's critics are always more certain than they have a right to be. If the true life is indeed hidden, its invisibility contains both the promise and the enigma of the delayed second life. Only those who already know can know, and the speaker is not among them. The secrecy resembles that of Mark's parables in which the kingdom of God is rendered so that "seeing they may see, and not perceive; and hearing they may hear, and not understand" (4.12), which is a way both to have and to withhold omniscience. The ending depends on a distinction among degrees of certainty and the parties who speculate. It acknowledges the unanswerable question, "What happens to ambition once tangible goals are denied and a new goal is placed beyond the most energetic and wisely directed effort?" The apostles had the satisfaction of gathering a greater flock, which was their occupation. Once conversion narratives grow routine and evangelical fervor slacks, it becomes more difficult to tie personal exhalation to the collective course or to believe that history itself is making headway. Nothing about *The Temple* suggests that its speakers are on a mission to justify their being "eager, hot, and undertaking." "The Church Militant" renders a panoramic vision of a mission but places no real hope in it. Peter's justification of the interim between comings as the time of conversions is sometimes used in seventeenth-century commentaries on Revelation but is not exploited by Herbert, despite his interest in the Virginia Colony and the exportation of religion to the new world. Neither this speaker nor his critics can say what they know until they discover the relation between service and the end. The shedding of other desires is comparatively easy, and the skyward thrust is clear; the question is, what happens when one has to keep starting over again? Is the answer simply the recurrent story of Christian "progresses," an answer to the historical question that the absent Messiah generates by the key departure that Herbert locates in "Redemption" at the precise moment of "*Your suit is granted*, said, & died"?

We could probably provide other answers to the answer from round about *The Temple*, but the point of many of them would be equally baffling to the mind even where they bring the heart into line more firmly than "The Answer" does. "Affliction 1," for instance, realizes after much vacillation that service is none other than the heart's duty: "Let me not love thee, if I love thee not," which I have tried to explain elsewhere as a forestalling of further questioning and endorsement of the sincere heart (*Lyric Provinces* 132–36). The passivity of love's recipient in "Love 3" is qualified by a participatory ritual in "I did sit and eat." And of course "The Quip" and other retort poems put the thrust and parry of world and God in dialogic terms and expect at some point a decisive victory of one over the other.

The skepticism of "The Answer" argues a distinction between biblical omniscience, which sometimes comes in veiled form, and the certainty that must await the end. Interim certainty takes forms other than knowledge, such as sacramental assurance. That distinction is common enough in Herbert's mystery-oriented church, which depends less on a rationalized analysis of Scripture than the Puritans tended to do. We can glimpse something of what being caught between dulled perceptions and omniscience means in Donne, for instance, who provides a useful parallel to Herbert to contrast with the Baconian emphasis on progressive knowledge and ever-nearing union of natural history and revelation. As Donne puts it, the large difference between *nunc* and *tunc* belies the one-letter difference in the abrupt Latin and acknowledges that although the ministry has its ordinances, its knowledge is at best "but in part." *Here* we know the things of nature and of men directly but the things of God only *per speculum et aenigma*; *there* in the last phase whose manner is not yet revealed, it will be different: "He that asks me what heaven is means not to hear me, but to silence me; he knows I cannot tell him; when I meet him there, I shall be able to tell him, and then he will be as able to tell me" (*Sermons*, no. 23).

No doubt "The Answer" itself awaits some such moment without stating a principle to cover it. The speaker's reply is not that he knows nothing but that he knows less than some think he should and perhaps more than they think they do. What saves such limited knowledge from agnosticism is what can be known at least darkly, or in Donne's words: "So this sight of God, which our apostle says we have in a glass, is enough to assure us that a God there is." Donne actually assumes much more than that—such as that heaven too exists and that the church, Bacon's and Herbert's as well as his, is the delegated body for the founding and enforcing of ordinances. The suggestion of "The Answer" is that the speaker is subject both to the limits of knowledge and to the attraction of the unknown, even as he realizes that "it is impossible to love anything till we know it." The best anyone can do is to "shoot at that which *Is* on high," but "The Answer" backs away from even a minimal retort.

In "The Quip," a companion poem in many respects, the reply to antagonistic critics is more encouraging and the damage done to worldly troping comes closer to general havoc. After repeating confidently to a battery of charges *"But thou shalt answer, Lord, for me,"* with all the biblical echoes Chana Bloch finds in that phrase (16), the speaker backs away from demanding divine intervention without ceasing to expect it or predicting what it will accomplish:

> Yet when the houre of thy designe
> To answer these fine things shall come;
> Speak not at large, say, I am thine:
> And then they have their answer home.

Up to this point, the poem has proceeded as another life-story allegory that personifies the merry world's most tempting resources—beauty, money, glory, quick wit, and conversation. In an actual life, these could come in any order and no doubt one or two of them would repeat their visits to one's dying day. They keep stepping across the way in front of Bunyan's Christian or walk beside him and suggest that no stage of spiritual advancement is free of basic temptations, until, as Fish suggests in *Self-Consuming Artifacts*, the very idea of progress seems suspect; here the challengers and taunters are arranged as an abstract cross section of the best that the world has to offer. They all know how to turn a phrase as well as a profit. The final stanza switches to a climax different from the one heralded by the four refrains. Its answer awaits an unspecified time beyond the retort but is nonetheless set for *some* literal hour, when "I am thine" will announce the sacrificial gift of God to the sinner and herald the reversal of "Love 3." Herbert guarantees "the rest" as saints and angels know it. Like the answer of a patron to one's debtors, he capitalizes on a general parallel between the realm of manners and spiritual conditions. But of course, as is almost always true even in his strong closure poems, that reply is not actually delivered, merely anticipated; it shatters the resemblance even as it establishes it. When patronage is the Lord's, being taken under protection is as unlike anything in the usual round of exchanges as celestial treasure is unlike earthly pleasure. The poet is again reduced to coaching the dramatic entry of the Lord, anticipating a retaliation distantly akin to swordplay and the vengeance of YHWH.

"The Quip" is quintessential Herbert both in casting the human story in the form of a concise and idiomatic parable and in rendering what seems a complete story on one level while leaving everything up in the air on another—finished as a statement of faith but caught in duration. Also left unsettled is the office of the victim, either now or at the last moment. "Home" has the finality of "rest" but makes no pretense to understand either the plan or its timetable. "The hour of thy design" falls in the general category of the "at hand" of Peter's promised kingdom. It allows no midlevel axioms and gradual ascents. In this riddling mode Herbert puts momentarily out of mind other means of immanence and separates Christian vengeance from the interventions of the Lord of Hosts whose hand can actually be seen in the destruction of a Sodom or the wry afflicting of Philistine cities that pass the captured ark among them. Patience and provisional answers to the merry world take the place of usable wisdom and marked but always-temporary victories. We are reminded that the answer to Job, coming grandly out of a whirlwind, never justifies the trials the loyal servant has undergone; instead, it stresses power and the futility of anyone's trying to answer either the world's tribulations or its merry quips, which is why the mind must sooner or later be put in abeyance. This may seem extreme for the gentle "they have their answer home"—until we remember the conclusion to "Vertue," the answer in "Decay" ("all things burn"), Herbert's frequent apocalyptic concern, and the biblical mockery of those who, like Job, try to answer for themselves.

Twisted Courses: Intricacy and Confession in "Affliction 4," "Dialogue," and "A Wreath"

Stationed together in a sequence that makes a hopeful run through "Man" to "Antiphon 2" before pausing, "The Pearl" and "Affliction 4" are more circumstantially confessional than the poems I have just examined or than

"Love unknown." They are among poems of *The Church* that present a crooked course through self-assessment while throwing themselves on the simplicity of the contrite heart. They present formal tangles that seem to run against the interests of the devotional simplicity they imply or call for. Similarly, "Dialogue" and "A Wreath" present the detours and reversals en route to unconditional self-surrender.

Some of the questions that such poems raise I considered in discussing "The Pearl" earlier, but there Herbert marks the turn from that intricate charting with a decisive choice, "Yet I love thee," a reply of the heart to the manifold cleverness of the brain. In the other three poems—and they are typical—the formal entanglement does not come to anything like the vertical lift of the silk twist, which presents a solvable riddle to the decipherer of a parable that virtually explains itself. A residue of ambivalence clouds them even though it is clear where the heart should be. The decision of "The Pearl" is both wiser and harder than those of "The Quip" and "The Answer." As it turns out, the speaker's learning has no bearing on the main purchase, which the simplest, poorest man could make as well as the most astute scholar and courtier. Nor is learning how to climb the silk twist the same as actually doing so, any more than coaching the Lord's answers is the same as actually having them. Where attention falls on teaching and learning, the mind has more to do in assessing wit before the heart makes its crucial choice.

If "The Pearl" poses alternative and contrasting ways of self-deconstructing, "Affliction 4" reverses its assurance and poses a broken lyric of disturbances that result when the "elements are let loose to fight" and one can only call out psalmlike "Oh help, my God!" Both poems suppose that one's own labors are useless in the work of salvation and helpless before "powers, which work for grief" in "the space / Betwixt this world and that of grace." Daily living is mainly a torture to one whose thoughts

> are all a case of knives,
> Wounding my heart
> With scatter'd smart,
> As watring pots give flowers their lives.

Although these are internal matters that should fall under one's own surveillance if anything does, the speaker is ineffective against them, and the heart's roots have nowhere else to go for water; they receive their sustenance entirely from tears. Doubling the metaphors, Herbert first encases the heart among knives of thought and then plants it and waters it with a rain of remembrances and self-incriminations. The latter figure is especially complex in the light of Herbert's "Posie," "Life," and "The Flower" and their association of rhetorical flowers with poems. Recollection brings forth the stuff of such flowers, and poems would not grow without it; but they are also heart-shriveling tears that, in this compounding of figures, "wound and pink" the soul. All these figures are incorporated into a master trope of redemption, first by God's dissolving the "knot" between heart and head and then by his coercing the wounding powers to work for him, partly by changing complaint to praise:

> Then shall those powers, which work for grief,
>   Enter thy pay,
>   And day by day
> Labour thy praise, and my relief;
>   With care and courage building me,
>   Till I reach heav'n, and much more, thee.

The end as always is to reach heaven; the means is the use of the mind's powers, which now "work for grief," to "Labour thy praise." Where the restless mind continues to work against the heart, its "smartness" is scattered, and the smarter it is the more it smarts. "Nothing performs the task of life" or controls the fury of thinking too much and deciding too little. Whether or not the answer to a way that tosses pilgrims between hope and despair is an especially Anglican one, it makes a concession to the usefulness of gradually acquired inner strength. That it sounds trite suggests that Herbert feels his doubts and suffering more intensely than he does his comforts, or has simply arranged the poems to postpone the latter.

In any case, as I suggested earlier, he does not often dwell on the autumnal flavor of regretful recollection or heap it full of Keatsian earth-poem images. It amounts to acknowledged sessions with grief and self-mortification. Nearly all the personal past in *The Church* is afflicted, or a puzzling, random sequence of vernal and wintry seasons without much slow and savored passage through their decline. This too has the effect of removing transitions and seasonal balances, either of Keats's odic variety or Wallace Stevens's intricate dialectic. It cuts short the exchanges of imagination and reality. It is not finally the imagination at all that provides access to the cure for affliction but biblical scholarship and the reliving of the tropes it extracts from typological parallels and their culmination in the triumphant affliction of the antitype.

Perhaps because it evens out in the final stanza after a ragged course that gasps and churns through a stanza that can be flexibly rough or smooth, "Affliction 4" is the least satisfactory of the affliction and employment poems. It is conceivable that a stable mind could be built up by daily successes specifically in versing, which is probably what Herbert means by laboring praise and gaining relief. It is also conceivable that this would constitute a useful vocation after all, a prospect that better poems consider. The "till I reach" assumes such a progress, which could finish the self-construction at a logical point, when translation to heaven would come effortlessly. But as Bunyan's Christian discovers, the River of Death comes at a time not necessarily coincident with finished preparation. *Grace Abounding* too has what looks like definitive changes of heart followed by backslidings and hard-won renewals of assurance. Suspended in an indefinite duration, Herbert pairs "care and courage" as the chief building materials. Having begun with the recognition that he is "Broken in pieces all asunder," the speaker certainly needs the courage, but "care" could cover a multitude of things: dedication to a task, craftsmanship in the rendering of praise, the self-respect that comes of prolonged diligence, and care in devotions after certain powers have exercised their capacity to "pink" the soul. Whatever it is, it makes an uninspired contribution as it nestles down in rhyme that sounds uncharacteristically mechanical. Herbert musters some resolution in "Then shall those powers," but the conclusion to which he comes hovers between purposeful self-making ("until I've built myself up enough to warrant heaven") and waiting ("I'll keep at this until my time comes").

Perhaps the best contribution of such poems to *The Church* is to show the narrow room for compromise between the mind's industry and the all-or-nothing heart. In expecting gradual spiritual betterment, the speaker errs as far in one direction as the self-effacing speaker of "Dialogue" does in the opposite. The word "care" appears again in the estimation of worth that "Dialogue" comes to, but it adds up to nothing—"the way" being no part of the speaker's efforts, merely a name for a spiritual deprivation that lies beyond all accounting:

> But as I can see no merit,
>> Leading to this favour:
> So the way to fit me for it
>> Is beyond my savour.

> As the reason then is thine;
> So the way is none of mine:
> I disclaim the whole designe:
> Sinne disclaims and I resigne.

Here again one senses that these short declarative sentences have been mechanically fitted to the design of alternating rhymes, but in this case the very rapidity of the closed units carries a lively exasperation. It is the covenant-renouncing dismissal of a speaker thoroughly put out. The feminine near rhyme of "merit" and "for it" and the oddity of "savour" suggest a self-mocking belittlement that accords with the simplicity of word and syntax in "To fit me for it." The "way" shifts from "means" to *the* way. Punning on the abyss between his way and Christ's, the speaker finds the latter beyond his "savour" but obviously not beyond the "savior," another of Herbert's ingeniously twisted figures that cancels personal experience (taste on the tongue) with the key to the marring and mending history.

The rephrasing from "I" to "Sinne" for the subject that does the disclaiming uncovers what is often a doubleness of mood in Herbert. It shifts from something like helplessness to a hint of rebellion. Stiff-necked pride it is that wishes to command the way and go by merit. Sin takes up that aggression against the "whole design" gleefully, apparently pleased to find a function in the antiplot and a partner in conspiracy. An acknowledgement of grandeur in the scope of God's way accompanies its disclaimer, while the self gives up the effort to salvage respect in the face of providential mystery. Recognizing the partnership between sin and self and yet forcing them a little apart is perhaps a gain. It is the most the speaker can manage in a situation far beyond his scope. He cannot taste such a vast scheme and could never be content with Bacon's confession of it, which only serves to frame a belief to hang on the wall while the philosopher scientist goes about his work. That scheme escapes reason and human estimate—requisites for appropriate emotional coloration and "savour." On this occasion he doesn't yet gain a sufficient triumph of hear to overrule the insistent need for merited favor and knowledge of the design. Formal abruptness and impatience leave no openings for praise or even piety. The speaker is defined by his movement between hoping for recognition and an emotional conviction that comes with only love. Obviously, the moved resignation of the final gesture in "I did sit and eat" is not yet forthcoming in the resignation of "Dialogue." The rhyme hammers at the mine/thine distinction and the rising up of resentment in "I disclaim" before the revised statement modulates into a quieter rebellion.

The possibilities between a tormenting whole design and one that answers "home" or gives "rest" are numerous, but they all presume an interim whose turns require frequent rededication and something more than ritual and ceremony.

In the company of these moments of frustration, so nicely sculpted and timed by Herbert's colloquial mood shifts, poems like "Temper 1" and "The Flower" seem all the more impressive for their insights into the dilemma of those who would like to put their careers under their own management and act decisively but cannot do so. Those poems conclude with the discovery of new attitudes and a new patience. Unlike the speaker of "Affliction 4" their voices rise to the occasion after questioning the place of affliction and the very possibility of rendering praise. Unlike such illustrative parables as "Love unknown," they speak with a first-person emotion that suggests a greater overlap between Herbert and the speakers, something we obviously cannot assume in a poem like "Dialogue," despite its convincing imitation of exasperation on the rise.

In "Temper 1," rather than achieving the poetic exaltation that the regenerate heart would like, the poet is alternately raised up and cast down. He is stretched and contracted in a manner that defeats calculation but leaves him a middle region of "love and trust" to live in, between the high poetic pitch he would like and the plunges to hell he fears. The piety of "This is but tuning of my breast, / To make the musick better," like the moralizing last stanza of "The Flower," does not assume either permanent improvement or self-direction. It merely acknowledges the poet as an instrument. Both poems settle for a moderating attitude suitable to a suspended interim. The speaker salvages a partnership of sorts with God in "Thy power and love, my love and trust / Make one place ev'ry where." The equating of all times and places removes the need for spiritual exercises or a way that can be traveled. God contributes the most to their union, but the speaker contributes love as well as passive trust. That relative stability counteracts, without changing, the violent extremes of soaring with angels and collapsing into dust. The extremes belong to the world of daily projects and career courses; the newly balanced attitude spans all states and is ready for anything. It carries the assurance of the whole design without understanding a thing about it—hence "trust" in place of knowledge. The rounded deliberative style and a vocabulary of entities drawn from theological heights to the personal level engage the mind in the settlement if only marginally. This too is obviously an altogether different resignation from that of "Dialogue"—a tempered one, but overbalanced on behalf of the heart.

However, the heart manages to come forth too in the last stanza of "The Dialogue," goaded out of the pouting "I resigne" by a timely reminder of the sacrifice, which in moving closer reveals the special power of the design in the voice of Christ telling what true resignation is and showing how little reason has to do with it:

> *That is all, if that I could*
> *Get without repining;*
> *And my clay, my creature, would*
> *Follow my resigning:*
> *That as I did freely part*
> *With my glorie and desert,*
> *Left all joyes to feel all smart—*
> Ah! no more: thou break'st my heart.

We can only speculate what the last line would have been had the speaker not been interrupted, but it would have continued in an instructional mode and proposed a creaturely likeness set up by the model of costly heartfelt love. Presumably the emphasis for the creature too would fall on choice, on the "free" submission, and on a sacrifice of his pittance of glory. Christ's kenosis would thus mark the way for the clay creature's surrender ("Follow *my* resigning"), except that by resigning, the former pays and the creature receives. As is the case in "Hope," which also ends "no more, no more," the exchange is a game of wits until that breaking-off shows the speaker's unreadiness to accept the full gift or even contemplate it, because it only increases his unworthiness. Not nostalgia for earthly things, which we could more readily understand, but acute sorrow over the slain god is what would open the heart if it were not broken first. Realizing that he has been ransomed in this way is almost as painful as the sacrifice itself. The heart again and again sticks on that realization in *The Church*. In this case the speaker breaks off the rhyming game to insert his own best word, retrieved from "The Altar."

In "The Flower," Herbert might be said to affirm rather than disclaim "the whole design," but he does so very wistfully in

> We say amisse,
> This or that is:
> Thy word is all, if we could spell.

Even for those who already know that the word is all, the "this or that" continues to intervene, not as a cross section of the whole but as everything within experience that all stories mistell and that must be discarded. Equivalents would be the "Old" Testament canceling itself in the New, science sacrificed on the altar, pleasure quitted, the ways of honor left behind. The poem is caught between the certain necessity for such rejections and doubt that the speaker can do more. It reflects the tension between the Herbert who turns away from the "lord of the inductive method" and the one who eventually finds himself beyond conflict in the post-*Temple* message to Ferrar. "*We* say amiss" would presumably contrast the words of normal men (poets and scientists, for instance) to the Gospels. "We *say* amiss" would hint at the inevitable reproach that any speech incurs in asserting something, as whatever Job says will be wrong (he can count on it). Having undone the language that theology supplies and having suggested that we do not really command *any* language, Herbert leaves the speaker in the quandary of a deconstruction that knows the indeterminacy of endless saying but cannot forbear saying more and still more. The whole is conditioned by "*if* we could spell," the conditionality of which is akin to that of "Affliction 1" in its giving up of service without yet finding "perfect freedom" ("Let me not love thee, *if* I love thee not").

"A Wreath" adds one further complication to the search for either intellectual settlement or respite for the heart. I'll conclude with it as a last if somewhat minor piece of evidence of how the self-estimating wit that looks about the world becomes reconciled to the absolutist heart which refuses to attach itself to anything except the sacrificial figure, breaking it as it breaks all tropes. Although this poem is not an allegorical narrative as some of the previous examples have been, it does twist through a formal equivalent to the life of a poet who cannot take the straight way to "a crown of praise." It models a nomadic life and implies an interaction of mind and heart as a creative process that "weaves" a poem before our eyes:

> A wreathed garland of deserved praise,
> Of praise deserved, unto thee I give,
> I give to thee, who knowest all my wayes,
> My crooked winding wayes, wherein I live,
> Wherein I die, not live: for life is straight,
> Straight as a line, and ever tends to thee,
> To thee, who are more farr above deceit,
> Then deceit seems above simplicitie.

The "crooked winding wayes" paradoxically avoid the heart's desire while making progress toward it and in some sense fulfilling it enroute by the always-more-satisfying rephrasing. The speaker's saying that he lives and dies therein is both a delay and a tactic to show the second course that leads toward the hidden life. God already knows those intricate ways, which needn't be written out. Hence the reiterated call for the plain style:

> Give me simplicitie, that I may live,
> So live and like, that I may know, thy wayes,
> Know them and practise them: then shall I give
> For this poore wreath, give thee a crown of praise.

To "like" the labyrinth would obviously be to affirm it. To know and like God's ways and yet not practice them amounts to rejecting them. Just as fatal to the poet if not to the man is that knowing *and* practicing them would mean the end of writing, as would following the stylistic advice of "Jordan 1." To arrive at the crown, the one meant here, would be to discard the wreath. Poems that yield to the heart right off must do exactly that. Disentangling a program from experience, they would see it entire and render it in a phrase, or perhaps not bother to render it at all. In contrast, life as lived, as opposed to life thus charted, is all complex wreathing and storied progress, as artistry winds the self into the sense. If anything takes precedence over faith and its end, it is that inescapable moment-by-moment experience. It requires renewed investigation and explaining just to determine how God's ways would work if one could get at them.

The rephrasing of "A Wreath" can work in more than one way, however. It is a constant issuing of correctives, a release and regripping of thought that either winds down or starts to go astray and needs correction. Or it is a formal device imposed from without as a set of hurdles to test agility. The former reading—the issuing of correctives—would be compatible with the unpacking of an ever-more sincere heart unwinding the skein not to claim it and use it but to sacrifice it. The latter meaning—the setting up of a palpable device to force poetic leaps—is more firmly entrenched in cerebral levels of a psyche that would not know what to do if not this. The poem starts as though intent upon converting both the oblique and the straight movements into a formal declaration, almost a special covenant for poets. But the grammar is peculiar in its introducing of the confessional element in relative clauses, as this very nonperiodic sentence spins itself out as one increment piled upon another. Crafted and tight in formal terms, that sentence, after delivering its main elements in just two lines, ends up filling the entire octave. With each corrective and supplanting turn, simplicity is set back another step. The result is a wreath that serves at best as a training exercise for true praise. If "for" in the last line means "in place of," the wreath will have to go: knowing and practicing the straight way will reduce it to a heartfelt outburst.

Whatever the poet does now—and he must do something—full delivery awaits the future. But the wreath is a repeatable gesture, to some degree renewed in many poems of *The Church* that put their formal artistry on display. It is likely to be as deceiving as the reiterated offerings of "Love unknown" or as the horizontally slashed-through body of "Coloss. 3.3" and the lopped vegetation of "Paradise." As though turning an upward spiral while recalling former phrases, the poet wants to emerge at a poetic height that could both see and conclude the way. Only then presumably would the mind and heart blend into the celebrant-writer of the true hymn or maker of the crown of praise. To imagine that movement more fully, *The Church* must eventually reduce the entire wreathed way to love's ritualized courtship of the reluctant sinner, the ultimate (almost thoughtless) experience of God's ways. "Love 3" finds the self-judging mind still holding back and the way still twisted, but the heart attends to what it has all the while hoped for and makes its concession to grace into a positive act. "So I did sit and eat" stresses the deed and doer and cancels futurity in a definite preterit. Before he allows that moment, Herbert has to wreathe his way through a good many other trials of the interim that his rejection of Bacon's regard for secondary goals and for the book of nature has left largely without intelligible purpose.

3
POSTPONEMENT

Estragon: I was dreaming I was happy.
Vladimir: That passed the time.
—Samuel Beckett, *Waiting for Godot*

"The Pilgrimage"

It would be difficult to duplicate in any period since the Middle Ages the collective poetic otherworldliness of the seventeenth century. Yet I am concerned here not with why Herbert or his contemporaries rejected the energetic advances of the Renaissance but with how Herbert negotiated the divide between the secular and sacred realms. In this chapter I want to work somewhat broadly and thematically across *The Church* to sample his mapping of the means and direction of a spiritual "advancement," which can be read in some ways as a rebuttal to the restlessness he classified variously as ambition, giddiness, and vanity. "The Pilgrimage" offers an opportunity both to judge Herbert's elimination of detail in the parabolic mode and his capacity to vary the landscape and through it either suggest or deny progress "toward my journie's end" (Herbert, *Complete Works* 3.485). Compressed enough, an autobiographical narrative can become lyric, but of course never in Herbert at the tune of Shakespeare's "That time of year thou mayst in me behold." Herbert's regrets are balanced against prospects of hope. Behind him lies "Adam," ahead, but not in sight, a recovered paradise. Those are the common boundaries of everyone's story; the lyric project is to work toward the common types they enclose from the particularities of personal waywardness.

The impatience of the speaker of "The Pilgrimage" derives as much from the desolation of the landscape as from his failure to realize any particular goal, and in that respect its compression is fixed more in the wasted phase than in the forward view, although it is the latter that drives the progress. Such poems of impatience are in good supply in *The Church*. Together with Herbert's unemployment poems, they explore the personal side of the "first fruits" problem once various consuming enterprises have been suppressed— interest in the court, in science, and in this case in the topography of certain kinds of poetry. Without calling the end itself into question or growing especially concerned about election, they begin to question not only how far knowledge may extend but what sort of signs a pilgrim reads and to what extent Providence places omniscience at his disposal. (The formal implications of segmented progress and divided phases of attitude change I will reserve for later attention.)

The poems of impatience seek to balance confidence in the end against the fact that exile is often justified. In the Old Testament the stubbornness of an errant people is its cause. According to Hebrews, the pilgrimage figure under the Law resembles the enigmatic landscape and the condition of spiritual doubt that persists even after the Incarnation: "These all died in faith, not having received the promises, but having seen them afar off, and were persuaded of them, and embraced them, and confessed that they were strangers and pilgrims on the earth. For they that say such things declare plainly that they seek a country. . . . But now they desire a better country, that is, an heavenly," so the anonymous writer of Hebrews remarks generally of the wandering ancestors of Christianity (11:13–16). For Herbert in *The Country Parson*, the modern condition of the Jews speaks to the same issue, and it tells a remarkable story of Providence, which has left a forlorn and homeless people to fend for themselves until they return to favored status:

The Jewes yet live, and are known: they have their Law and Language bearing witnesse to them, and they to it: they are Circumcised to this day, and expect the promises of the Scripture; their Countrey also is known, the places, and rivers travelled unto, and frequented by others, but to them an unpenetrable rock, an unaccessible desert. Wherefore if the Jewes live, all the great wonders of old live in them, and then who can deny the stretched out arme of a mighty God? especially since it may be a just doubt, whether, considering the stubbornnesse of the Nation, their living then in their Countrey under so many miracles were a stranger thing, then their present exile, and disability to live in their Countrey. And it is observable, that this very thing was intended by God, that the Jewes should be his proof, and witnesses, as he calls them, *Isaiah* 43.12. And their very dispersion in all Lands, was intended not only for a punishment to them; but for an exciting of others by their sight, to acknowledging of God, and his power, *Psalm* 59.11. (*The Works* 281–82)

Herbert takes the passage from Isaiah ("therefore ye are my witnesses" and "beside me there is no savior") as clear evidence of an intended providence and a chosen people to demonstrate it, and the psalm as the intentional reprieve from annihilation so that a scattered people will show God's power. If justice is manifest in the contemporary condition of the Jews, the course of a church militant does not promise much more for Christians, who are also scattered: all holy people are pilgrims, as we are told in 1 Peter 2:11 and Matthew 7:13–14.

In "The Pilgrimage," a poem that urges our careful reading of it as a story of abandonment, Herbert is more concerned with the psychology of delay than with its theological implications. Critics are often uneasy about the indeterminacy of the poem and about its remoteness from literary and emblematic coordinates. To Helen Vendler (92–98) the pilgrim's disappointment over what he thinks is to be a gladsome hill is bitter beyond recompense, in keeping with Herbert's other self-revising poems. Louis Martz compares this to the *Via Dolorosa* and other "Roman" associations (306). Bart Westerweel (200) is forced to extend the pilgrim's journey past its stopping place in the poem in order to anticipate the equivalent of Bunyan's arrival at Mount Sion. The difficulty lies in part in the unphilosophical speaker himself, who does not define his trek in terms of long-range goals. His journey does not recall the Exodus or the Exile; he employs no new-covenant sacraments or rites. Indeed, he breaks free of every institutional support or guide. Unlike

Bunyan's pilgrims he pauses neither for devotions nor instruction. Without a house of interpretation, he is on his own in reading the signs of the way. He is tempted to murmur but does not fall into apostasy, and he is not openly chastised for his errors. In that much he is distinguishable from the Jews Herbert sets up as exemplars of diaspora and from other murmurers of *The Church*. His story has neither beginning nor end, merely an undesignated origin and a projected ending, both lying outside the borders of the poem.

Initially, this determined pilgrim simply announces "I Travell'd on" as though already well into an episodic journey. If he had started from a memorable occasion, he might have taken a direction from it. As it is, he is prompted by the illusion that the hilltop ahead is his goal:

> I Travell'd on, seeing the hill, where lay
> My expectation.
> A long it was and weary way.
> The gloomy cave of Desperation
> I left on th' one, and on the other side
> The rock of Pride.

Unlike Buyanesque pilgrims who control their optimism and despair only with difficulty, Herbert's speaker gets past Desperation and Pride without so much as pausing to assess them. So stark and rapid is the exchange of one place for another that we may begin to think Herbert engaged in a strenuous naming exercise whose regimen is to put certain labels and areas of experience behind the pilgrim so that he can get on to something of value. Each rejected stage says little about what lies ahead, nor is there an evident reason that a copse should come after a meadow, or a hill after a wasteland. Without a start or finish to define direction, the sequencing cannot be said to be either right or wrong. The enticement for both the pilgrim and the reader is to draw nearer and investigate.

What the pilgrim approaches is of course in no way a Spenserian or Miltonic place that combines scriptural, classical, and actual location, nor is it even the intangible place of spirit where Vaughan's pilgrim in "Regeneration" hears "*Where I please.*" It does us little good to associate Herbert with Renaissance pictorial or mythological lushness, romantic imagination kindled by the visitation of natural places, or mysticism embedded in landscapes. Alexander Grosart, sometimes voicing a perversity that pushes us in a better direction, misunderstands Herbert's imagery in defending him against "purblind critics" who have "ignorantly said of Herbert that he knew and cared little or nothing for the signs and sounds of outside Nature" (Herbert, *Complete Works* 2.xcii). That opinion parallels Grosart's belief that Herbert was the first poet to see "the central position of man to the universe," as "microcosm to the All." Herbert's combined human-centered and Christocentric universe requires that nature shrink to usable symbols, or again as Grosart puts it, more appropriately this time, "It was only a grotesque grandeur to make Earth (as old astronomic science did) the centre of the universe, and the huge sun to wheel in attendance on it; but it is grand, without touch of grotesqueness, to recognise thus in Man the centre of the vastest and remotest circumference, with all the visible world 'to attend him' " (2.xci). That attendance means linguistically the adopting of cryptic shorthand to betoken spiritual states, but in Herbert's case without Vaughan's sense of an immanent being in the sounds and shapes and rushing wind of dreamlike places.

But therein lies the chief problem of Herbert's pilgrim—the reading of meadows, copses, and hilltops in a way that salvages progress from process. They are neither natural places nor distinct biblical types or expressions of advancing divine/human relations. Herbert has deliberately simplified the way, avoiding sacramental foretastes of regeneration and avoiding eventful conversion crises (he was himself born into the church and had no need of a personal reversal). Obviously he is staying clear also of stations of enlightenment reminiscent of St. Bonaventure and does not suggest a dialectical organization of a Perkins style of chart. This is not properly speaking even a service or employment poem that carries Providence down to the vocational level, although it makes oblique reference to poetry as a possible interlude. Elsewhere poetry has the more captivating capacity to offer praise and greet special occasions—Easter, the Eucharist, baptism—with hope for sample ascensions; here Herbert gets down to the bare essentials in the search for a destination, or *the* destination.

Nor does "The Pilgrimage" suggest a coincidence in tropes between the individual journey and the transition from Old Testament to New found in other poems, as "Easter-wings," for instance, compresses the entire *mythos* into a single chart. Nature remains stubbornly enigmatic despite the clear designation of certain landscape features—the rock of Pride, the cave of Desperation, the gladsome hill. It has its comforts, but the pilgrim is determined to get past them. All normal symbolic means of anticipating paradise and restoring the divine presence are unavailable. Certainly the pilgrim has not moved appreciably closer to his goal on arriving at his hilltop, which lacks any special reception or revelation, as its brackish water denies spiritual cleansing. Figurative reduction becomes spiritual disillusionment and hard experience, as though the tropes had diminished to epithets devoid of predication and systematic definition. The stops along the way lack even the shadowy prefiguration that give typological stories their momentum, which is especially disappointing to the pilgrim once he passes by potentially rich rhetorical and poetic fields to get to what from a distance he hopes will be better. The result is an enforced postponement that resembles the stalled and unrevealing moments of poems concerned with the lack of calling.

"The Pilgrimage" is extreme in its lack of guideposts, but its very extremity shows Herbert's divorce of spiritual pursuits from actual societies and topographies. What it replaces these with primarily is a fast pace, measured by stanzas and narrative stages. Herbert uses the shortened second and last lines of the stanza to interrupt the movement. In the first stanza, the second half injects new resolve and lists accomplishments as though obstacles were mere cobwebs to be brushed aside. The pilgrim bypasses the temptations to substitute lament, analysis, or praise for narrative and to rationalize the way with deliberation and meditation. In that too the stanza imposes an abruptness that cuts off recital. In the second stanza, for instance, the equivalent to Bunyan's Bypass Meadow is an especially tempting spot for psalmic expansion. After a glimpse of potential copiousness, the stanza turns sharply to denial and moves on quickly:

> And so I came to Fancies medow strow'd
> With many a flower:
> Fain would I here have made abode,
> But I was quicken'd by my houre.
> So to Cares cops I came, and there got through
> With much ado.

A poem that rejects fancy's meadow and gladsome hilltops is applicable both to life in general and to the reduction of poetic and rhetorical resources. Herbert uses the short lines to underscore not naming the flowers and to dismiss the ornamentation that would ordinarily accompany both songs of praise and laments, were there time for such. The landscape contains almost none of poetry's usual pastoral or sylvan imagery. The logic of narrative must prevail: "my hour" sets the limits, quickens the step, and leaves the reader to fill in the blanks. In this bypassed moment one could conceivably do just that, using bits and pieces of information from Herbert's situation, other stories of exile and pilgrimage, or the context of *The Temple* generally. The more amplified allusions could be used to fill in an educational track, for instance, and allow the flower-strewn meadows a glance at Herbert's years as Cambridge orator or the poetic vocation. Care's copse could be said to encapsulate what "Affliction 1" takes longer to spell out as shadow biography. But the haste of the poem and the shortage of detail discourage such excursions, and whatever the temptation to specify equivalents, the labeling operation is truncated. Brevity prevails in the copse as well as in the meadow, with no hint of what the "much ado" of the second short line might contain.

Although they are opposites that keep before us the likelihood that the way is not totally random, both pleasure and tribulation get the same short shrift. We can speculate that the reason for this foreshortening is that ultimately it does not matter whether one has gone an easy or a hard way; pastoral places and worrisome copses are equally suspect from the vantage point of the greater *mythos*. Nor does Herbert have Bunyan's types and fellow pilgrims to suggest better or worse ways to choose among. The rejection of stopovers goes with the pilgrim's isolation. No society gathers in pleasure's byways; no Petrarchans or knights with cast-aside shields congregate in tableaux as they do where manners and morals count, as though we could have the entire *Faerie Queene* in a few stanzas. Like other speakers of *The Church*, the pilgrim must drop any concept of the self as the product of alliances or accumulated experience.

This is especially true of the next phase, which packages medieval allegory in a lyric form:

> That led me to the wilde of Passion, which
> Some call the wold;
> A wasted place, but sometimes rich.
> Here I was robb'd of all my gold,
> Save one good Angell, which a friend had ti'd
> Close to my side.

In contrast to amplified "feeling and experience," as William Empson remarks about this pivotal stanza, the tone "gives a prophetic importance" to flat writing (147). It is as though the woods had been swept clean of human agents and the history of cultures reduced to an anonymous blank. The stanza nonetheless suggests a literary ancestry, as again Empson suggests: it rejects the meandering through mazy woods found in romance, but "the wold" has medieval resonance, as does the *cursus* of the allegory generally. Even a denied association with romance can suggest, as it does quite properly

to Empson, "vast and inhuman wildernesses," "the portentous luxury" of
the missing enchanted castles, and perhaps again Herbert's own "long and
painful process of judgment" in choosing a way of life (148). The one positive
sign is the good angel. Whether some purchase can be made with its coinage
we never discover, but it shows that the speaker has not always been alone.

By this juncture Herbert has used cave, rock, meadow, and copse to
discipline desire in several phases—sensuous, poetic, social—without stalling
the wayfarer or defining him by allied types of pilgrimage. The landscape
possesses no usable fertility. As I suggested, nothing of Traherne's or
Vaughan's gleaming emblems or Milton's spirit-dwelling groves appears in it.
The meadow is antiparadisal not because it is a devil's corner but because it
is not permanent, and perhaps not quite real. Desperation, pride, delight,
and care are more or less pointed passions, and the wild of passion is their
bleak collective home. Such a wild is a synedoche for the world as the
opposite of paradise, the primal matter and source of passions, at once the
vaguest and most powerful of deterrents and most suggestive of the phase
labels. That the wold was once, or has been now and again, "rich" is
disheartening, as if the speaker had arrived after the exodus of all those who
might give company and instruction. We get the impression that many take
this track if no two at the same time, yet any intelligence that might have
been responsible for charting it has long ago departed. Both the wold and the
angel suggest a history now unavailable to investigation and a future that is
beyond imagining.

Such a path does not require choices, since it has no branches or habitations. The speaker accepts what turns up as what it seems. But with his
arrival at the mistaken goal, the gladsome hill that surpasses fancy's meadow
in promise (it seemingly belongs to the realm of theophany rather than
rhetoric and poetics), he realizes the emptying of hopes and the signs they
depend upon:

> At length I got unto the gladsome hill,
> Where lay my hope,
> Where lay my heart; and climbing still,
> When I had gain'd the brow and top,
> A lake of brackish waters on the ground
> Was all I found.

Where courses are normally educational (as in "Peace" and to some extent
"Love unknown"), signs here, quite against the expectations of both the

pilgrim and the reader, are not ways to approach the word. Nearly any seventeenth-century catechism or spiritual instruction holds out some promise of clarification. As John Robinson remarks concerning the growth of converts, their advance is tied to sentence-by-sentence instruction and learnable doctrines, since the spirit makes no revelations without the word (*Of Religious Communion* 126, cited in George 122). Although not arranged by the convert himself and not necessarily a straightforward advance, each stage moves toward *some* gladsome point, however distant. Here both the way and the mistaken end undo pilgrimage logic and its customary language. The hilltop lake has no depth and makes glamour seem a function of distance. Almost any pleasant surprise could dwell at the top of such a hill: a company of saints to receive the victorious climber, a vision, a contemplative guide of the kind that educates the Red Cross Knight, a gateway. Even a house of correction and purgation would be something. Instead, the pilgrim finds an emblem of stagnation and pollution without so much as a trickle of living waters flowing in from elsewhere.

At the top of this ungladsome hill, Herbert for a moment seems on the verge of agreeing with modern discreditings of those who make literalist readings of religious tropes. As Douglas Berggren argues, science and religion alike avoid literal nonsense by using tensional metaphors. Idolatry results from people naively thinking, for instance, that they will be spiritually transformed by eating the bread of communion, the equivalent to a scientist mistaking mathematics and theory for reality (Berggren 537–38). So one might think that labels in a mythic landscape will translate into reality once one gets to the appropriate spot in the journey of reading; but not so. The way that leads to the end goes through paradox and surprise; what seems a happy prospect from a distance turns into its opposite, which is the way of history generally and especially its central marker, the Crucifixion. Triumph may be in some sense "in" the sign or the event enigmatically but never literally or immediately. Human expectation provides no predictive basis unless one comes to expect the opposite of what one desires.

But Herbert is not prepared to deny the literal truth of such phenomena as incarnate divinity, virgin birth, or a physical body ascending to a spiritual heaven (Berggren gives exactly these as examples of literal nonsense, 544). Nor does he allow such a decisive dichotomy between the natural and the supernatural that no messages from the latter appear in the former. The pilgrim may not find his destination right off, but he never stops assuming that he has one and that the crooked way leads to it. The mistaken destination might ordinarily extract an outcry and a complaint or supplication from a

Herbert persona; here it only goads a resumed search and a prediction of a
still more extreme departure from accomplishments and missions. Having
brought his pilgrim to this anticlimax, Herbert can now turn to the psychology of frustration, and it is an extraordinary one if we come from either
scriptural murmurers or romantic lamentations:

> With that abash'd and struck with many a sting
> > Of swarming fears,
> > I fell, and cry'd, Alas my King!
> > Can both the way and end be tears?
> Yet taking heart I rose, and then perceiv'd
> > I was deceiv'd:

Unlike the first trek, the direction the pilgrim next chooses has some bearing
on the timing of delivery, although the new hill he sees in the distance will
not likely be a place of visions:

> My hill was further: so I flung away,
> > Yet heard a crie
> > Just as I went, *None goes that way*
> > *And lives*: If that be all, said I,
> After so foul a journey death is fair,
> > And but a chair.

The speaker's function is not to illustrate the paralyzing fear of murmurers,
since he takes heart immediately and resumes his quest fearlessly. Having
dropped into anxiety and the typical way of the abandoned, "Alas my King!"
he rebounds as the prophets and psalmists seldom do. A personal destination
is just that and nothing more, and so the journey is evidently to have no
meaningful stations before its culmination in death. His recognition of that,
in defiance of the caution that comes out of nowhere, takes the form of a
retort tossed over the shoulder. This most abrupt man-angel or man-God
dialogue has no motivating hope or instruction, because this pilgrim needs
more. Implicit in it is a warning that poetry itself cannot locate revealing
semblances of a proper end, much less achieve transcendence. Beyond copses
reduced to care and wilds reduced to passion, can there be anything except
abstraction or the emptying of the metaphoric journey? The parallel between
the mind's way through symbolic modes and the pilgrim's through emblems
strikes us with renewed force. The triumph of the visionary, the discovery of

divine presence and its "treasure," would just as surely bring an end to landscape visualization, albeit a positive end. This onward-rushing pilgrim must be transformed to get "off the track." Such residue from the natural world as the vehicle commands prevents arrival even as it advances the progress, and it is the pilgrim's vow to continue that "ends" a poem that can have no conceptual end within the limited knowledge of the narrator.

The pilgrim is no man for nostalgia or lamentation or even Bunyanesque hand-wringing. Not at all fearful of the mysterious voice, he puts aside whatever exasperation he has accumulated. "If that be all" is as though to say, "I'm not surprised, given what I've seen." The last part of the labeling is to replace bleaker adjectives for death with "fair" and to draw out of the traditional supply of tropes the surprisingly domestic and comfortable "chair," which the defiant speaker puts forth as though claiming the right to provide his own names for things. Whoever has designed this obstacle course, he implies, has had a time of it, placing temptations, erecting illusory hilltops, erasing potential stopping places. Death at the last stop is meant to discourage him further, but whereas "ground" and "found" bring the spirit's and the poem's *melos* to earth, "fair" and "chair" let them rise a little. They compose an antiphony in plain grammar, set forcefully against the biblical warning *"none goes that way / And lives."* Whether or not the "chair" is a chariot conveyance to heaven (Morillo 271–75; Westerweel 201), death at least collapses the distance between the "now" and the true end of scriptural pilgrimages. A sedan chair or litter suggests that without bodily encumbrances the soul could virtually ride the rest of the way.

Neither concluding statement encourages the copiousness that fancy's meadow or care's copse ordinarily would. Because of this and the concluding warning, the poem does not return to where it began to begin again in the biblical manner (in which, what Numbers renders, Joshua repeats, because history has been virtually eliminated. Down to the bare minimum, the pilgrim is spared cycles even as he is denied a place to rest. With renewed will he seizes upon the contrast between the end and the living struggle "after so foul a journey" and adopts the seasoned attitude of one who has been through the mire, has been tricked, "struck with many a sting," and "abash'd." His hopes have been disappointed not through any obvious mistake he has made (except in thinking that a gladsome hill might be gladsome) but by the nature of the landscape. He refuses either to give up hope (Westerweel's point) or to conceal his bitterness (Vendler's point). No doubt the Sion we assume he desires exercises a powerful attraction, but the poem emphasizes little more than his persistence. That the reader may view the terrain as a reminder of one who underwent a still more bitter way on the cross (Martz's point) does not seem to weigh heavily with or against him. All things considered, he copes well with a bad situation, which is no less than the temporal life abstracted into a few selected images—copes well, but only if we grant his otherworldly premise and do not hold him responsible for the lack of favorable signs. To go along with him fully we would have to agree that the energy of those who are moved by the prospect of a better place would be wasted in interim measures of a Baconian kind, draining the brackish water to make the ground produce, for instance, or arranging into rows the rhetorical flowers of the poet's meadow.

Even without our concurrence in its sturdy pessimism, however, the poem works well as a certain kind of reductive exercise in troping the world. The style is, for Herbert, unbiblical; the poem has no repetition, parallelism, doublets, or commandments. In Herbert's rewriting of the wilderness episodes, the landscape becomes dreamlike and the pilgrim must be all heart, there being nothing else to go on. Having set in place the outfittings of spiritual changes of state, Herbert psychologizes them as distilled experience. The irrepressible pilgrim is impelled basically by the way things are in this solitary, nasty, and (he begins to hope) short life.

Decay

One reason that the Hebrew Bible's diverse chronicles sometimes seem to Herbert less in need of translation than Pauline thought might suggest is that they are no further from 1 A.D. than he is. Like the anticipatory prophecies of the post-Exilic period, Christian historical thought becomes stretched between an exemplary period and an indefinite future, as the later Hebraic prophets are suspended between a past monarchical glory and an expected Messiah. However, a major difference separates the two in the redefinition of the "kingdom." The laws of pentateuchal and deuteronomic history are social instruments and shape public attitudes as well as devotional life. They are administrative, and their interpreters and redactors either were or were close to judges and monarchs. Although the prophets of the Exile are shut off from national life, they still remember it and look forward to a reunion of monarchy and priesthood. The difference in both the expectation and retrievals of the past is summed up in the presence and removal of the antitype, and it bears upon the text/life relationship and the degree to which

Providence can now be located in events. As Sanford Budick argues with respect to midrash-oriented typology in the final books of *Paradise Lost*, "Many Christian typologists (especially Protestants), struggling to understand the radically unfulfilled status of divine reality in the interval between Christ's Comings, could and did make use of [two] figural modes, one within the other." One remains strongly Christocentric and absorbs previous figures as foreshadowing; the other is an open-ended and variable typology that has broken loose from the center. As the nucleus of any Christian interpretation, even Christ can prove to be "gloriously fissionable" in the latter readings (Budick and Hartman 208). Thus from two sides—the complex association of secular and sacred things in Hebrew thought and the pursuit of secondary causes—the hold of the salvation story is loosened.

Virtually the last thing we would expect of Herbert is any great concession to either version of this historical variability. He reinserts the sacrifice into consciousness at every spiritual crisis and again and again interprets current life in the light of scriptural types. But we have come to realize, especially in the readings of Helen Vendler and Stanley Fish, that many of his poems are neither liturgically based reenactments of the center nor fully stabilized salvation paradigms. As Jonathan Goldberg reads his view of the Old Testament in poems such as "Decay," they too become "fissionable," if not so gloriously. "Decay" in particular remembers and rehearses a "generative line of texts that gloss and regloss each other. Citation, retextualised; allusion, made indeterminate; narrative, redistributed and reorganised. . . . Figurative and figural possibilities in the text keep history open to the possibility of meaning in their refusal of determinate finality" (17). No specific indebtedness to midrashic interpretation need be established to justify such uncertainty. The extended events since the Incarnation and the remoteness of the promise cause the middle and the end to drift apart, not only in Herbert but in several variants of seventeenth-century otherworldliness in Donne, Andrewes, and Vaughan.

Herbert is well aware of the conventional parallels between Christian typology and the incidents and figures of the Hebrew Bible and their earlier messianic anticipations of later sacred writings. The difficulty is less the absorbing of that previous history than the application of Christ's prophecies to what follows. In "Decay," when recent days and unenlightened contemporaries carry the poet back to older types, the poet, for once nostalgic, is struck by YHWH's intimacy with his people:

> Sweet were the dayes, when thou didst lodge with Lot,
> Struggle with Jacob, sit with Gideon,

> Advise with Abraham, when thy power could not
> Encounter Moses strong complaints and mone:
> Thy words were then, *Let me alone*.

This familiar Lord (primarily *J*'s rather than *E*'s) enters the biographies of the leaders at such junctures as the issuing of the Law and the passing of the command from Moses to Joshua. He converts familiar places into scenes of revelation and transforms the geography on both sides of the Jordan into a litany of cherished names. When pressed hard by a faltering humanity, he withholds his wrath and retreats, as though a badgered family member. Not everything gets subordinated to him or to proper devotional practice or he would not have to retreat; but when he wishes to he applies himself directly to the governance of Abraham's people. Such incidents are what the deuteronomic historians use to guide reapplications of the Law to a still-intact and recurrently "stubborn" people. Anecdotal narratives are helpful to establish models and enforce the law.

In contrast, history since the Incarnation has fallen onto the hard times of the *deus absconditus*. Herbert's poem "The Jews" expresses sympathy for the altered condition of Abraham's people, since in the Pauline framework the Law is now dead and the new spiritual life is an offshoot of apostles ("our scions") who in spiritualizing history on the Pauline model have sapped the strength of the parent plant:

> Poore nation, whose sweet sap and juice
> Our cyens have purloin'd, and left you drie:
> Whose streams we got by the Apostles sluce,
> And use in baptisme, while ye pine and die:
> Who by not keeping once, became a debter;
> And now by keeping lose the letter.

That desiccation, which is strangely like a Christian theft of oasis or Jordan water, does not prevent Herbert from wishing a Jewish restoration, but he believes that it will come only at the blast of the angel's final trumpet. As that breaking off of his sympathy and substitution of something more apocalyptic suggests, he does not look for a conversion by human means, any more than he expects a successful reunion of civil and religious authority in a militant church ruled by saints:

Oh that my prayers! mine, alas!
Oh that some Angel might a trumpet sound;
At which the Church falling upon her face
Should crie so loud, untill the trump were drown'd,
And by that crie of her deare Lord obtain,
      That your sweet sap might come again!

The wish is no doubt sincere, as the break in the first line suggests. But *The Country Parson* is more mindful of the Jewish betrayal of Christ than of either the old sweet days or the final conversion (Katz 185–86). In the passage I cited earlier, Herbert makes of the Jews examples of God's just punishment of disbelief. Their homelessness is equivalent to the divorce of God's administrative power from spiritual life. The new chosen people are now a militant church that will never be exactly equivalent to a homeland. The real location of Jewish watering places has become the symbolic and transportable rite of baptism. Hebraic symbolism cannot bring real places into such hellenistic symbolism, which makes of the old holy land a (fore)shadow of what is to come. The letter that pulls the reader into the detailed stuff of geography and politics and leaves the Jews there gives way now to the spirit that drops all details in pursuing a new relief. It will take the collective cry of the militant church and the extremity of final moments to bring about the total prophesied conversion and bring the Jews "home" again, only now to the new Jerusalem, not, for instance, to England for the millennial rule of reformed saints. For Herbert final events are not as imminent, or at least not as predictable, as they were for millenarians and, later, those Cromwellians who developed a hopeful Jewish policy to complement their campaigns against the antichrist and supposed an actual geographical relocation as a preliminary. $2\overline{5}973\,6$

In "Decay" the contrast works against modern Christianity as well as against the "Poore nation" exiled from the holy land (and not incidentally from England). In these lengthening days, Herbert suggests, the Lord is straightened on all sides and so retreats to a corner of the heart, the only location accessible to him when even the Church betrays him. In the days of expectation that follow the failure of an immediate *parousia*, the temper of the times alters radically: the demands on the people are great and the enticements of holiness are faint. The last phase of the fable and its divine reentries into time through meditation and sacrament are impressive in their own right, but they have lost the leisure of the old anecdotes. This is not because the Lord is no longer willing to show himself but because a new

breed of stiff-necked people give him even less civil space than Gideon or
Jacob did:

> But now thou dost thy self immure and close
> In some one corner of a feeble heart:
> Where yet doth Sinne and Satan, thy old foes,
> Do pinch and straiten thee, and use much art
> To gain thy thirds and little part.

The cause of this alienation is that sin has followed the course of types from
public figures into the Christian heart; it counters Pauline spiritual abstraction with its own universal ambitions. It is everywhere, Herbert insists in
several poems and conclusively in "The Church Militant": it preempts
places, vocations, ambition, surfaces, and interiors. Virtually nothing in the
temporal world is exempt from it, which is no wonder, since Paul has defined
everything worldly as corrupt. As I suggested earlier, a pious people can no
longer unite against identifiable foes condemned by God (or by his represen-
tatives) and defeat them on a real field of battle; one cannot go up against
Midianites to restore the holy land. The inner enemy is subtler and more
pernicious. What has been lost in the detaching of sacred texts from the
collective life is the sociability of a deity who appeared not merely in the
private heart or the inner sanctums adjacent to the court but in the fields and
tabernacles. He once participated in the wanderings of the people and
directed the construction of their temples and their towns. In that regard, at
least in prosperous times, he forestalled the emphasis on the future characteristic of the prophetic texts, which are quite vague in comparison with the
historical chronicles. It is somewhat easier intellectually to shape a national
course either in prospect or retrospect than it is to unite private hearts in a
single collective narrative. That is one of the disadvantages of the Protestant
situating of personal life and the seat of reform in the heart.

Taking up Herbert's topic as though in mid conversation, equally remote
from a united churchfolk, Vaughan in "Corruption" agrees with this diagno-
sis of ancient and modern times:

> Sure, It was so. Man in those early days
> Was not all stone, and Earth,
> He shin'd a little, and by those weak Rays
> Had some glimpse of his birth.

One main point is tellingly different, however, the neoplatonist turn Vaughan gives to Jewish history itself. Except for Eden, he drops the proper names and places and the familiarity of the holy land (Herbert's main point) and makes heaven the natural home of humankind from the outset. Ever since Eden, humanity has yearned for a nongeographic location and cultivated its alienation along with its hope. The human spirit quarrels constantly with "murmurers and foes," which include even the vegetation. Hence for Vaughan to say *"Ah! what bright days were those!"* is to yearn not for the old tribal and cultic religion but for a preexisting paradise that in its historical recollections could never be anything but a shadow. The contrast is not between olden days and now but between the darkness of incarnation (or the curtained light that thickened around Adam) and the brilliant light no mortal has ever lived within. Texts for Vaughan glimpse that light in figures that make even sacred stories fables, at best tangential to truth. For Herbert, narrative is suspended between the two testaments as an account first of works and laws and then of faith. The latter makes events into imperfect enactments of a spiritual paradigm that only the new Joshua, the high priest, fulfills. Since all temporality is equally shadowy, Vaughan makes that division less decisively, and for him both testaments record the fall from light.

Vaughan's departure from Herbert in that regard underscores the special quality of Herbert's conception of the time between the Incarnation and Judgment. Given Vaughan's devaluing of incarnation and historical time, his Jesus is not a forceful historical presence, and so one does not come to the Crucifixion with a sense of the far-reaching reversal that Herbert's speakers discover in "The Thanksgiving," "Redemption," and other poems. Vaughan's lost interval stretches all the way from Adam to doomsday and for individuals, from birth to death. The poet has less compelling reasons to retrieve the historical center in either rites or memory, and the interplay between poem and biblical source has fewer repercussions for the act of writing. When Vaughan does return to the holy land in "The Search," the savior is already absent from it; whether old or new, all objects are but "The Skinne, and shell of things." Thus too in "Corruption" when the God of wrath returns in imitation of Herbert's in "Decay," he assumes a power that has not been felt on earth since the creation:

> All's in deep sleep, and night; Thick darknes lyes
> And hatcheth o'r thy people;
> But hark! what trumpets that? what Angel cries
> *Arise! Thrust in thy sickle.*

The harvest truly begins for Vaughan at that point, and the difference between Herbert's old/new historiography and his neoplatonism ceases to matter. The Messiah becomes once again a figure of power. When the wrathful God of Herbert's "Decay" returns and calls out *Justice* and "all things burn," he will not so much be taking vengeance or repenting his creation as claiming a right he once exercised through the commandments and the Law. Again showing a side that he once revealed frequently, he will be returning to a more public life.

If spiritual experience is domesticated in YHWH's early relations to the Hebrews, God's absence becomes all the more a source of grief—much greater grief, Herbert sometimes feels, than those of conventional elegies that expect something less than a full divine presence. *The Church* does not treat definitively this concern with the emptying of time, and we need to cross through several of its spiritual zones to test them. In "Grief," which follows "The Search," sorrow for the absent God outruns "measure, tune, and time" and is both the grief of the passion (which the poet cannot match in "The Thanksgiving") and an accumulated spiritual attrition. "Keep your measures for some lover's lute" the speaker advises poets who wish to strum elegiac tunes; grief for this suffering is beyond cording (or discording). In "The Search," too, only a complete reversal of divine policy will suffice to placate universal grief over God's absence:

> When thou dost turn, and wilt be neare;
> > What edge so keen,
> What point so piercing can appeare
> > To come between?
> For as thy absence doth excell
> > All distance known:
> So doth thy nearenesse bear the bell,
> > Making two one.

Herbert characteristically thinks of such divine returns as unexpected but not completely independent of human influence—if supplication is to have a function. Short of the final trumpet, nearness is the best answer to the condition of "Decay." It cancels historical distances and the need for recounting other and better moments.

The question of where to look when "thy nearenesse" does not "bear the bell" (catch the prize) and make the human the divine One proves unanswerable in "The Search" itself, where both Scripture and nature—again Herbert's nature of enigmatic spiritual signs, not Bacon's footsteps traceable to a clearing—are inadequate substitutes. In place of actual presence, the first offers words and the second mere objects. Deciding for the moment to ignore words, "The Search" looks for sign-bearing herbs and stars and finds that although their evidence does argue for divine favor, nothing definitive actually appears. This much is as Bacon says: similitude is of less use for vertical ascent than for parallel material instances and the axioms that are derivable from them. The speaker looks up and presses his knees down but sees nothing. Several stanzas evaluate nature's possibilities and conclude with the questions, "where is my God? what hidden place / Conceals thee still?" Such concealment, which must after all be willed, frustrates any search and any invocation. As "Home" laments in a similar mood, "Nothing but drought and dearth, but bush and brake, / Which way so-e're I look, I see." Such a researcher is in no better condition than the dispersed Jews, and the reason is not disbelief or impiety but simply the global condition once the Messiah has left history and has not permanently returned to immediate presence through sacraments.

A similar impatience pervades too many of Herbert's grief poems to be passed over as lightly as the concentration on the serene Herbert—the Herbert of the subjected will and liturgical consolations—once encouraged. Sacraments *are* an effective way to overcome textual distance with ritual reenactment, and church calendar days permit God to reenter the historical stream. But these come only on a momentary devotional basis. The fable must make contact with all the days of the poet. Nor do sacraments stifle awareness of the distinction between historical life however devotional and the ultimate promise. Similarly, although Herbert never closes off hope, neither does he indulge in specific prophecies and expectations that might reinsert sacred narrative into historical experience outside the church. In "Hope," a speaker with a history similar to those of the affliction poems disputes with the guard at a gate who denies his progress. Their emblematic exchange is governed by riddling evasions. The anchor, optic, and green ears with which Hope answers the speaker's watch, well-used prayer book, and vial of tears are all reminders that the time is not yet full and that "prayers . . . alas!" are ineffectual. As an expectation perpetually put off, Hope freezes time in an awkward stage. The suppliant's reaction in this case is not to rediscover patience but to break off the exchange, since none of his works unlocks the reserve of bliss that faith tells him is there.

One alternative for Herbert as poet is to fill the interim with poetic production, or what "The Dedication" calls "gain," which includes good

works as well as praise and mimetic participation in Christian charity and
teaching. By modeling himself on the actual deeds of the first advent, the
good servant gains a sweet semblance to Christ, when, in the metaphor of
"The Odour. 2. Cor. 2. 15," he is pervaded with a spiritual perfume:

> How sweetly doth *My Master* sound! *My Master!*
> As Amber-greese leaves a rich sent
> Unto the taster:
> So do these words a sweet content,
> An orientall fragrancie, *My Master*.
>
> With these all day I do perfume my minde,
> My minde ev'n thrust into them both:
> That I might finde
> What cordials make this curious broth,
> This broth of smells, that feeds and fats my minde.

The Pauline text that he draws upon presumes the earning of the sweetness
through such evangelical works as the writing of the Epistles themselves:
"Now thanks be unto God, which always causeth us to triumph in Christ,
and maketh manifest the savour of his knowledge by us in every place. For
we are unto God a sweet savour of Christ, in them that are saved, and in them
that perish" (2 Cor. 2.14–15). However, even here Herbert's own savoring of
the words "my master" and "my servant" is qualified by the fact that words
alone fill him with sweetness; their application remains hypothetical until
God in fact answers *"my servant"* and causes the two odors to mingle:

> For when *My Master*, which alone is sweet,
> And ev'n in my unworthinesse pleasing,
> Shall call and meet,
> *My servant*, as thee not displeasing,
> That call is but the breathing of the sweet.
>
> This breathing would with gains by sweetning me
> (As sweet things traffick when they meet)
> Return to Thee.
> And so this new commerce and sweet
> Should all my life employ and busie me.

Until that meeting happens, or unless it happens, the word are as insubstan-
tial as fragrance, and what really fills the interim is not "new commerce" and

busy employment but dreaming. Entitlement has no substance unless the service is called for, and we know from "Love 3" that it will not be—that real presence is based not on reciprocal titles (master and servant), duties, or devotional forms, but on something else entirely. Personas who wish new commerce and new employment are too persistent and too eloquent in *The Church* for us not to take them seriously, although they are never the wisest fronts for a Herbert who cancels personal grievances in the move toward submission that climaxes in "Love 3."

Hope's companion faith, in Herbert's lexicon of temporal assistants and counselors, is just as future-oriented as hope is, but it allows significant deliveries here and now, as does love, deliveries not of instructions for behavior but of actual delight. By remembering ease, meat at the table, forgiveness of debts, bliss, light, and glory, the faithful actually produce these things, or reproduce them, since divine gifts and momentary presences are based on biblical precedent. Reviewing the old narratives tells us that divine promises are kept sooner or later, and so in a certain frame of mind Herbert's more confident speakers suspend the anxiety of hoped-for employment and the protocol of master/servant negotiation. In that frame of mind, the lack of accountable tasks to be performed is no longer a frustration, and faith can be substituted for the way stations of pilgrimage:

> Faith makes me any thing, or all
> That I beleeve is in the sacred storie;
> And where sinne placeth me in Adams fall,
> Faith sets me higher in his glorie.

Faith virtually equates the anecdotal nature of the Hebrew Bible with the new gospel's higher glory, it makes the latter much more immediate. In this comparatively early poem, the moments that it governs cancel the disadvantage of the always-waiting servant. Whereas the speakers of "The Pilgrimage" and "The Search" take to heart their inability to get through the tangled way, faith's narrative is perpetually "there":

> That which before was darkned clean
> With bushie groves, pricking the lookers eie,
> Vanisht away, when Faith did change the scene:
> And then appear'd a glorious skie.

This kind of filled time, which cancels cause and effect, circumstance, and the wait for apocalypse, is as unlike that of "The Pilgrimage" and "Decay" as it is unlike Estragon and Vladimir's as they wait for Godot, and not surprisingly, three of Herbert's more buoyant lyrics follow "Faith" in the Bodleian rearrangement and expansion: "Prayer 1," "The H. Communion," and "Antiphon 1." Together these constitute perhaps *The Church*'s greatest spiritual confidence short of liturgical reassurances and end things themselves; they certainly contain a buoyancy beyond that of "The Flower" and the poems that follow it. They treat moments of confidence not as mere changes of circumstance or mood but as encouragement from outside the church calendar. As the ultimate substance of both faith and hope (preeminently narrative virtues and attitudes from in the midst), they are not only based on end things but reach almost to them with proleptic figures and the high diction of "glorie" and "glorious skie."

Representations of an Absent God

For whatever reasons—reasons that perhaps include the tenuous spirituality of faith, the lack of specificity in the glory tropes, or simply the recurring momentum of a history that makes consolations evaporate—faith's solution does not govern all moments, any more than sacramental assurance carries over into murmuring and impatience. The tug of war between experience since the Incarnation and the two advents is recurrent: experience and tribulation gain some days; the blessings of the sacrifice and its promise gain others. Where faith says that God is a kind father, one who longs for him in his absence remembers human parents behaving with compassion toward their children while God seems indifferent or cruel. As "Longing" asks, how can a parental protection based on trust be an appropriate trope for God, when

> Thou tarriest, while I die,
> And fall to nothing: thou doest reigne,
> And rule on high,
> While I remain
> In bitter grief: Yet am I stil'd
> Thy childe.

Like sections of several complaint poems, "Longing" is cast as a prayer of complaint and places the imperative mood between the promise and the speaker's desperation. "Stil'd" is a telling word that incriminates whatever proponent of the trope the passive mood tactfully avoids naming. As a writerly word for masters who arouse the envy of their servants while treating them abysmally, it points up the discrepancy between text and experience. The alliterative lingering and resentful complaint of "reigne / And rule on high" sets up a bitter contrast to go with the insolence of the final rhyme. The conventional narrative tells us that the Lord Jesus bowed his "dying head upon the tree." How then can he be "more dead to me!" the speaker wonders, thinking in the terms of diaries of spiritual dessication: "*Shall he that made the eare, / Not heare?*"

Such appeals in *The Church* acknowledge a generally incurable, troubled context but cannot move toward a change. Even doctrine is subject to psychological states dictated not by capricious changes of mood but by the lack of connection between the events that sacraments reenact and extended time. The desire nonetheless to overrule experience by doctrine or by faith and hope is evident in "The Discharge," in which a similarly beleaguered speaker admonishes himself to forget inquiries into the past and the future. Curiosity implies lack of confidence. It encourages human reason to encroach bit by bit into the heart's domain and what belongs properly only to God:

> Busie enquiring heart, what wouldst thou know?
> Why dost thou prie,
> And turn, and leer, and with a licorous eye
> Look high and low;
> And in thy lookings stretch and grow?
>
> Hast thou not made thy counts, and summ'd up all?
> Did not thy heart
> Give up the whole, and with the whole depart?
> Let what will fall:
> That which is past who can recall?

On several occasions Herbert opposes prying, but seldom does a speaker show as much scorn for it as the first line does. Where Herbert subtly denies curiosity in "The Pearl" and "Vanity 1," he turns the wrath of the preacher loose upon it here. No one grows spiritually by snooping into divine secrets, as the rhetorical questions reiterate. The decision to "give up the whole"

seems final; and although its overstatement begs a response, none is forthcoming. In "prie," "turn," and "leer," equivalents to the need for certainty
are seated in firm metrical units, cumulative disgust, and anger.

If Herbert establishes a broader domain for forbidden knowledge than
either Donne or Milton does, the reason is surely in part that one is not well
employed in devising ways to help out Providence or to explain it when the
whole question of works is unresolved. His concern is not merely distrust but
lack of concentration on the present and the anxiety that comes of being end-
minded. Whatever is not controlled by faith—that is vaguely futuristic or
nostalgically past—drains the life out of "things present":

> God chains the dog till night: wilt loose the chain,
> And wake thy sorrow?
> Wilt thou forestall it, and now grieve to morrow,
> And then again
> Grieve over freshly all thy pain?
>
> Either grief will not come: or if it must,
> Do not forecast.
> And while it cometh, it is almost past.
> Away distrust:
> My God hath promis'd; he is just.

The tone is curious after the excess of the heart's chastisement earlier, as is
the oddity of the speaker's talking of the heart's heart as though he could not
decide what part of him is so ill-advisedly discontented. We now understand
more clearly that the violence of the diction has been self-directed, that it is
the scolding of a tempted heart. Applied to collective and social matters as
well as to personal pain and grief, such violence actually counsels patience
round about. The upshot is that in the midst of grief, or in anticipation of it,
trust is difficult to hold but must be held, and that usually means passivity.
The chained dog will be unleashed soon enough ("God chains the dog" only
"till night"). To go toward it or await it without fear would be presumptuous.
Faith must somehow be strong enough to make one ignore both scriptural
chronicles and personal experience wherever a grief-laden past seems to bode
a grief-laden future. Death itself is as much of the present as it is of the
future, "For death each houre environs and surrounds." That being so, one's
personal future goes "through a Church-yard" that doomsday will empty at
last. Such a future shrinks the present with its awareness of what after all

requires no very close inquiry to see—the ever-pressing lessons of flesh, falling to nothing while God prepares for final moments.

Another hitch in Herbert's attempt to stop the leakage of faith in some personas despite heartening renewals, is suggested by the echo here of the first line of Donne's poem "The Sunne Rising": "Busie old foole, unruly Sunne." Besides their opening lines, what the two poems have in common is the dismissal of a social world that has no regard for the heart's desire. Donne's brash lover addresses a solar alarm clock imposing its schedule. His answer to the regulated world is that lovers can make themselves oblivious to anything outside if they choose to. In both poems, the more forcefully the speaker strikes rival interests off the list, the more aware of them he becomes. Remembering not to remember is a psychological trick comparable to recalling God's promise without thinking of his absence or to finding certain associations in metaphors such as "father" and "child" without thinking of the holder of the dog's chain. The obvious difference between "The Sunne Rising" and "The Discharge" is Herbert's substitution of God for the mistress. His speaker cannot fasten upon God as Donne's can upon "her sight." She is actually present, in a bed that can be imagined the sun's center; God in "The Discharge" is nowhere in sight, the negative side of Herbert's rewriting of secular love conventions. Yet to remember that God owns everything ("Thy life is Gods, thy time to come is gone, / And is his right") requires inattention to the present. Even though a discharge is a release from such obligations and in a legalistic context the present is one's fee or reward, the present cannot bring satisfaction if faith is everything and works nothing, which is another way of saying that the future is everything, the personal present and past merely fleeting. Yet again, exclusive focus on the present, even if one could manage it, would only bring the fable to a standstill. As it is, longing causes it to evaporate moment by moment.

Like "Decay" and "Longing," "The Discharge" exposes the dreary underside of faith and its draining away of life-as-lived. It reveals another cost of the pearl and the rejection of the Baconian pursuit of secondary causes, which we can begin to see as something greater in sum than inventories of learning, honor, and pleasure in "The Pearl." If God's presence is the fullness of time, his absence must empty it. If Jesus is the only high priest, as the hellenic writer of Hebrews argues, then the Holy of Holies and the mercy seat are paradoxically always and never occupied. Assurance of salvation, although comforting with respect to the future, does not change the details of personal narratives, which will be as deprived or as luxurious as their social and bodily life dictates. Inquiry into any secular field competes with the absolutism of that narrative. "Counting" and "summing" up in "The Discharge" are relegated to the time when the heart first gave up the rest. Given the fact that the hound will be turned loose eventually, the best consolation the speaker can offer his anxious heart is that however hard it bites *that* pain does not last long.

Rewriting the Past

Obviously, these impatience poems are not among Herbert's happier ones; and if they were isolated or their attitudes were not present also in his best work—"The Flower," "Temper 1," "Vertue," "Church-monuments," and others—it would not be justifiable to give them such prominence. As it is, however, they go hand in hand with lyric moments placed in a historical waste that Herbert shares with many of his contemporaries, and within the metaphoric sedimentation of the dominant Reformation and seventeenth-century doctrines. Drawing upon conventional emblems and iconological traditions, Herbert's vocabulary is predefined by the given semantic field and an aggregate of tropes that stress expectation and supplication while ignoring or dismissing the bulk of the past and present.

I have used Bacon's confession of faith primarily to suggest that Herbert's degree of world-denial need not have been as extreme even within that aggregate field and its institutions. (With some adjustments, Milton might help make a similar point.) As the scriptural passages that Herbert uses show, he need not have turned to Genevan theology for much of his version of temporality. It is already well-represented in the synoptic Gospels, the Pauline Epistles, and a Messiah who, though represented by the spirit and the word, does not keep reentering history and working actively, as YHWH does. Bacon's achievement was to develop an alternative terminology for empiricism with a method that he could keep from open conflict with his confession. He imagines state, church, and scientific establishment coexisting harmoniously, not merely in utopia but in a realizable future. His employment of what Stephen Daniel calls "literate experience" contrasts to Herbert's use of parables and sacred language in that respect. For Herbert only language that delivers sure instruction for climbing the silk twist is worthy to be set beside sacramental presences. Bacon's "mythic thought provides the context for specifying the prerational and prephilosophic structures upon which a theory of discovery can be based" (Daniel 219). Those storied constructions conduct us to a mastery of such subjects as the ones Herbert finds suspiciously enticing to the fleet astronomer and his nimble and subtle company. But Herbert's rejection of natural history is only the first step in clearing the way for the exclusive study of parabolic and sacramental tropes. In the intersection of the sedimented language and its institutional rites, current historical moments encounter the overall salvation narrative again and again. His poems take root in that meeting, in which nature plays only a minor role—and that at an entry level. When he turns his attention from the grievances of the moment to the writing process, he realizes both the mutual pressure that the moment and the framework exert on each other and the limitations of nature's storehouse of metaphors.

The proper place and function of longing, grief, hope, and faith is by and large a psychological question in the postponement poems, but it brings with it an ontological concern with nature as well. The impatience poems are often convinced that the weightier reality here and now is that of tribulation. In "Dotage" Herbert lists quantities of false hopes without suggesting a frame of mind to lighten their impact:

> False glozing pleasures, casks of happinesse,
> Foolish night-fires, womens and childrens wishes,
> Chases in Arras, guilded emptinesse,
> Shadows well mounted, dreams in a career,
> Embroider'd lyes, nothing between two dishes;
>   These are the pleasures here.
>
> True earnest sorrows, rooted miseries,
> Anguish in grain, vexations ripe and blown,
> Sure-footed griefs, solid calamities,
> Plain demonstrations, evident and cleare,
> Fetching their proofs ev'n from the very bone;
>   These are the sorrows here.

Hammered into place by an emphatic trochaic measure, elaborately balanced, these two itemizations propose contrasting definitions of what is illusory and what is woefully true. Pleasures lie concealed or indirectly represented in art and in figments of imagination dangled in trailing rhymes. Anyone who bothers to lift the veils of "false glozing pleasures" finds that happiness stored in casks leaves hangovers; hunts portrayed on tapestry are not proper substitutes for the feel of a horse at full gallop; women and children imagine what their gift bearers will bring and reach out to find nothing. Each of these instances reduces hope to illusion. Sorrows meanwhile have no such ontological difficulty. Substantial in quantity and sharp in presence, they fetch "their proofs ev'n from the very bone."

Herbert makes these points with an unusual emphasis on adjectives, with something close to a cursing effect, which suggests that we pronounce the word "dotage" with contempt. The brisk movement through the so-called pleasures and their dismissal gets us quickly into the sorrows, which are slowed down a little by their superior weightiness. "Fetching their proofs" nails down that weight with a certainty that is difficult to avoid. It is a tribute to Herbert that these are not remarkable stanzas by his standard and that nothing particularly noteworthy climaxes them in that painful final line, yet many another poet would be thankful to have written them. Much of the secret lies in the reinforcement of attitude by vocal gesture, another topic for a later consideration of his mastery of formal devices. The double stresses of the adjectives "true earnest" and "sure-footed" plant the sorrows and griefs squarely in the way, so that the reader cannot brush by them casually. Having used a trochaic hammer to break up the frail pleasures, he uses it again to set misery and calamity in place. This is typical of Herbert as a poet of complaint and suggests a certain conviction in that mode.

The third stanza for equally characteristic reasons (unfortunately) answers this imbalance between pleasures and miseries with moralizing piety and a less convincing case for patience:

> But oh the folly of distracted men,
> Who griefs in earnest, joyes in jest pursue;
> Preferring, like brute beasts, a lothsome den
> Before a court, ev'n that above so cleare,
> Where are no sorrows, but delights more true
>   Then miseries are here!

Herbert repeats that commonplace sentiment elsewhere as well, as in "The Size," which concludes, "*These seas are tears, and heav'n the haven.*" To be "distracted" (on the wrong track) is to swerve from the ending "above so cleare." The more telling matter, however, is the limpness of "Where are no sorrows, but delights more true" compared to the corresponding lines in the preceding two stanzas. The present refuses to be written off in favor of so vague a future. *It* falls solidly into place; meanwhile "that above so cleare" is not at all clear in image or in the substance that is to be put into the "true."

The difficulty is that denouncing one's dotage ends lower pursuits without necessarily empowering better ones. Meanwhile we are treated to a subtle modulation of rhythm that combines features of the two previous stanzas, as Herbert allows a subdued ambivalence to linger. "But of the folly" triggers an elegiac note in the aftermath of the vigorous list of follies at the outset. If the parade of false pleasures has passed by at a fast tempo and the sorrows have staying power, here the caesura of the second line balances earnest griefs and jesting joys with fine irony before attention shifts to another setting beyond any that can actually be witnessed. Wielding alliteration as keynote and counterpoint, Herbert uses the last of the vigorous rhythms on "brute beasts" before appropriating the same alliteration in "before" and "above" in the countering high court. No full movement in that direction is possible from within the present-dominated distress. The trailing construction of the last sentence silently concedes the highest magnitude to folly, using truer delights mainly as judgmental leverage and basis for enduring.

In its open approval of longing, "Dotage" appears to reverse the advice of the preceding poem, "The Flower." In "Dotage" men do not actually see the earnestness of sorrows and absurdity of joys, and so they persist. The speaker of "The Flower" finds no alternative to enduring the cycles of God's returns and departures and cautions himself to stay within them. As both poems indicate, the future and the immediate past differ from the distant past. The memory of recent frosts intensifies the return of divine favor; late quickenings intensify God's "least frown." In the flourishing present, the poet can scrutinize that recent memory and take it to heart. Yet Herbert takes a cautious way in assuming that vacillation is designed to make us see that "we are but flowers that glide," where "glide" means to go with the times and sit patiently in humility—or in negative terms, not to swell, "shoot up fair," or yearn for heaven. What the best of moments brings forth—an inspired poetic blossoming—is the very thing one must guard against. Reaching the final garden depends on "finding and proving" the reiterated truth of a powerless frailty: "Which when we once can finde and prove, / Thou has a garden for us," where "once" means "if we could ever *really* find." Achieving paradise depends on a balanced philosophical attitude in which one is ready to leave but is not so eager to go that one becomes presumptuous. That is a less orthodox observation than the conclusion of "Dotage" but psychologically sound when set against romantic nostalgia. That the garden Herbert hopes for in "The Flower" may be a paradise within (Strier, *Love Known* 252) seems unlikely. "Thou hast a garden" sounds like the paradise past changing. For the time being, occasional flourishing—

unpredictable in its coming and going and disturbing in its foretaste of paradise—seems the only consolation, certainly the one the poem as such must settle for, given the limitations of the flower metaphor. Its satisfactions are more personal than liturgical, more connected to the psyche's inner trials and discoveries and to the poet's coming forth with tropes.

By Way of Purchase

When Herbert looks for ways around the impasse of such poems, what he often settles for is a rearguard defense of poetic works, a defense vital to the writing of *The Temple*. The poems that employ it are not as forceful as those which dramatize the difficulty of enduring patiently, the denials of proffered service ("Love 3"), and the visionary canceling of temporality ("Vertue," "Death"). For want of a more timely moment, I will consider one such defense here, "Obedience," as a complex counterstatement that combines an implied personal story with a different sort of scrutiny of writing. From "The Dedication" through "Love 3," to render service generally and service as a poet specifically is a recurrent desire. Herbert would obviously like to honor the production of *The Church* if a way could be found to do so—or a variety of ways, since justification for psalmic praise is less difficult than justification for poems of longing, complaint, or definition. "Obedience" illustrates the bargaining of one who is not backward in articling with God.

　　The first three stanzas request divine acceptance of the gift and offer reasons based on sincerity—which constitutes the chief enticement for God's acceptance of poem-offerings intermittently from "the Altar" onward. The fourth stanza retracts the poet's claim for ownership of his deed, although if love guides him his way becomes coincident with God's without ceasing to be his:

> My God, if writings may
> Convey a Lordship any way
> Wither the buyer and the seller please;
> Let it not thee displease,
> If this poore paper do as much as they.

> On it my heart doth bleed
> As many lines, as there doth need

To passe it self and all it hath to thee.
To which I do agree,
And here present it as my speciall Deed.

If that hereafter Pleasure
Cavill, and claim her part and measure,
As if this passed with a reservation,
Or some such words in fashion;
I here exclude the wrangler from thy treasure.

O let thy sacred will
All thy delight in me fulfill!
Let me not think an action mine own way,
But as thy love shall sway,
Resigning up the rudder to thy skill.

Inscribing himself in a work he says to be of transparent feeling (but is much too legalistic for that), he imagines himself justified in asking what he asks. The transparency is all but gone by the fourth stanza when we realize that the appeal permits two quite different readings: delight in *me*, or *thy* delight fulfill, as though to say "consummate the delight you already take in me" or "give me the unbounded delight that only you can give." In the third stanza too, "thy treasure" could be either the treasure offered by the speaker or the hidden life awarded by the Son. The alternative favorable to personal achievement is not necessarily incompatible with what follows, but the poet's act of bestowing is to say the least under a shadow. One could surrender the rudder and still ply the oars; or one could be a passenger in both a Son-powered and a Son-directed craft.

Other doublings parallel these, as for instance in a later stanza, "Besides, thy death and bloud / Show'd a strange love to all our good," where "good" could be possessed by "our" or the purpose of the showing. Still more crucial is the governing clause of the deed, which finally forces a choice among these hovering possibilities:

Wherefore I all forgo:
To one word onely I say, No:
Where in the Deed there was an intimation
Of a gift or donation,
Lord, let it now by way of purchase go.

The reading proposed by Richard Strier finds the speaker retracting his attempts to bargain and makes the purchase what Christ paid for in the Crucifixion. The stanza as a whole then becomes a "genuine conclusion, summing up and resolving the entire movement of the poem," a movement toward the unconditional surrender of claims to personal merit (*Love Known* 95). Such a surrender drops the speaker into a thoroughly stalled history and reinstates the partnership of faith and patience, besides keeping Herbert firmly in the Genevan camp where Strier wants him.

A consequence of that reading, consistent with the surrender of self, is that the last two stanzas become an afterthought, in the manner of Calvinist preachers whose encouragement of moral conduct contradicts the predestination they assume (*Love Known* 96). Apart from the inadvisability of discarding two stanzas of a poem, "to one word onely I say, No" more naturally suggests what must after all be a strong temptation for a poet who day after day returns to his desk to write. The preceding lines have conceded that Christ's grace is offered in "earnest" (paraphrasable as seriously, in grief, and in pledged prepayment): it is not superficial and cannot be turned down, at least by this speaker. But since realizing that requires a retraction of what he has hoped to convey by deed, he takes back the "all" and puts "by way of purchase" in place of "gift or donation." Although he has not actually used either of these latter words, he has summed up his heart and passed the deed and "all it hath" to God. If the "No" serves any purpose, then, he clings to what the heart has offered as his purchasing power.

Just how passive or active anyone must be toward a divine covenant is always debatable. Before entering into league with YHWH, Moses questions the conditions and is shown evidence of the Lord's sincerity and power, and when he weakens, he is confirmed in his purpose. How much of his patriarchal role he owes to his own qualities as a leader and how much to this reiterated support is not easily determined. Indeed, this is a question that could be asked about Joshua and the several protagonists of Judges and Kings as well. In "Assurance" Herbert looks upon the certainty of earlier covenants into which have crept a "spiteful bitter thought" and gnawing pensiveness. In seeking a renewal of assurance, he recalls the clear sign of God's intent in the willing issuance of the text: "when the league was made / Thou didst at once thy self indite, / And hold my hand, while I did write." Does this mean that the human hand moves of its own accord, with God's guidance? Or that the cosigner is a puppet sustained by God's forcefulness? It is impossible to say, and the position of "Obedience" should perhaps be stated just as tentatively. One way or another the covenant ends up with the agreement of both parties, and the poet from his end knows only that he has made up his will, worded it as best he can, and thrust it forward.

If one person's sincere heart *can* be exchanged for divine favor, so may another's. The will-maker's gesture, which sends forth several tropes for the divine/human agreement, has the rhetorical power to attract others of like kind, so that the parties to the deed may expand from the poet to readers—specifically, as it turns out, from Herbert to Vaughan. When poets thus claim an evangelical mission, as Herbert also does in "Praise 3" and "An Offering"—the specific work of a verbal vineyard—they construct a small church history within literary history. Their collaboration forms a kind of genealogy among producers of deeds, which forges a bond between one person's insight and another's. Both the first and the second parties "thrust" their hearts in, where they stay until they fly together to "heav'ns Court of Rolls." Reading the poem more or less straightforwardly in this way (and I am not that confident that we should) avoids some internal difficulties and honors Vaughan's reaction in "The Match" as well as the line from "Praise 3," where the speaker proclaims, "O that I might some other hearts convert." The poet of heartfelt lines withstands the cancellation that seems unavoidable in poems such as "The Thanksgiving," where a baffled speaker finds no proper trope for the sacrifice and no other entirely satisfactory work. Despite his doubts elsewhere and despite the ambiguities of "The Dedication," Herbert anticipates at the outset that those who "turn their eyes hither" will "make a gain." Presumably if he did not think so, he would not have sent the manuscript to Ferrar or gestured to all those with pure hearts to come and make an offering:

> O that within us hearts had propagation,
> Since many gifts do challenge many hearts!
> Yet one, if good, may title to a number;
> And single things grow fruitfull by deserts.
> In publick judgements one may be a nation,
> And fence a plague, while others sleep and slumber.
>
> ("An Offering")

Whether or not Herbert himself is equivalent to his bargaining speaker in "Obedience" or the hopeful begetter of offerers elsewhere is of course debatable. Although the immediately surrounding poems do not question his ambition and the writing of the manuscript says much for it, purchasing God's favor by such a bestowal contradicts the passivity of "The Holdfast,"

"Love unknown," "Love 3," and other poems. Perhaps the most one can say is that collectively the poems are searching and restive, and that what appears in one is contradicted in another.

The most interesting piece of near-contemporary opinion comes from Vaughan, who in meeting Herbert's offer halfway in "The Match" is also open to the idea of usable works. He readily gives up all *"Thoughts, words, actions,"* probably worldly ones, but the verbs of his equivalent deed describe a project that, inflamed by Herbert, he prosecutes vigorously: "Here I join hands, and thrust in my stubborn heart / Into thy *deed.*" Once he makes that commitment to self-conveyance, certain moral repercussions follow. He expects to be "from no *duties*" freed:

> And if hereafter *youth*, or *folly* thwart
> And claim their share,
> Here I renounce the pois'nous ware.

Contrition produces seedlike tears that through Christ's agency grow into grain and become *"new* and *quick,"* which is to say that they too become fruitful works. Vaughan thereby grants that a man like Herbert does "much good / To many," including himself. We may distrust a poem that scatters so many metaphors about, but a statement such as "Here I renounce" is obviously a speech act of some confidence. If the lifelines of poets prepare for the final pleading of their cases, they are not totally wasted; and the entire business of postponement gains a purpose that does much to quiet impatience.

The language of covenanting in both "Obedience" and "The Match" parallels the emergence of regulatory agreements from YHWH's encounters with the prophets. But where conditional agreements make a highly mediated patriarchal application of divine will to a people, obedience to these unilateral commitments by Herbert and Vaughan is individual and tentative. Neither receives direct instruction or participates in the consensus-making signs and displays of good faith that accompany the covenants as codified in Leviticus and reiterated throughout pentateuchal and deuteronomic history. Both have much less to go on; yet if what they are writing into the record accompanies them all the way to "heav'ns Court of Rolls," something significant is obviously at stake. Where reward for service ordinarily becomes an outmoded concept once the reward is totalized and made unconditional (on the grounds that nothing can earn it), "Obedience" testifies to how hard it is to eliminate metaphors of account keeping and exchange. Even the sale of all pearls to purchase the great one suggests that the merchant has stored-up personal wealth to contribute to it. Somehow the incommensurability of resources and reward does not disable his purchase. The twist lies in the fact that he cashes in his accumulation not for actual salvation but for a belief that requires discarding rival interests before he can then receive salvation as a gift. He cannot earn it either; what he does is initiate a personal history that sweeps him into a defiance of logic that would connect all moments to the end. That obliterates lesser, time-serving goals but threatens also to cut him off from social and natural history. It is this isolation in the construction of a personal identity that removes meaningful civil and scientific projects of the interim, drastically reduces the dialogue exchanges and addresses that fill the secular work of a Sidney or a Jonson, and gives pilgrimages stark symbolic landscapes concluded by death or apocalypse.

4
FILLED INTERVALS AND ABSTRACT TOTALITY

Now the children of Reuben and the children of Gad had a very great multitude of cattle: and when they saw the land of Jazer, and the land of Gilead, that, behold, the place was a place for cattle: The children of Gad and the children of Reuben came and spake unto Moses.

—Numbers 32.1–2

Stopping This Side of the Jordan

As the poems of impatience and limited knowledge discussed in the previous two chapters teach us, the lighted way of Scripture can be weakened by intrusions of personal experience. It is also obscured in Scripture itself by the several roles a universal God must assume in taking over the functions of corn gods, battle gods, fertility gods, and gods of the weather, the heavens, and the underworld. The deciphering of sacred texts reveals other Hebraic "equivalents" to the Christian way that on the surface are not quite exact, such as the journey to Canaan, the destruction and restoration of the Temple, and the davidic Messiah. Too much of this cultural pluralism falls outside the

Pauline fable to allow its easy assimilation through allegory. Renegade elements intrude into the lives of even fairly exemplary leaders and heroes such as Saul, Gideon, David, and Solomon.

In this chapter, which resembles the previous in considering the effects on Herbert's lyric moments of an enforced wait, I want to insert into the fable and its master tropes the principle of randomness and narrative loops. It is after all a social and political history that biblical authors work with, full of divergences and interruptions in the progression. One example is the settling of the children of Gad and Reuben east of the Jordan, a story of unexpected opportunism that comes back to hamper the unifiers of the Exodus story in a slightly different manner from that of the murmuring rebels of the "bunch of grapes" episode. The Reubenite diversion opens the way for parallel deflections from the trek to Canaan, which unifies both the pentateuchal narrative and its typological parallels. The appropriation of that overall narrative to the reading of the Bible that links the Old Testament and the New prepares the way for the movement from a national to a universal covenant. Such breaks in the momentum of the story offer precedents for local alliances and self-initiated works. In effect, what the Reubenites turn to is the cattle business when the Lord of Hosts is bent on conquest. This sets a pattern for escaping the rigors of pilgrimage that Herbert's personas, especially the wayward and rebellious ones, can convert into their own agendas.

In narrative terms it comes to this in Numbers 32: the tribes of Reuben and Gad find what they consider a suitable place short of the designated land and propose to Moses, Eleazar the priest, and the council that their settling there need not weaken the invasion of Canaan. Certainly it would not constitute anything like a return to Egypt, the always-condemned counter-movement of the Exodus story and indication of contamination by Egyptian gods, which amounts to abandoning providential history. The two opposed prospects, getting to Canaan and reverting to slavery, prove to be narrative types usable for Christian pilgrimages and their concepts of relapse. In hellenist readings, that usually means pitting spirituality and abstract philosophy against the material world and the appetites. The desire to turn back shows a lack of faith that Herbert uses to advantage, for instance, in the rebellion of the speaker in "The Bunch of Grapes." Yet to press on risks very real dangers and apparent penalties. In the land of Jazer and Gilead, the Gadites and Reubenites find what they consider a suitable compromise and see no reason not to build there. That their discovery comes as a surprise is suggested by the "behold." It substitutes geographical recognition for the theophanies that initiate and reaffirm conquest epic under Moses, Aaron, and Joshua. In effect it opens the national movement to the contingencies of an unprophesied and divided future.

Not until the Gadites and Reubenites agree to honor their military commitment before returning to their newfound pastureland does Moses accept their proposal. Numbers, Joshua, and Deuteronomy subsequently pay reiterated attention to that agreement and the prospect of schism that it raises. In effect, it leads not to an outright division but to a troubling religious and cultural variety that plagues the centralized monarchy later. Calum Carmichael finds long-term problems of law, military service, and transvestitism in the incident, problems that are not cleared up or forgotten (160–80). Certainly this episode complicates the yoking of national prosperity to obedience, since the deflection is neither permitted nor forbidden but simply avoids prophesied closure. It lowers the intensity of devotion and opens a humanist wedge in a society commanded otherwise to commit genocide in the name of religion.

As a chronicle, the Hebrew Bible has other diversions and attendant tales that cannot be said either to forward the Exodus narrative or seriously to impede it. They are interludes that concede that even a book devoted exclusively to the people's relations to God does not find clear commandments or rules for all occasions. (It may in fact, as Martin Noth speculates [52], have not been a unified account to begin with but separate tribal chronicles following different routes to different sectors of Canaan.) Some history slips under the explanatory guard and seems to sanction a multiplicity of interpretations. Yet whatever the verse-by-verse interpretation, the overall thrust of Hebrew prophecy is otherwise and undermines any such drifting away. Sooner or later the tendency for compromise will make concessions to foreign gods and neighboring cults, which remains very much a problem through Judges, Samuel, Kings, and Chronicles. It has already done so many times when the Reubenite story itself is being written, since the entire episode is interpreted after the fact from amid other deflections from centralized worship. That no grapes are on the vine or figs in the tree, that leaves are everywhere withered, becomes all the more telling in the lamentations of the prophets when they are thought to show a reverse providence, taking away the prosperity that the people regard as their right. The sadly wiser poet, after so many setbacks and under the cloud of the lost homeland, complains that "Thou has covered with anger, and persecuted us: thou has slain, thou has not pitied. Thou hast covered thyself with a cloud, that our prayer should not pass through. Thou hast made us as the offscouring and refuse in the midst of the people" (Lamentations 3.43–45).

The desire of the Gadites and Reubenites to settle outside Canaan does not warrant outright condemnation, however, and therein lies its attraction and its enigmatic place in the context of narrative totalism. It gains its blessings without either the assistance or the wrath of Moses and the high priest. It singles out of YHWH's multiple personality the part that is interested in animal husbandry rather than in the slaying of Amalekites. One would expect New Testament equivalents to this episode to be rare, since eschatology absolutizes the promised land. The pearl parable indicates Herbert's support of that commitment. Even so, the Christian eras, like the eventful histories of the Jews, are sure to produce comparable "things indifferent." The question becomes what to make of them in weaving the various into the unitary. Byways like "Fancy's meadow" in "The Pilgrimage" are largely temptations to be turned down, except that the poet in considering them in verse is already pausing to write about not pausing in them, and sometimes to write about not writing about not pausing in them. This paradox is very much like the one that Fisch points out in the Jordan poems, in Herbert's use of extended and often clever devices to condemn such, or again in the "A Wreath" winding slowly to a conclusion that demands the straightest way possible. Is some randomness still possible even for a poet who binds everything to the single configuration of "H. Scriptures 2"? Can one pass in and out of providential zones? These questions parallel the question of language's relation to the aggregate Christian language: can a Christian lyric poetry explore climate changes and collide various languages with the single language of devotion that the poet hopes to master?

The storied detail of the Hebrew Bible is a critical test for Herbert because it gives episodic history a prominent place, with all the sanctions of canonization. The allegory encouraged by Hebrews (a thinned-out version, according to Gabriel Josipovici and Gerald Bruns) argues against one's passing in and out of providential command. That Herbert should discourage freewheeling invention might seem to follow from his plain-style declarations and from "The Pearl" and "The Holdfast" as, among other things, policy statements. But attention to complaints and nostalgic glances at Jewish narratives suggest that he could not consistently put aside all lingering glances at equivalents to the settlement of Jazer and Gilead.

The main obstacle to a completely closed narrative is the difficulty of discovering purpose within an arena of secondary causes that effectively screen off the First Cause and leave interpreters with what Bacon calls Pan's footsteps. The length of the interval between the First and Second Comings compounds that problem. As Christ has built upon Daniel, Peter upon Christ, and John of Patmos upon a by-then considerable genealogy, so Tudor and Jacobean expounders of many accumulated texts (expounders such as John Napier, Thomas Brightman, Hugh Broughton, Henry Burton, Joseph Mede, and James I) attempt to assimilate an ever-increasing Library of materials into world history. But they do so without notable success, especially when, like Richard Haklyut, Sir Walter Raleigh, and Samuel Purchase, they expand the scope of those texts geographically. In retrospect, whatever has already happened can perhaps be considered in typological terms, but it is less convincing to say that what *will* happen is already prewritten and timed, or to predict an end to time by a certain date. Yet practically every historian/prophet who thinks of world history, including Bacon, Browne, Milton, and Marvell among the more cautious ones, concede that the world's term is nearly expired, and that what Providence has all along intended will soon be clear.

The question of intervals that fall outside such interpretive schemes sheds light on the structure of *The Temple* and the spiritual progress that some readings impose upon it. Although I will not pursue the architectural side of the question here, the placing of the lyrics in the single-book model established by "H. Scriptures 2" reiterates the problem of assimilating Herbert's recurrent "now" into a master pattern. Thanks partly to his rejection of natural and civil history as an abiding interest, not a good deal works free of the governing *mythos*, but well-grounded, everyday language is itself a deviation of sorts. Constantly locked in battle, the abstract vocabulary of Christian philosophemes and colloquial speech measure each other, perhaps in no other poet as in Herbert. If "progress" is the right word for the movement toward the "mystical repast," it is obviously a much-impeded and devious one, full of Reubenite defections. Despite that, critics have been tempted to program *The Temple* as though it is not only destination bound (which it is) but mappable. Thus the first group of poems from "The Altar" to "The Crosse" resembles we are told the temple's forecourt. A middle group up to "The Flower" resembles the sanctuary. Poems from there to the end of *The Church* reach an inner sanctum. Unfortunately, the first group is by nature open and the last group does not fit snugly into a pattern of spiritual achievement. It is also questionable whether the sacramental resolution implied by "Love 3," which draws back from the eschatology of the preceding poems, can be made into more than a model case of self-submission, by an Everyone created for that poem, a typical wayward soul personally "mastered." Finally—a point to be pursued later—it is a poem and not a sacrament.

That "Love 3" sets several vocabularies side by side—drawn primarily

from the courtship situation of Renaissance love poetry and the Bible—allows
Herbert to subdue a certain amount of ordinary usage to an extraordinary
redeeming love. But that in no way answers the problem of a self otherwise
occupied. Nor do the poems from "The Flower" onward lead to the end as
the climax of an implied spiritual development. The last word of "The
Watercourse" is "Damnation"; the keynote of "self-condemnation" is appropriately enough self-condemnation; the bitter matches the sweet in "Bitter-
sweet"; "The Answer" as we noted earlier offers no answer; "The Foil"
could be placed almost anywhere in the volume, as could "Discipline,"
which renders a suppliant's appeal to the God of wrath. Even "Dooms-day,"
after a promising beginning, returns to the anxiety of the postponed end.
"Heaven" hears in a distant echo a voice that renews the promise but lacks
the force of immanence. It consigns reverberation to abstractions—light, joy,
leisure, eternity. In several lyric pressure points, Herbert seems comfortable
with the large scale, as he is in "Vertue" and "Dooms-day," but not with the
mantle of the prophets or their rhetoric. Thus we do not approach even the
final group in the heightened vocabulary of Revelation or Donnelike anxiety,
a point I will explore further in the final chapter. The loftier moments of *The
Church* are not very numerous or particularly featured. The translation of the
soul in "Vertue" and the collective ending of "The Church Militant" are
brief and relatively quiet. In their most sustained concern with the end, the
last several poems prefer the muted tone of "Death" and "Love 3" to
Revelation's radiance of the Lamb. Only occasionally does Herbert develop
the amplified exaltation of Psalms. When he wants to be all-encompassing,
he is more likely to use a miniaturist's technique, in a language of interchange
in which the sacred and the secular jostle each other without allowing the
universal God very far into the role of a god of corn, animals, weather, or any
specific place.

The Whole World at Once

The better lyric opportunities tend to come at strained points of impatience
or in the midst of new realizations when the instrumentation and timing of
the promise are suspended but no Reubenite alternative is at hand. Herbert
draws upon a conventional typology, biographical narrative, and psalmic lyric
intervals to handle them. Before exploring the principle of intervals further,
however, I want to establish one highly abstract "coverage" poem as an

opposite but related case. In contrast to both intense lyric moments and things indifferent, "The World" is just such a synoptic poem. It uses allegorical animation to present the history of Love's stately house, which may be also imagined to be the scene of the final poem of *The Church*. It is primarily in this poem that Herbert connects general history with the mastery that love is ultimately given. How love enters history and what it does is here put in comprehensive terms, with reference to types of forces at play throughout the course of things from beginning to end. "The World" uses fixed-essence abstractions of a kind also illustrated by both the titles of many Herbert poems and certain lines that stop internal movement, such as "Softnesse, and peace, and joy, and love, and blisse" in "Prayer 1." Reducing the entire world to a single trope and all its major forces to builders and wreckers, Herbert manages not merely a single-volume universal history but a twenty-line synopsis of it. However large the panorama, this poetic globe can be held in one hand.

When nothing can save the house, Herbert sets love, grace, and glory against the Lord's enemies and has them construct a "braver palace":

> Love built a stately house; where *Fortune* came,
> And spinning phansies, she was heard to say,
> That her fine cobwebs did support the frame,
> Whereas they were supported by the same:
> But *Wisdome* quickly swept them all away.
>
> Then *Pleasure* came, who, liking not the fashion,
> Began to make *Balcones*, *Terraces*,
> Till she had weakned all by alteration:
> But rev'rend *laws*, and many a *proclamation*
> Reformed all at length with menaces.
>
> Then enter'd *Sinne*, and with that Sycomore,
> Whose leaves first sheltred man from drought & dew,
> Working and winding slily evermore,
> The inward walls and sommers cleft and tore:
> But *Grace* shor'd these, and cut that as it grew.
>
> Then *Sinne* combin'd with *Death* in a firm band
> To raze the building to the very floore:
> Which they effected, none could them withstand.
> But *Love* and *Grace* took *Glorie* by the hand,
> And built a braver Palace then before.

Into this one parable, which rids paradise of all interest in what corn and animal gods normally supply, Herbert collects some of his most representative assumptions and narrative strategies, to go with an idiom that marks a sweeping cancellation of the alternatives, seen here as architectural frills that fortune and pleasure add to the original house. Were either the chronological story or the church foremost, sin would no doubt come first and give fortune and pleasure their moments. The reforms of wisdom and law would come later, although progress from the Old to the New Testament, barely visible here, would still require their replacement. The poem follows a logic similar to that of Hebrews and the concluding books of *Paradise Lost*: so universal are the ravages of the Fall that not only are fortune and pleasure helpless but so also are the authors of the Law. Ornate building in the Lord's house is diversionary and dangerous in its heterodoxy. Fortune has no final say in the matter. Pleasures derive from human meddling and run toward display.

Included in what Herbert consigns to these abstractions are the multitude of human stories that in the long run amount to nothing. The comprehensiveness of "None could them withstand" takes care of each and every human effort. Were personal experience a serious concern, the proper order would be that of trial and discovery, and the final phase might include an anxious projection of a still-uncertain future rather than hints of an apocalypse. Instead, "The World" pairs programmatic opposites, giving dialectical charting priority over chronology. It then resolves their contest in the celebrational brevity of "built a braver Palace." But the diminution is not precisely that of a summary. It subdues not only the chronological story but dialectic to the art of troping, especially personification, which gives the poem both its measured distance and its energy. The assault of those forcefully applied acts of "working" and "winding," and the wreckage of "cleft," "tore," and finally the razing itself put spin on the globe.

Where Assyrians, Greeks, and Romans razed the sacred houses of the Israelites historically, sin and death combine in this succession of scenes. Since as "The Church Militant" illustrates, no national institution can stand against them, Herbert does not bother to include historical epochs. The key to the world is not the collective empires people have built but inner motives. Only certain temporary safeguards draw upon human resourcefulness. Wisdom and law, for instance, fall within ordinary education and require nothing beyond a prudent observation of what sustains the edifice, nothing beyond the received institutional codes. "Menaces" is an odd word for what constrains pleasure, but discipline has to use force. The final gesture finishes the bickering of the contestants with a display of unity that goes beyond human prowess but does not preclude human participation. The personification would be less compelling were it not for wisdom's, law's, and grace's dismissals of subterfuge, but finally it is the combination of love and grace that prevails both here and in the conclusion of *The Church*. Where biblical storytellers and psalmists might have resorted to amplitude, Herbert restricts himself to a concluding tranquility.

It is after all glory that love and grace bring forth, and glory is achievement raised beyond human triumph. In the psalms and Hebrew battle hymns, it attends upon and follows vengeance, but in this greater triumph it passes straight into eschatology, as it does in Perkins's ambitious world diagram. In that respect, Herbert's narrative maintains some contact with the kind of events that the chronicles and lamentations respond to while compensating for their lack of omniscience. The gain overall is a braver palace than the stately house of the beginning, which amounts to a *felix culpa*. Herbert may also be banking on the relative strength of other emblems besides the transformed house trope: the emblems of sin and death make lesser stays seem mere props, while the combined strength of love and grace draws upon a Providence quite different in its finality than anything the prophets could foresee.

The technique of enlivened riposte in "The World" resembles that of "The Quip," and like that poem this one does not have to gather allies to defeat the world. The struggle is over what commands the upkeep and future of the entire salvation house, the making and the maintaining of which require diligence but not a Mosaic (or a Puritan) campaign. The allegory pays its highest dividend in the arrival of the future seen as already accomplished. Given the source of love, grace, and glory, Paradise is not still to be constructed; it already is—all the more reason to disallow both holy warfare and any comfortable accommodation on the humanistic side of the Jordan. Whatever the house's pitiful condition at a given point, this certainty of paradise precludes a partnership of volition and grace. If fortune is impersonal, grace shares with it an unaccountability that sidesteps the apparent capriciousness of disasters and prosperity in historical chronicles. Whether a given era flourishes or declines, it is governed and pointed. Even wisdom and law come from divine dictation before they are given over to magistrates and priests. In any case, the entire history is over so quickly that the poet never pauses at a crossroads to deliberate.

Whereas "The World" sweeps aside complications, Herbert more customarily foregrounds acts of choosing, sometimes switching from the striving of the middle to closure. No poem does so as abruptly as "Redemption," perhaps Herbert's most effective straightening of a crooked course. I'll reserve comment on its technique until the next chapter (on Herbert's formalism), but it is pertinent to note here that like "The World" "Redemption" sets a pattern for Everyone and the discarding of contingencies in an uncompromised salvation. Like "The Pilgrimage," it is staged as a first-person search. The speaker must make an effort to get to the right spot before he can intercept Christ and hear "Your suit is granted." In that working of the transition from law to grace, love and grace in effect take glory once more by the hand, but this time from in the midst of a historical trauma. The word "suit" links personal complaint to the redemptive covenant and at the same time converts a Hebrew-style narrative to eschatology—decidedly not the kind of revised contract that Gadites and Reubenites wished to negotiate. The proclaiming of redemption is finished with the concluding statement under the most ironic of circumstances. The success of the petition has nothing to do with personal merit or spiritual alertness or even divine power operating within the framework of the world. Length of service under the old lease is no more at issue than are hours in the vineyard or degrees of merit in "Faith," where we are told that "by Faith all arms are of a length; / One size doth all conditions fit." The suppliant's long-suffering is important only to him. The turn at history's center cancels types of pursuit by an antitype who paradoxically rescues by dying helplessly and thereby shows the irrelevance of power. The human race reaches a reversal at the same moment, long prepared for despite its surprises for the speaker. As Chauncey Wood points out, the reader must reconcile the first-person story not only with the Crucifixion but with the long possession preceding it, realizing that God buys the world even before Christ takes possession of it ("George and Henry Herbert" 299–301).

"Temper 1," "The Flower," and "Josephs coat" keep before us the more stubborn difference between the redemptive moment and the experience of those who can never fully extricate themselves from their circumstances to reach the granting of the "suit." These poems are similar despite making quite different responses to affliction—which tunes the breast to make the music better ("Temper 1"), qualifies songs of joy and praise with cautionary wisdom ("The Flower"), and by variety prevents what would otherwise be a fatal obsession with one grief ("Josephs coat"). Meanwhile, the indefinite extending of the "exodus" makes a settlement recurrently desirable. Wisdom and the Law are not rendered totally useless merely because something beyond them is required for the ultimate defeat of sin and death. In less synoptic narratives and in different moods, Herbert reopens the case for them and, along with them, for the possibility of byways and loops.

"Josephs coat"

Of all Herbert's poems concerned with divine disfavor, "Josephs coat" is perhaps the most closely tied to the compensations of poetry that constitute his main diversion and way to fill intervals. The possibility of consolation in writing hovers about several poems but is secondary to poetry's capacity to make a personal offering and to praise. "Josephs coat" pairs offering with grievance. In technique, the implied story of Joseph goes in the opposite direction from the parabolic abstraction of "The World." It sets the present case in the context of at least one historical parallel, and criticism has raised the prospect of a New Testament parallel as well. Rosemond Tuve, for instance, sees Joseph as a forerunner not of the Hebrew nation (initiating the Egyptian period and thus preparing for the Exodus) but of the antitype. Most prominent on the surface of the poem is the psychology of the speaker, for whom writing perpetuates both relief and torment. The intrusion of Providence determines the significance and direction of joys and griefs, which would not sing if it were not for their showing of God's power.

Except for the "once did bring" (which implies that joys and griefs do not rotate in and out in cycles but have taken a single critical turn), the poem is in present and continuous past tense:

> Wounded I sing, tormented I indite,
> Thrown down I fall into a bed, and rest:
> Sorrow hath chang'd its note: such is his will,
> Who changeth all things, as him pleaseth best.
>   For well he knows, if but one grief and smart
> Among my many had his full career,
> Sure it would carrie with it ev'n my heart,
> And both would runne untill they found a biere
>   To fetch the bodie; both being due to grief.
> But he hath spoil'd the race; and giv'n to anguish
> One of Joyes coats, ticing it with relief

> To linger in me, and together languish.
> I live to shew his power, who once did bring
> My *joyes* to *weep*, and now my *griefs* to *sing*.

The framing story of Joseph and his coat basically likens the speaker to Joseph and thus implicitly God to Jacob and the coat to poetry. How much further we are meant to go is not clear. Joseph's tribulations and eventual success in Egypt do not apparently apply, given the immediacy of the tormenting and the singing precisely of griefs. Even the coat contains an apparent contradiction: it is not something that marks Joseph for persecution but a flashy sign of Jacob's favor. Indeed, Joseph is doubly blessed, by Jacob and by a Lord who sends the prophetic dream of eventual dominance over his brothers, and we cannot totally avoid that prominent difference. If Joseph arose from the pit, the speaker can perform no such miracle.

A still greater accomplishment belongs to the conventional emblem figure to which Tuve points as a tropic "garment" torn in the Crucifixion. Where Jacob's grief over the apparent loss of Joseph is inconsolable, the torn coat of humanity in the Son is both worse and better. Grief and joy are inextricable in both instances but on a scale that "The Thanksgiving" knows no poet can match. Where the brothers run to fetch Joseph's body and find it missing and where the deposition of Christ's body is followed by its resurrection, the speaker is saved only momentarily and consoled only by the song itself. Thus neither story provides an exact equivalent to a poet who can never become such a force to be reckoned with. The Hebrew and Christian parallels also stress the bond that unites the rescuer to his people, in Joseph's case the bond of genealogy; but kinship is not relevant to Herbert's speaker.

In several respects, the poet is closer to the typical sonneteer than to biblical precedents. This secular parallel is implied by the use of the sonnet form and the concern with vocation. The slightly varied parallelism of the opening sentence promises a careful formality, and Herbert does in fact respect the form throughout. The pairing of anguish and joy gives the poet time to "indite," in the manner of sonneteers aware of their writerly task. As a Petrarchan complaint, "Josephs coat" becomes a kind of sacred parody, or as Bruce Wardropper prefers, a *contrafacta*. "The Forerunners," the Jordan poems, and the three poems on love show more openly Herbert's general intent in rewriting secular love traditions, but "Wounded I sing, tormented I indite" does so as well. After taking the complaint through three quatrains, the speaker manages an epigrammatic neutrality marked by sobering wit. To be given the coat, one has to be dear; to be sold into slavery, chosen. Linking joys that weep to griefs that sing extracts a final irony from the realization that he is favored not by long life but by song, and no ordinary love sonnet, Herbert implies, expects so much. Yet lyric outcries are an age-old relief to be set beside songs of praise, especially when the singer cannot say, along with Psalm 105, "and he brought forth his people with joy." Such stalled lyrics, unable to proceed to a resolution, account for much of the book of Job, Lamentations, and Psalms, and *The Church* itself. In that company, "Josephs coat" comes finally to another justification of first fruits. Like the servant songs of Isaiah (Isaiah 42.1–4; 49.1–6; 50.4–9; 52.13–53.12), it concedes omniscience to the tormenter and ignorance to the tormented. The latter may be part of some still-unfinished story such as Joseph's, but for the time being his story is more limited.

In the context of "The World," "Redemption," and other poems that take in a longer span, "Josephs coat" is the product of a circumscribed focus. If the impersonality of "The World" suggests the aloofness of near omniscience, the intensity of "Josephs coat" is the product of a suffered groping for a single illuminating trope or a scriptural parallel that will find out the individual case. It suggests even more urgently than "H. Scriptures 2" does that locating constellations and configurations and seeing one's personal life in this or that episode is not equivalent to farsightedness. One could almost say that the stronger the "I," the less the narrative scope. "Josephs coat" is an exercise in controlled tangential similitude; its hints of "renaming" in the light of the sacrifice remain no more than that, which is perhaps why it has much more the sound of a conventional sonnet than "Redemption" does. In psalms, the individual voicing would be used as a means to make suffering a preliminary to lyrical supplication. Herbert stops in the midst, as though the speaker of Psalm 77 were to say, "Is his mercy clean gone for ever? doth his promise fail for evermore" (77.8) and not proceed to "I will remember the works of the Lord: surely I will remember thy wonders of old" (77.11–12)— except that, pursued far enough in the Joseph story, wonders do follow.

Faith, Giddiness, and "The Bunch of Grapes"

Joseph's coat applies an enigmatic set of parallels to the singing of grief and raises the question of the carry-over of detail from an extended narrative. It does not go into possible causes for the speaker's suffering, which are not likely to be explained by the Joseph story or by Hebrew parallels generally.

In the reigns of Israel's prophets, judges, and kings, what ordinarily brings God's disfavor is a failure to prosecute domestic and foreign policies rigorously enough—as when YHWH commands Saul (through Samuel) to "go and smite Amalek, and utterly destroy all that they have; do not spare them, but kill both man and woman, infant and suckling, ox and sheep, camel and ass" (1 Samuel 15.2). When Saul nonetheless spares Agag, paranoia, necromancy, defeat, and death are the result.

The loss of specific curses for specific crimes comes with the suspension of the Law and its replacement by a transcendent reward. Both suffering and guilt become diffused in Herbert and leave the speakers of poems like "Affliction 1" and "Josephs coat" groping for explanations that can be tied to the personal record. Divine absences and moments of disfavor are less subject to such eventful explanation once the doctrine of sufficient faith under Herbert's kindlier but much vaguer taskmaster has dismissed nationalist and institutional obligations. As "Faith" suggests, nothing more than faith is required to hold off the punitive figure of the judgment. The dullest of faculties is capable of bringing forth miracles merely by reentering the pages of Scripture and finding there emblems of the Son's presence:

> When creatures had no reall light
> Inherent in them, thou didst make the sunne
> Impute a lustre, and allow them bright;
> And in this shew, what Christ hath done.

"Shew" and "hath done" make a powerful combination, not as finished preterits but as past tenses still extending. As Christ performs his sacrifice again and again, he makes up for the weaknesses not only of human mind and body but of a deceptive history that seems full of inexplicable good and bad fortune.

In "Giddinesse" Herbert goes to the opposite extreme in maintaining a distinction between man's blind participation in God's designs and the logic of those designs. Faith assumes blindness also and in a certain frame of mind, moments of confidence under faith can come to seem the products of self-deception. But the lack of certainty that sponsors trust one moment spins the mind around and produces terror the next. Each man then becomes "some twentie sev'rall men at least / Each sev'rall houre." He "counts of heav'n, as of his treasure,"

> But then a thought creeps in,
> And calls him coward, who for fear of sinne
> Will lose a pleasure.

Filling in for certain knowledge, imagination feeds both extremes. It retrieves scenes that bolster faith and yet blows griefs up into portents and evidences of divine wrath. Embedded in the labyrinth, states of mind can generate almost limitless episodes of self-questioning. Any narrative suddenly seems possible; both the past and the future open up to variable readings. Faith may move mountains, but pitiful man

> builds a house, which quickly down must go,
> As if a whirlwinde blew
> And crusht the building: and it's partly true,
> His minde is so.

In terms of the polarity I discussed earlier, faith belongs to the heart's arrival at a preliminary closure, vicissitude to the restless and inventive mind. In terms of the Hebrew/Christian relations and the current settings of complaint, faith joins with the spiritualizing of texts under christianized troping, whereas giddiness and uncertainty betray an overbalance of returning circumstantiality in all its resistance to interpretation. The stately palace that love, grace, and glory build returns to the ramshackle structure of everyday semantics.

Where such poems as "Giddinesse" must head is not much in doubt, since their view of radical instability counsels the seeking of an unchangeable foundation. Their technique is to plunge into the maelstrom and then return to the omniscience of "The World," where the whole story is already written. Herbert's way of combining giddiness and faith is to use the first perspective to prompt the second and to conclude, "Except thou make us dayly, we shall spurn / Our own salvation," which rephrased slightly means "gather every event of our biographies into the master pattern" or "trope every natural and therefore catastrophic event." To "suffice our turn" means "to last our duration." It also implies that stories of fickle change will continue, whatever immunity the world in abstract claims. As giddy men take up and discard role after role in a frantic search for the word that makes "this or that" into nothing, the ever-laboring Lord cannot afford a leave of absence. Having once set forth on the enterprise of eschatological translation, he must keep constant vigil.

A more complicated example of groping, in the context of a Providence that should sustain but seems forgetful, is "The Bunch of Grapes," a poem that suggests why Herbert is often at his best when he goes to neither extreme but intertwines faith and giddiness, Hebrew and Christian settings, doctrine and experience, personal narrative and a typology that fits the instances into an overall coherence. When he turns to certain moments of Hebrew history for examples of giddiness, he finds there a different balance of current moment and what is now to be interpreted as foreshadowing. Thus "The Bunch of Grapes" sets a personal story across from two parallel moments, the murmurers' challenge to the Exodus leadership and the Crucifixion. It is typical of the poem's critics, Joseph Summers (*George Herbert* 126–28) and Laurence Lerner (60–61), for instance, to find the speaker's struggle being converted into those types. The poem begins on a personal level but moves toward a realization of a pattern now countless times reinforced by the daily vigilance of Providence. Barbara Leah Harman (*Costly Moments* 71–81) keeps more prominently in mind the speaker's foreground meditation, but virtually all readings of the poem associate the speaker's complaint with types of deliverance that reflect on it from the poem's more panoramic viewpoint.

Anticipating both Summers and Harman, Rosemond Tuve links the rebellious children of Israel to modern criticism's romanticized Herbert. Reaching into previous representations of murmuring, the allusion to the grapes of Eshcol and the Crucifixion's "pressing" generate a resonance beyond personal emotion:

> A reader . . . made sensitive to the full meaning of the figures will perceive that there is another dimension to the subject of this poem, beyond the mere conveyance of a particular individual's emotion at a given time, that thin subject with which modern readers have come to be content but which Herbert throws to one side with his "A *single* deed is small renown." Herbert is seriously interested in the idea that his case too is covered, taken count of, in an eternally true series of events that preceded him in time; in other words he reads history and biblical story as one great web of metaphor. . . . The poem widens to include us too, our Red Sea, our Canaan, our grape-cluster. (Tuve, *A Reading* 117)

Precisely. The web of metaphor is the sedimented language of centuries of hermeneutic work seizing upon mountains, paths, labyrinths, seas, many-colored coats, Abraham and Isaac, women at the well, battles, theophanies, houses, beds, crops, and journeys and giving them a place within a movement toward a promised closure. Nothing in the book of creatures or the various texts of history and fiction is immune to that "eternally true series of events." This massive troping operation in effect cancels personal stories once the sequential experience of first one episode and then another gets placed. As Hebrews says, "sundry times and diverse manners" by which God "speaks in times past unto the fathers by the prophets"—are summed up in the Son whom God "hath appointed heir of all things" (Hebrews 1.1–2). Tuve's reading is criticism's equivalent to the reduction in Hebrews of the great cloud of witnesses—Abel, Noah, Abraham, Sarah, Isaac, Jacob, Joseph, Moses, Joshua, Rahab, Gideon, Barak, Samson, Jephthah, David, and Samuel—to examples of faith.

As I suggested earlier, that habit of typological forecasting and reduction is already well embedded in pentateuchal historiography itself. The assimilation of types is assisted by the Joshua historian's awareness of both the Red Sea and the grapes episodes and by the psalmists' recollections of these and foreshadowings of the victory they portend. Awareness of an emerging Jewish story from tribal dispersal capitalizes on hindsight in accounting for the already-known possession of Canaan. Similarly, by an assimilation of previous episodes, suffering at any time can be accounted for as expiation for forsaken vows, or as a test of faith in what is to come. By making so many instances parallel, the gathering fable gains confirmation in one instance from the interpretation of another. It rises toward the Pauline Epistles long before the final hellenist turn.

Tuve is thus on solid historical footing in having Herbert use the standard judgment of murmuring as grounds for chastising the speaker's lack of confidence in Providence. The "one great web of metaphor" and the individual story form a tension that gets underway with an account of the recent personal past:

> Joy, I did lock thee up: but some bad man
>   Hath let thee out again:
> And now, me thinks, I am where I began
>   Sev'n yeares ago: one vogue and vein,
>   One aire of thoughts usurps my brain.
> I did towards Canaan draw; but now I am
> Brought back to the Red sea, the sea of shame.

It does not particularly matter who the bad man is. The basic model is an Israelite type. Trying to get to a point at which joy will be secure within giddy possibilities is futile, no matter how diligent the poet is in trying to enter the systematic web. The various types of Exodus recurrently draw near their respective Canaans only to be cast back into the wilderness, or if they succeed they are soon undercut by further broken covenants and captivities.

In this case, Tuve's admonitions to modern criticism notwithstanding, the speaker clings to his grievances. His complaint is not only comparatively shortsighted but close to the heart of Herbert's placing of lyric moments. The question is not so much how long the personal grief will last as how completely it is answered and defined by the biblical parallels. Although the speaker does find that "his" journey is not really his own, the episode of the grapes resists becoming merely an illustration of uncalled-for timorousness or in some way a preliminary to the Crucifixion. Clinging to the distinctiveness of one's life may be equivalent to refusing grace, and the speaker may acknowledge his own excess in "one vogue and vein"; but the point at issue is precisely murmuring, and it always breaks out in the context of a very limited foreknowledge. What does suffering mean to the complainers themselves, and how does it affect the quest for a homeland? The doubters of Aaron and Moses wonder how much they may have to pay in blood for the land that has produced such grapes: how much can be logically inferred from the spy reports and how much must be taken on faith? It occurs to some of the hesitant group that to "reach the promised land" may be a euphemism for invading a well-armed, already-occupied territory. It takes productive land to grow such fruit; it takes farmers, wives and children, a developed economy, and cities. They themselves are a struggling civilian population, not even an organized army. Personal experience and an already prolonged wilderness trek teaches them that one may be pious and wish well and still face every hardship without notable divine assistance, over very long periods.

In that fairly circumstantial narrative, before it gets reduced to exemplary uses and psalmic citation—the first stages of typing—the grape crisis thrives on contrasting reports and intertwining with the previous experience of the people. They are now being asked to interpret mere grapes as a promise of the Lord of Host's unleashed wrath against idolatry. Caleb acknowledges the fearful presence of the Children of Anak, the Amalekites, Hittites, Jebusites, and Amorites, but thinks that with providential help all these can be overcome. That belief transforms the means by which significance is extracted from emblems, which become not a part representing the whole economic system but a "systematic" metaphor and a wonder, that is, part of the marvelous sign system YHWH has used to guide the entire expedition out of Egypt. Into one trope the text crowds virtually the entire Exodus

story; and into its subsequent New Testament interpretation, biblical hermeneutic crowds much of the Christian equivalent.

The doubters feel nonetheless that, faced with giants before whom they
are but grasshoppers, an invasion will bring retaliation rather than the
complete victory that YHWH's "ban" commands. Indeed, the lingering fear
of retribution is precisely what calls for the annihilation of the resident
Canaanites and thereby sets another type featured by Deuteronomy, Joshua,
and Judges. These texts under varying circumstances all repeat the injunction
first issued as a battle plan: "Then ye shall drive out all the inhabitants of the
land from before you, and destroy all their pictures, and destroy all their
molten images, and quite pluck down all their high places: and ye shall
dispossess the inhabitants of the land, and dwell therein: for I have given you
the land to possess it. . . . But if ye will not drive out the inhabitants of the
land from before you; then it shall come to pass, that those which ye let
remain of them shall be pricks in your eyes, and thorns in your sides"
(Numbers 33.52–55). Almost every chosen leader, in subsequently voicing
similar doubts, must be reassured by a similar promise that the enemy will
be delivered into his hands.

The murmuring in Numbers is thus a hint of greater distrust to come of
both YHWH's promise and the leadership of the patriarchs. It is retrospectively interpreted as part of a general mandate for the promises of complete
victory wherever subsequent Israelite hosts prove to be obedient. For the
time being, however, some of them ask, "And whereof hath the Lord brought
us into this land," "to fall by the sword, that our wives and our children
should be a prey? were it not better for us to return into Egypt" (Numbers
14.3). That final phrase will also be remembered by priests and historians
when they encounter the reluctance that each new generation breeds. The
covenant under which this recording and remembering people define their
relations to YHWH and to the patriarchs goes backward and forward a long
way. They bring into each decision the entire movement toward and away
from Egypt, the social and political structure, and the military policy it uses
to gain and hold a homeland. The credit not only of the prophets in the
wilderness but of church fathers and kings later is at stake in the making of
parallels and collapsing of episodic incidents into the recurrence of fabulous
narrative. The new curse of forty years in the wilderness to which the Lord
sentences all but Caleb and Joshua is the culmination of many episodes and
herald of more, a stock of repeatable common places, ritualized and made
lyrical for the choral reunifying of later temple worshipers, confirming a
collective identity.

Stories of tribulation punctuated by intervals of doubt and complaint are bound up in a genealogy that goes from immediate elders to the patrimony of Abraham and Jacob. That true devotion will thrive best in a homeland is a presupposition of the story. It is maintained until the destruction of the Temple and the Exile and the discovery that even as YHWH worship could survive in the wilderness, so it can survive in the diaspora. But for the developmental period leading to the monarchy, the continuity of the patriarchy depends particularly upon the fulfillment of the covenants. It is this aspect of the vineyard metaphor that Bacon exploits in building the bunch of grapes into the ceremonial fatherhood of the *New Atlantis*, where the temple, now the established house of Salomon, rests upon ancestral respect. (The senior male, the Tirsan, designates the Son of the Vine and seals the family's loyalty to the king and the state charter in a display of grapes in number as many as there are descendants of the family [*Works* 3.149–50]). The genealogical issue is built into the type-antitype succession and into Christ as the sacrificial son of the vine, the inheritor of his father's house.

The lack of fruit in the speaker's own life in "The Bunch of Grapes," in that context, has the added effect of deracination and apparent disinheritance. It can be countered only by awareness that the speaker too is an inheritor, but in a specially converted sense that breaks the territorial imperative and the enticement for invasion, which from a Pauline perspective becomes a literal and therefore darkened view of deliverance. But let us continue Herbert's lyrical use of the story:

> For as the Jews of old by God's command
> Travell'd, and saw no town;
> So now each Christian hath his journeys spann'd:
> Their storie pennes and sets us down.
> A single deed is small renown.
> Gods works are wide, and let in future times;
> His ancient justice overflows our crimes.
>
> Then have we too our guardian fires and clouds;
> Our Scripture-dew drops fast:
> We have our sands and serpents, tents and shrowds;
> Alas! our murmurings come not last.
> But where's the cluster? where's the taste
> Of mine inheritance? Lord, if I must borrow,
> Let me as well take up their joy, as sorrow.

The thing to be avoided in both Bacon's ceremonial new Bensalem (or New Jerusalem) and Herbert's speaker lacking an immediate remedy for his suffering is moral and spiritual drifting. Whereas Bacon urges the establishment of a better state, Herbert's solution is otherworldly and depends on a redefinition of the tent-tabernacle as the place not of high priests but again of the Son who replaces them. The speaker of "Temper 1" wishes a place to roost (perhaps somewhere like the Holy of Holies, where the wings of the cherubim are at rest), but he knows that he cannot command such a haven. In "Anagram," it is the Lord himself who comes in the tabernacle-tent of incarnation. In the Crucifixion and ascension poems, he departs on Easter wings and in "Whitsunday" returns on "golden wings," as the mystical spirit descends in holy fire to the apostles. The point in "The Bunch of Grapes" would seem to be that because God's works are wide and the new Canaan now has no earthly setting, the Christian "nomad" is left without a foretaste or a harboring sanctuary. This is equivalent to saying that he must get along without both the prefigurative types of glory and the perils of the conquest epic, although he has the Eucharist to replace that glory. In Herbert's final figure for temporal prosperity, the fruit is transformed into a communion symbol:

> But can he want the grape, who hath the wine?
>   I have their fruit and more.
> Blessed be God, who prosper'd *Noahs* vine,
>   And made it bring forth grapes good store.
>   But much more him I must adore,
> Who of the Laws sowre juice sweet wine did make,
> Ev'n God himself being pressed for my sake.

In place of a bountiful harvest the new covenant offers the slain Son, whose fate confirms the worst fears of the Numbers murmurers: the way to Canaan is obstructed by the utmost peril. In the symbolic feast of the faithful, the New Testament joins the reluctant followers of former spiritual leaders, but not on earth, which thereby becomes all the more a prolonged wilderness.

By equating the Valley of Eshcol to heaven, the old covenant to grace, and the grapes to the Eucharist, Herbert's New Testament revisionism falls in with the general Protestant adaptation of types. In "But much more," Herbert sums up the compensatory logic of that category change of "rescue." In place of the disciplining priesthood of Aaron and Moses, he has the successor to priests, and in place of tangible fruitfulness, the imitation of the squeezed Son. "I *must* adore" nonetheless suggests a not entirely purged individual rebelliousness. Although it is possible also to emphasize "I" and to produce virtually the opposite meaning—or to stress "*him*," in contrast to Noah's blessing of God for the new race to descend from the patriarchal vine—the tone is less than ecstatic. The meanings are something like "I too—along with the sons of Noah," and "him especially, far above any of the Jewish fathers and sons." Either of these transforms the need for war against the holders of Hebron into Christ's sacrifice. But the speaker's comforts are still being postponed at the moment of writing, and it is difficult to determine the degree of piety he feels in that unfinished story. The machinery of translation is in place, and piety this surely is, but the ending is not cast stylistically as a hymn of thanksgiving. It remains partly a self-rebuke for the remembering of grievances and failure to gather in the full returns of the conversion from the old covenant to the new.

If this residue of disquiet is as serious as it sounds, Tuve's confidence in sacraments and alignment of Herbert with a total victory over individualism and perhaps even Harman's lesser submergence of the individual in the type are not entirely to be trusted, at least not in this still-preliminary stage of discontent, so far from "Love 3." The tension between the typological patterns and the anecdotal level of personal experience continues. Counsel for self-discipline is built into Christian conformity, but that a wholehearted stifling of doubts and of self-concern goes with it seems doubtful, which is why one might legitimately associate these examples of the interplay of Hebrew, Christian and personal motifs with the impatience poems. Gratitude for something actually delivered is seldom an unmixed emotion, and if the followers of Moses are any indication, gratitude ahead of time for something foreseen with so little certainty is even less sustainable.

Another reason for caution is stifling the individual complaint is that one can scarcely even speculate on the conceit that carries the main burden of violent troping. In equating the Crucifixion with wine pressing, Herbert substitutes for an example of prosperity a stunningly paradoxical image that leaves the poet uncertain of the "gains" of "fruits." The work of the Son disqualifies work in the vineyard and the products that make up stories of effort and reward. The press squeezes bodily sin from humankind by way of the Incarnate God and transforms the whole into wine, a figure predicted by what John Smith in *Mystery of Rhetoric Unveiled* (50) calls catachresis in Deuteronomy 32.14: "And thou didst drink the pure blood of the grape." The association of tribulation with the pressing is still more radical here. It could be spoken with a dropping of the voice to fit the trailing clauses and the passing of the event beyond human reach. We know from "The Sacrifice" and "The Thanksgiving" that other reactions to the pressing are possible, depending on the interpreter's state of mind. The main differences among the Hebrew trek, Deuteronomy's blood-red wine, and Herbert's winemaking are that Noah's vines produce tangible fruit that goes to family tables, and the journey is across a real terrain to a geographical place; in the extremity of this catachresis, the antitype again loses that regional flavor and the social matrix.

When the speaker asks "where's the taste / Of mine inheritance?" he may also be remembering that some of his contemporaries take current prosperity to be a sign of election. The speaker's future condition and the promised delivery stand far apart, not just because of what is still needed to make him conform but because no text can be more than advisory about a state that not even sacraments can produce. Some of this gets compressed into the somewhat grudging phrasing if one hears in "must" (as I do) a quite different tone from what could just as easily have been a devotional or psalmic "him I *do* adore." Herbert makes it difficult for the reader to leave such poems of rebellion feeling that their speakers have arrived at much more than a sense of self-reproach and renewed obligation. From one standpoint, such modest conviction is to be not only expected but welcomed as part of his larger project of finding accomplished songs in narrative parallels and pressure points. Unlike Milton, his speakers never really expect a calling directed specifically to them; they do not see an army already on the move, certain of its mission. Unequivocal songs of praise are few in *The Church*, and calls for specific action are fewer.

A further comment upon that relative passivity is evident in the second of Herbert's two antiphons, which makes a distinction between angel and human contributions to hymns of delivery:

> *Cho.* He our foes in pieces brake;
> *Ang.* Him we touch;
> *Men.* And him we take.
> *Cho.* Wherefore since that he is such,
> *Ang.* We adore,
> *Men.* And we do crouch.

We might expect an antiphon to be an exaltation, as the first one is, but a true antiphon can be as difficult to produce as a true hymn. Grace and glory have belonged to angels from the beginning; to men they come only "in th'end." Angels touch God; men receive him in communion. Angels adore; men crouch. These two sides of devotion may join in choral praise, but built into the human portion is the abject posture, which derives from reiterated and persistently humbling experience as well as kneeling for prayer and communion. The most positive thing Herbert can do while working toward "Love 3" and the several assessments of end things that precede it is state the better thing second, as he does in "Bitter-sweet":

> Ah my deare angrie Lord,
> Since thou dost love, yet strike;
> Cast down, yet help afford;
> Sure I will do the like.
>
> I will complain, yet praise;
> I will bewail, approve:
> And all my sowre-sweet dayes
> I will lament, and love.

To write poems greatly different from angelic antiphons is to place lamentation beside praise and leave an emotional and logical gap, spanned here by commas and the "and" that allows both sides of a powerful ambivalence. Stripped of the psalmists' concluding appeals for vengeance, sparing in communal voicing, Herbert compresses everything into a brief acknowledgment of "love." He ordinarily retains doctrinal justifications and their biblical footing but dampens the exaltation. He does so in the antiphons and hymns, in the Easter poems of the outset, and even in the doomsday, judgment, and love poems of the conclusion. After the most convincing unfolding of love's dynamics, the voicing lapses into the conventionalism of

> *Glory be to* God *on high*
> *And on earth peace*
> *Good will towards men.*

But by then the psalmic resonance and the transformation of glory from that of a victorious Israelite nation to that of the nativity and the ascension help make this more than perfunctory. It is brief and abstract but for that very reason universal and self-surrendering. This last voice in *The Church* is in effect the choral voice of hymnists summoned from the annals by formulaic phrases, replacing the voices of individual speakers that emphasize the "I" in "I will complain, yet praise; / I will bewail, approve." Eliciting ritual repetition from the first person awaiting the end, the antiphon establishes a poetic program that can be repeated as often as it needs to be.

5
HERBERT AT PSALMS AND SONNETS

For a thousand years in thy sight are but as yesterday when it is past, and as a watch in the night. . . . For all our days are passed away in thy wrath: we spend our years as a tale that is told.

—Psalm 90.4, 9

Lord, how long shall the wicked, how long shall the wicked triumph?

—Psalm 94.4

My subject in this chapter, although it concerns form, is the area where sound combines with idea and where smaller structures of stress and duration play out their intricacies of thought and feeling. When Herbert stretches sentences across the frame of lines, and thought across the form of stanzas and sonnets, the problems in measurement are obviously different from those of fixing individual poems into the larger frame of *The Church*; but the effect in both cases is to divide attention between the passing moment and the fuller context, which Herbert adeptly summons by repetition, echo, and the use of abstract diction. It is not a new or particularly difficult act of reading that this divided attention demands (or this attention to division); the eye after all has peripheral vision, and the ear takes in sentences both a little at a time and as a whole. The difference in *The Church* is the extreme extent of the whole and the causal relations of various spans to it. Many of the structural problems he shares with the Bible as he read it, which also combines chronological development with typological cross-referencing. As Donne remarks, sentences in Scripture too are "like hairs in horsetales"; they "concur in one root of beauty and strength; but being plucked out one by one, serve only for springes and snares."

As critics have noticed, form often constrains in *The Church*, but the question is not so much whether it straightens or protects (as Huntley, Pahlka, and Lull, *The Poem in Time*, 119–36, would have it) as whether it is expressive. Any formal division, like any metaphoric container, in a sense both expresses and belies its subject when the latter is inexpressible. Any epochal closure or episodic narrative must be interpreted in the light of an indefinite span; and the place of any formal segment of *The Church* from the smallest unit to the whole volume depends on its relation to eschatology. Yet the connective logic cannot be additive—it cannot contribute to a closure that is brought about by its own internal elements. Narratives are subject to abrupt breaking off, as when a speaker seeking to finish his quest for an improved life, finds his Lord perishing and hears "Your suit is granted." Against all expectations, he suddenly sees the death of the Redeemer as a substitute ending of the story he had initiated, sorted into phases, arranged as sonnet pieces, and perhaps expected to close in another kind of couplet.

Narrative and dramatic units, in sonnets, stanzas, and linked sequences, are subject to just that kind of pressure when the poet attains a realization of the whole or when a key part falls into place. Not even sacramentally repeated patterns and dialectical questions and answers sponsored by catechismic learning can cross the gap. What to do about the artfulness of smaller units, figures, meters, lines, and stanzas, is thus understandably one of the recurrent questions of Herbert criticism. Merely to list the components of the formal problem is to see the difficulty of doing justice to them. They include influences set in place by echoes and allusions, patterned repetition in refrain and stanza, the relation of sacramental repetition to the end, and the linking of subgroups and sequences to *The Church* as a whole. Nor can we ignore image repetition and *mythos* as it shows in the several different lengths of story—the speaker's struggles, the global narrative, Christ's life, the reader's encouraged and guided progress, the writing of *The Temple*, the history of church militant, and compressed fables contained in such poems as "Love unknown" and "The Pilgrimage."

After a brief general comment on formalism and historicism (which seldom get along peacefully), I want to turn primarily to the stress that the overall narrative, conceived synoptically, places on formal measure, remembering that this stress parallels the wrenching of similitude into the more strained figures that populate Herbert's rhetoric—oxymoron, catechresis, prolepsis, and metalepsis. The nature of this undertaking is not only to be somewhat selective, given the many sides of the formal problem that *The Church* poses, but to require adequate quotation, since Herbert's interest often lies in local units of line and stanza and in the interplay of sound systems and sense. Reconciling aestheticism with rhetorical, polemical, instructional, religious, ideological, and historical substance is at best a sensitive operation in any period, but Herbert aggravates the problem by practicing very intricately designed forms while arguing for simplicity and plainness. He is fearful that beautiful objects and craft cannot maintain their worth and be simultaneously subordinated to the fable. This issue he brings to bear on church ceremony and the Anglican middle way in "The British Church," where we discover that far from being merely an internal problem of decorum, determining what is fit and proper overlaps the determination of church policy. In "Prayer 1" it also creeps into the style of personal address. How to clothe God and what temporal tropes and what art best express divine beauty are thus by no means incidental or occasional questions to Herbert: they begin with "The Altar" and figure in the persistent metapoetic and ecclesiastical concerns of *The Temple* virtually to the end.

But let us turn to a couple of preliminary examples that will speak to the special task the sacred poet undertakes. I deliberately select two of Herbert's more ingenious exercises but in order to concentrate more on the ear than the eye, not diagram poems where printed shape gives us a folded or doubled effect. The examples are "Charms and Knots" and "Justice 1," the first a series of proverbial sayings on the order of "Who reade a chapter when they rise, / Shall ne're be troubled with ill eyes." That poem does not require extended sampling, but "Justice 1" must be seen entire:

> I cannot skill of these thy wayes.
> *Lord, thou didst make me, yet thou woundest me;*
> *Lord, thou dost wound me, yet thou dost relieve me:*
> *Lord, thou relievest, yet I die by thee:*

> *Lord, thou dost kill me, yet thou dost reprieve me.*
> But when I mark my life and praise,
> Thy justice me most fitly payes:
> For, *I do praise thee, yet I praise thee not*:
> *My prayers mean thee, yet my prayers stray*:
> *I would do well, yet sinne the hand hath got*:
> *My soul doth love thee, yet it loves delay.*
> I cannot skill of these my wayes.

Herbert juxtaposes "Charms and Knots" and "Justice 1," perhaps as related riddle poems, but "Charms and Knots" is closer to "outlandish" sayings than to genuine riddle. In a series of couplets that could be extended or shortened—that has no affective curve or story to develop from a beginning to an ending—it offers moral sayings of a basic sort and dominates form by pithy statement: "Who shuts his hand, hath lost his gold: / Who opens it, hath it twice told," and so on. In "Justice 1," anaphora, antithesis, riddle, and what John Smith labels syncrisis (comparison of contrary things) work in the opposite direction. The self-estimating paradoxes probe a touchy relationship between speaker and divine judge in a mirror form that stresses the parallelism of the saying. Its dramatic address and focus on the self further distinguish it from the terseness of a true proverb or a riddle poem. Like so many of Herbert's poems, it is basically a *stanza* poem, moving through changes in two antithetical phases. Its repetition is governed by revision, and its progress is the fitting of the speaker into the fable bit by bit, as the evidence collects into its two neatly stacked containers. Bracketed by the "I give up" figure (aporia) stated in straightforward iambic tetrameter, the poem offers an itemized list of puzzles and attempted answers, and moves from reproach to self-blame. The first sequence falls into line chronologically and amounts to a life story shaped as a series of apparent contradictions in the Lord, each phase countermanding the one preceding and suggesting that how the series ends is going to be what matters. Justice will then be both manifest, and as "Justice 2" and "Judgement" make clear, averted or replaced. The elaborate parallelism is set off by a reiterated address marked by initial stress and balancing emphases on "thou" and the verbs, "make," "wound," "relievest," "kill," "reprieve," and finally "pays."

Ritualizing the two lists gives the speaker formal command where he claims to lack intellectual command. But of course the first doubt ("I don't understand you") is canceled by the second ("It is I whom I don't understand"). In the first, the Lord has answered tit for tat through a history of errors and correctives, which suggests why so many of Herbert's poems are dialogue retorts arranged as musical counterpoint. They put their refrains to dramatic use: for every event in one's life read providentially, there has been or will be an answer thrust forward in the briefest way. Herbert's recurrent imagery of circumference and circle carries the same conviction that God always strikes the mark, wounds the soul to the quick, relieves at the core—"most fitly payes." The concept of fit form, not as imprisoning containment or as divine protection but as decorum and a punctual intrusion of end into the midst, depends upon this providential taking over of what would otherwise be lacking in meaningful form. Not only does "Justice 1" concern such fitness, it formalizes it on a stringent principle of verbal economy and decorum. Seeming at first to waste words with its anaphora, it is actually quite efficient, as "I cannot skill of," as a colloquial phrase, is not only ear-catching but short and sweet for the bafflement theme. The first half assigns responsibility for active response to the Lord, the agent against the passive victim; the verbs of the second half all belong to the speaker, and they never strike home.

Herbert's poems are frequently working formulas and word magic of this kind. They retain a trace of narrative and a trace of drama to go with riddle and wisdom statement, as the speaker starts with a bill of grievances and in the very stating of them realizes the whys and wherefores and reverses himself. He does so not in the manner of searching dialogue or autobiography but in what is also partly a musical form. The form again matters: it reflects the greater symmetry and efficiently administered policy of the prime maker, the plot director whose scheme provides a macrocosmic frame. What is enacted in small in this case is the speaker's personal rehearsal of the race. He has been made like Adam, wounded and relieved by Christ's sacrifice, but will be killed nonetheless as the world reaches apocalypse, and then reprieved—almost exactly Bacon's scheme for nature in "Confession of Faith." If the second set of riddles is harder to account for and remains in doubt in the final line, it is because of human, not divine, illogic. The abstractions and the acts—praise, prayers, charitable deeds, and love—could be substantial and fixed, but they get eroded by the insincerity of the corrupted heart. The foundation words that should head off divine wrath do not mean what they should, and each line wastes itself in contradiction. For every godly stratagem in the first half, the speaker has managed a countering dissonance and therefore a threatening formlessness. He it is who delays and expatiates, and thus lacks the "skill" to phrase himself fitly. The result is the ironic twisting of what starts out seeming like a sure form and ends formally complete but open as statement. The solution to the riddle that is the speaker himself lies in the sacrifice and the testament that will be substituted for any personal account of grievances.

The theme of justice will return and find better answers, not only in "Judgement" but in "Justice 2" and "Love 3" ("know you not . . . who bore the blame?"). But the formality of "Justice 1" meanwhile has placed in the midst of *The Church* one of several counterpuntal structures and a bridging abstraction that, by means both of its lexical range and its place in the fable, constitutes an overarching device. Its bounded shape can claim a place in the volume's memory links. By hanging its ornate portrait of justice under a broad title, it prepares for inclusion among related general entitlements (peace, grace, etc.) and thereby reinforces overall coherence. It is invested with meaning by the intellect out of theological premises, and it is set in place by skilled workmanship. It almost totally removes the issue of justice from the civil realm and from the Hebrew context of the Law and is thus all the more a subject for the I-thou negotiations of lyricism—the basic source of duplicative structure, retorts, and dramatic changes that discover in antithesis the grounds for reversing first readings.

The inherent collaboration of minuscule melodic techniques and narrative, interpreted by governing ideas, makes Herbert's lyric sequencing unique among predecessors and later imitators. Nothing in the two testaments, the medieval lyric, or Renaissance sonnet sequencing quite prepares us for it. He thus gives us every reason to keep form and historicism together; certainly *The Temple* has both agenda material *and* an articulated architecture. The repetition of themes and acoustical schemes is equally prominent. Optical and aural figures are nearly always found in the company of a linking *lexis* and interweaving of abstractions, which are evident not only in Herbert's titles but in the defining function he gives to lyric. The major themes and images that stretch across his structures of repetition include the cross (thorns, crown), wilderness, paradise, flowers, seasons, altar, music, center and circumference, court, furniture, temple, house, tombs and monuments, stars, treasure, the bag, the coat, the pulley, and the watercourse. The chief abstractions are familiar to all Herbert readers, many of them best defined in theological and doctrinal contexts.

The refrains that Herbert can make of these interwoven strands are numerous, and many of them he manages to point toward the poems on end things and "Love 3." Indeed, the repetition of these and other elements constitutes an architectural formality that matches on the book level the intricacies of verbal repetition and sound patterns of individual poems. This in turn parallels the Bible's use of type narratives and insertion of cycles in history's events-of-a-kind and the church's reenactments in ritual, which at the institutional level function like ceremonial repetends. But it would be a mistake to assume that the patterning at any level is unproblematic or that symmetry always serves analogy and parallelism. Even in "Justice 1" Herbert ends with semantic puzzles, the soul's love of delay, and what in other contexts become endless darkened "ways." Within poems that use repetition and refrains, he tends to bring back the semantic elements in ever-new contexts that can both augment and erode their earlier meanings. In distant echoes across the breadth of *The Church*, the same reconsideration and fretting holds true. Metaphoric networking can serve not only to link one verse to another but, in its sheer abundance, to create a maze, the implication being that anything assigned to "my skill" is likely not to arrive at its destination. Prayers go astray; deeds get taken over by sin and reversed in their intention. The wreath that the poet would make into a crown goes round about. The love we hear mentioned so often never gets fixed on its object until Love personified takes matters in hand.

Such unfinished patterns characterize *The Church*, whose finely wrought units sometimes end resoundingly and neatly only to deny, in psychology or statement or by implication, the certainty of statement and doctrinal realization that should accompany them: what they extend formally with one hand they take back thematically with the other. As Janis Lull has shown, even in significantly revising the statements that certain poems make, Herbert usually keeps the same line and stanza forms, which in effect makes form a given and denies its organic growth from content. For Herbert the form of nearly everything is a given: the shape of history as "Easter-wings" diagrams it, the ladder of natural forms, the events of the sacrifice that yield sacraments and place a strong element of ritual recurrence in the militant church, the dialectical shape of human statement and divine retort. The simultaneous establishing and breaking of form is perhaps the best guide to a concept of the interaction of form and content in Herbert. Whenever something begins to seem fixed and defined, awareness of an always-unfinished business and the failure of individuals to conform are likely to break in. Only where the retort is definitive, as it is in the rhyming corrections of "Heaven" and the dialogue progress of "Love 3," does a relatively firm closure succeed in stopping the career of human error and deformity.

As I suggested, formal principles have their figural parallels in oxymoronic, metaleptic, aporetic, and catachretic metaphors. These metaphors often come abruptly into play to eclipse tropes drawn to mere human scale. What we are to do about history and such things as social agendas is implicit in this: they should be subordinate to doctrines that philosophize the fable and give church sacraments precedent over church and state policy. I will reserve that matter for next chapter, however, where the nature of the church itself can be raised as an issue; my interest here is the more minute breakdown of units whenever the discrepancy between an intervening divinity and human rhetoric gets noticed—precisely the discrepancy that disturbs the formal neatness of "Justice 1." It is central also to such poems as "Temper 1," "The Flower," "Vertue," and finally and most definitively in "Heaven" and "Love 3."

All manner and measure of periodicity is challenged by both an intervening providence and the need to pass from sequential logic, in history, to another state if the fable is to be finished. The phases of any story governed by eschatology are comparable to gaps in the great chain that agitated Samuel Johnson: if one cannot approach infinity by gradations, the highest angel is no nearer the absolute than the humblest creature. Recognizing that difficulty, Bacon makes virtually the first article of his "Confession of Faith" the establishing of a mediator. Ostensibly, the Son prevents the Father's hating his own infinitely inferior creatures: "God is so holy, pure, and jealous, as it is impossible for him to be pleased in any creature, though the work of his own hands" (*Works* 7.219). But he is also required as a concept, a flexible source of the word and visible light willing to enter history and through allegorical accommodations give story form to the Father's will. Even that does not solve all the problems, however. If the good and the wicked cannot be nearer or further from closure, in what does an approach to the end consist? Divine prejudgment must be equally present at all times and cannot be more or less so. The last judgment has always existed and is no more or less at last than it is at first.

When Herbert takes up such discrepancies in scale, he tends to do so on a simulated personal level, within the limited knowledge of a first-person speaker attempting to bridge the gap between his experience and divine omniscience. In "Temper 1" disproportion in scale prompts a desperate attempt to end an unequal master-subject struggle:

> Wilt thou meet arms with man, that thou dost stretch
> A crumme of dust from heav'n to hell?
> Will great God measure with a wretch?
> Shall he thy stature spell?

One possible conclusion is that violent changes of state have a function in the writing of poetry itself: "This is but tuning of my breast, / To make the musick better." Paradoxically, tuned music is well proportioned and harmonious but must be produced by strain on the frets and a violent stretching of the strings. Having to forge a poetics of self-assessment, confession, and petition out of a human condition all too intimately measured by agitation, Herbert resembles the psalmists in his radical shifts of tone. The key to that fretted form is the mismatch.

Acoustics and Dramatic Voice

Herbert's concern with spiritual welfare and for the egoism of the poet weaving himself into the sense of his poems shows not only in metaphor (the focal point of his plain-style caveats) but in the marriage of voice to formal patterns. His uneasiness concerning craft in the Jordan poems and "The Forerunners" spills over into poems that practice what his self-admonitions find inadvisable. From both sacred and secular poets, he inherited not only a stock of conventions but a theory of harmonies and musical intervals, that as Louise Schleiner remarks, have the vitality of simulated movement; melodic patterns tend to take on a life of their own (70). His love of the lute and use of musical techniques allow some accommodation too of the Pythagorean heritage, as now and then he glances abroad at the harmonious cosmos, the parent of all symmetry. With that accommodation sometimes comes bardic amplitude, although he resorts to it surprisingly little compared to the Elizabethans and the psalmists. In the view he adopts in "Man" and "Providence," man is a composite world worthy of some celebration, not only the focus of the creation but its intellectual center. Man's source is visible in his own bodily shape, "all symmetrie, / Full of proportions, one limbe to another." Not only the human body but everything in the visible creation, "Man" says, displays divine proportioning.

But Herbert's emphasis falls more often on use than on beauty, and even his statements on the latter are more philosophic than rhapsodic. In "Man" the constraints of shorter syntactic units and a collaborating shrinkage of metaphor keep the tone sober:

> For us the windes do blow,
> The earth doth rest, heav'n move, and fountains flow.
> Nothing we see, but means our good,
> As our delight, or as our treasure:

> The whole is, either our cupboard of food,
> Or cabinet of pleasure.

Only a little searching in companion poems reveals the undoing of this inventory of blessings, as illustrations of abundance are undone by the broadening of the context to include the storied whole. Moreover, irregularity is often the more productive vein in Herbert, who prefers stanzas composed of uneven line lengths, variously halted and marked with rhyme. The moods that he stretches across these shapes can be as expansive as that of Psalm 90, as desperate for refuge as Psalm 91, and yet as intimate as the sonnet.

In ways reminiscent of Donne's sense of integrated pacing, psychological adjustment, and layered times, Herbert imitates the twists and turns of an ego overmatched by its opponent, denied both its own projects and any immediate divine presence. In the dramatic stretching of episodes within the greater story, he marries the meditative or dramatic voice to stanzaic form and speaking cadence, and he extends the struggle with ego beyond the single lyric as a linking problem concluded only in "Love 3." The general order and arrangement of *The Church* and the filling in of the Williams Manuscript outline show that he calculated both the making of the volume and that thematic conclusion early on. The dedication, the recurrent unemployment poems, and the many metapoems show that he thought frequently about the part that the vocation of poetry plays in the problem of self, as perhaps English secular and sacred predecessors prompted him to do more than his biblical precedents. From the former he could easily have justified a "George Herbert" volume by the corrections of amorous verse that he anticipates in his two earlier sonnets and carries through *The Church*. But as we have seen and as Herbert criticism has well recognized, undermining the entire enterprise from "The Dedication" onward are the dangers of weaving self into sense and attempting rhymes that will engrave God's love in steel, even in justifiable causes. Although tutored by Donne and Sidney in exhibitionism and perhaps tempted by Jonson to compile a collected works, he is denied their kind of authorial imprint by the need to reconcile all personas with the sacrificial pattern. That need charges *The Church* with a pervasive disquiet that strains against liturgical regulations of the self in recuperative moments. He locates some of his lesser rescues from personal entanglements in abstract diction, which has a way of lifting the personal into the typical and of tempering temper, as for instance in "Thy power and love, my love and trust / Make one place ev'ry where." The distinct combination of these elements—the idiomatic turn of phrase, the quickened rhythms within a metrical norm, the stanzaic pacing, the mirroring and echoing, and the locations of such philosophemes as this one from "Temper 1" constitutes perhaps his firmest sense of form.

Even so, not all of his songs and sonnets are greatly distinguishable from what, with a thematic change, some of his immediate predecessors could have written. "Avarice," for instance, uses a conventional English quatrain, couplet form, and prosopopoeia in addressing "Money, thou bane of blisse, & source of wo." It opens with the sound of Sidney building upon medieval homiletic:

> Money, thou bane of blisse, & sourse of wo,
> > Whence com'st thou, that thou art so fresh and fine?
> > I know thy parentage is base and low:
> Man found thee poore and dirtie in a mine.
> Surely thou didst so little contribute
> > To this great kingdome, which thou now has got,
> > That he was fain, when thou wert destitute,
> To digge thee out of thy dark cave and grot:
> Then forcing thee by fire he made thee bright:
> > Nay, thou hast got the face of man; for we
> > Have with our stamp and seal transferr'd our right:
> Thou are the man, and man but drosse to thee.
> > Man calleth thee his wealth, who made thee rich;
> > And while he digs out thee, falls in the ditch.

The moralizing couplet here is a habit, not entirely a good one, that Herbert inherited from the Elizabethan love of apothegms. The poem imposes a vocal pattern on the meter, but it is a conventional one that does not assume dramatic discovery or personal relevance.

"Avarice" does prepare, however, for what becomes a recurrent and more distinctive address to hostile patronlike powers in "Time," "Death," and God himself in certain punitive guises. This address can be profitably set across from the vocative presence of celebration, which also uses personification and a modified decorum of patronage. Thus Herbert opens "Sunday" with "O Day most calm, most bright," "Church-musick" with "Sweetest of sweets, I thank you," "Banquet" with "Welcome sweet and sacred cheer," "Vertue" with "Sweet day, so cool, so calm, so bright," and numerous poems with addresses to God in a variety of tones. Besides the slightly different look that "Avarice" acquires in this company of poems, which forge a compromise between dramatic voicing and songlike meters and stanzas, it also summarizes a storied history of the love of money that fits it into sin's seizing of rival empire in humankind's sad history. It thus wedges itself among Herbert's many adjustments of lyric to fable. Avarice in effect takes a way that rivals the soul's course and assumes a place among both visible institutions and the innermost recesses of sin. It begins in low parentage, underground, but men bring it forth and shine it up by fire, stamp it into coins with "the face of man," and give it the run of the world.

Such poems in the homiletic vein tend to put aside questions of aestheticism along with the more troubled first-person voicing that Herbert often uses. No one works at numbers and intricate symmetries and lays the sentence and its voicing across them more deftly or meaningfully than Herbert. He feeds into the unfolding of a stanza or pairs of stanzas both the slower and speedier pacing of music and the more or less emphatic speech that make simple stressed and unstressed notations of prosody inadequate for more than the basic meter. For instance, in "Praise 3" he balances two stanzas with an unusually detailed cross-referencing and a variety of syllabic weights and pauses:

> When thou dost favour any action,
> It runnes, it flies:
> All things concurre to give it a perfection.
> That which had but two legs before,
> When thou dost blesse, hath twelve: one wheel doth rise
> To twentie then, or more.
>
> But when thou dost on businesse blow,
> It hangs, it clogs:
> Not all the teams of Albion in a row
> Can hale or draw it out of doore.
> Legs are but stumps, and Pharaohs wheels but logs,
> And struggling hinders more.

"Praise 3" presents a collaborative *and* hindering but not predetermining Providence that allows good and bad to proceed with their own enterprises. Herbert thereby gives free will some scope but inserts the apparently mysterious matter of luck or fortune, obviously no light matter in the contrast between endorsed and opposed acts. The symmetry is as telling here as it is in "Justice 1," as enterprises fall into opposites set in lines that can be paired the more easily for their identifiable lengths and relatively heavy stresses. Thus "favour" and "blow" set up the basic contrast from different places in almost parallel statements, the second nailing down the contrast and setting up a rhyme. Each stanza read apart would tell its own helped or hindered story, but placed together in an unfolding argument they double the effects. It may come as a surprise that one dimeter line, "It runnes, it flies," with a semantic change can seem as heavy in "It hangs, it clogs" as it had seemed light-footed before, as though anticipating its pairing not only with the previous line but the crushing irony, "Legs are but stumps, and Pharaohs wheels but logs." In the combined structure of the two stanzas, the latter line settles into the ear as heavily as God's weight upon the muscles. It would be hard to find two better anchoring words than "stumps" and "logs" or a better figure to reinforce the irony than their hyperbole. That Herbert revised the contents of some poems without changing their outer form suggests an arbitrary relationship between the two, but "Praise 3" in an example of how pliable form can be in his hands. Whatever he pours into the form molds form to content in the dynamics of sound and sense. The relationship seems anything but arbitrary in the actual voicing of the poem.

In both stanzas here—it is difficult to say why—the trimeter of the conclusion seems inevitable, perhaps because by then we've heard nearly everything else (4-2-5-4-5). Part of the wit of these stanzas is just what sense of variation. Both propriety and stretched tropes reach toward amazement over Providence at work, the same amazement that stretches all figures and shapes eventually in Herbert's garden of formal word sculptures. Hyperbole twists the examples and gives some further gauge to the disbelief in "Temper 1" that God would measure with a wretch. It seems that he does, and with great delight, since it is he who crosses the distance in small releases of appropriate strength—never, fortunately, the full thunderbolt. Since nothing we could name has twelve legs and twenty wheels (three horses or six men would pull neither ten chariots nor a very large wagon), the numbers are capricious on purpose to suggest the mysterious boost God gives the more usual numbers. The reference to Exodus 14.24–25 and YHWH's removal of the Egyptian chariot wheels reinforces the impression that it is not the poet merely but the Lord himself who is humorous. He has ever been so if we consider the larger fable and its wrenching of self-generated momentum away from its wandering and into the punctual rescue of the granted (really preempted) "suit" of "Redemption." Above all, Providence, like "Love," is attentive, and it is this care that demands the poet's answer in regulating his own helped and hindered stanzas. The poet too is after all a maker and expediter, but of mimetic words rather than bustling activities entered into each day's ledger by people surprised at the ease or the obstacles.

As I suggested, our normal critical vocabulary is not fully adequate for exploring this somewhat technical area, where the need is to stitch together the semantic field provided by doctrine, its interplay with the more "normal" syntax of "Legs are but stumps," the drama of speakers in spiritual conflict, specific allusions to other literary forms and vocabularies, and the overall architecture of *The Church*. It is no easier to integrate these levels in matters of pacing than it is in their use of tropes and figures, especially once we move beyond stanzas and their duplicative mirroring to long-distance echoing. Neither theories of metaphor nor theories of poetic units have been as prolific on integrated levels and variable spans across sequences as they have been on the basic units and single-word tropes. The difficulty is that at any given point one needs to bear in mind, and hear, several different units, from the metrical foot to the chaptered story to echoes that can be quite faint and subtle. That applies pressure not only to diction but to the spiritual development of speakers and minor sequences. What we require is an alternation of short- and long-range focuses and a way to monitor the attention paid to foreground and background elements. Herbert keeps an acoustical balance between the dominant moment and counterpointing or harmonic instruments. *The Church* blends many voices, and the art of reading it is in part that of hearing several of them (not all Herbert's personally) while attending primarily to one.

Imitative Faltering

Herbert usually makes metrical pauses and rhyme coincident with syntactical pauses or periods and with the voicing that governs them, which is to say that like all good craftsmen in dramatic verse he works the interplay of formal pattern and meaning pinned to the sentence. As we have noted in several poems, he sometimes does so using abstractions that range far beyond structural boundaries to invoke the wider significance of the salvation pattern; at other times, as in "Miserie," he practices an eroded form, so that a drinking song that should be full of potential roistering and Gilbert-and-Sullivan cooperations of wit, melody, phrasal length, and mood—a song of foolery—becomes instead a song of halting foolishness. Meter parodies the form, and the moralizing voice of one who remembers Eden shatters its mood.

Two of the more familiar examples of Herbert's self-concern as a craftsman, "Deniall" and "A true Hymne," bear scrutiny here for their attention to the formal roughness that derives from that complicating of mood. In its acknowledgment of the disconnection between devotions and a far-off ear perhaps not listening, "Deniall" takes up the theme of "Longing" but adds to it the severance of thought from word and of word from recipient. The poem plays out as statement and theme what remains an unstated and less-obvious formal disruption elsewhere:

> When my devotions could not pierce
>   Thy silent eares;
> Then was my heart broken, as was my verse:
>   My breast was full of fears
>   And disorder:
>
> My bent thoughts, like a brittle bow,
>   Did flie asunder:
> Each took his way; some would to pleasures go,
>   Some to the warres and thunder
>   Of alarms.

What *should* chime with a poet's mind are words filled to the brim with some aspect of the one story and his enthusiastic participation in it. Poised to shoot thought's shafts to eternity, the bow—strained by the backward pull—does not merely break in two but shatters. When arrows aimed at that high target get nowhere, thoughts fall to the pleasures and the self-esteem that lie at hand, certainly one logical repercussion of struggling with a fable so disconnected at both ends. The target is all glory, the fall into the natural and social matrix all shame. Thoughts after all *will* be occupied with something, probably either devotional or poetic in Herbert's case, and if reason is of little use in divine affairs, it may turn elsewhere. No one is all heart, and the working brain is too curious for its own good.

The irregularities of the stanza mock the disorder of the futile man at devotions and separates him from the poet by a perspective-giving past tense and a self-critical attitude. The riddle logic of "silent eares" mocks the ineptness of the present as well, as do other failures of technique. The appeal in the final stanza to "defer no time" means in part "let the syllables fall in the right cadences,"with words that complete their meanings on the beat. The main request is for a united divine will and current skill:

> O cheer and tune my heartlesse breast,
>   Deferre no time;
> That so thy favours granting my request,
>   They and my minde may chime,
>   And mend my ryme.

Not until this point do we realize for sure that by "devotions" the speaker has meant versified ones, collapsing the distinction between churchman and rhymester.

The failure of poetic devotions is all the more obvious when the results are on the page for the critical eye to see. An extemporized private prayer or prayer-book recitation presumably has no such measure to betray it. The key to the clumsiness is timing, and it encounters basically the same difficulty that overtakes the impatience poems—the severing of applied divine power from human need, here reduced to the minimal mechanics of line-by-line composition. From the poet's perspective, the minute scale of momentary thought working its way toward praise requires a mended chiming just as much as larger events require the "favour" (or encounter the headwinds) of Providence. The possibility of manufacturing the appearance of good rhyme without making the mind actually accord with God underlies Arnold Stein's conclusion that "by the standard of Herbert's best poems the conclusion is a piece of arbitrary wit" (16). Richard Strier's notion is that the poet "cannot mend his spiritual state by mending [merely] his representation of it" (*Love Known* 191) and that the mending must therefore be of more than the poem. As Diane Benet also suggests, the poet's inner condition requires a significant change. Still, none of these observations explain the relationship between lame rhyme, good rhyme, and spiritual condition, a relationship that Janis Lull shows Herbert to have experimented with in revising the poem (*The Poem in Time* 92). These judgments refine that of Joseph Summers, who assumes that a granted request and an ordered prayer would provide evidence of an actual spiritual cure (*George Herbert* 136), as though a proper devotional attitude must coincide with technical mastery.

Perhaps something less definitive would be better: getting the form right is a first stage. Doing that *may* bring a fuller cure, but not necessarily. By the final rhyme, the speaker has recovered from his worst agitation and has put his verse in order. In the present tense of the writing, the untidiness has already been reduced to a mock imitation, a good sign of recovered spiritual poise. In better and more assured days, skillful execution in poetry and success in devotion line up as evidence of divine presence; this speaker is currently doing without these, but he is close enough that he can anticipate the feel of prosperity and see the humor of his ineptness. Unlike the psalmists, judges, and kings of old, he cannot expect extraordinary signs of favor, such as battlefield victories or success in desperate ventures. Anyway, the nature of writing and of personal devotions is to require inner dictation. God's intervention would show, he can only suppose, as competence in tropes and meters, in thought, and in their happy marriage.

What is a devotional poet without such favors, whether particularly given or not? As the body of "Deniall" demonstrates, he is an inept contriver of rattletrap stanzas. He sets a meter only to trip over it and sets a rhyme pattern only to require a tortured syntax and rhythm to prop it up. But paradoxically, we recognize that even these maladroit near-misses require skill. Someone intentionally a little off and limping through parody is performing a task no less difficult than one whose technique is entirely smooth. We might deduce from that a technical competence all along. As Mario A. Di Cesare remarks, "The prosody is intricate, subtle, demanding, and remarkably effective," although it does not follow from this that "the poem is fundamentally a textured narrative of spiritual dryness, with contrapuntal structures and ambivalent conclusion" (85). The humor evoked by deliberate error does not require metaphoric fireworks or even witty statement; it is basically slapstick, in this case by a verbal gymnast. It would not by itself demonstrate the spiritual state of estranged devotion if the poet did not say that it did.

"A true Hymne," which I glanced at earlier, is similar to "Deniall" in tampering as much with grammar and meter as it does with meaning. After longing gets the poet started, the failure of his project brings an example of his own cure: "As when th' heart says (sighing to be approved) / O, could I love! and stops: God writeth, Loved." It is difficult to tell whether, if God were actually to write "loved," the finished poem would be a result of faith or a gift of grace, but the speaker realizes that when a true hymn gets written, this will be how it sounds. From another angle, however, God has either always loved or never will do so, and saying so changes only the poem and the poet's mood, not the reality. Arriving at an exclamatory pitch of longing in "A true Hymne," the poet can again only prime the pump with a display of what the final finding of a form would produce. Certainly, as faith's formula, such a hymn would end the loitering, and it would receive, if not the ring that Hope's petitioner wants, a definitive phrase like the one that

consummates "Love 3." What "A true Hymne" as actually written offers
instead is a blueprint and a contrast of attitudes. It is neither quite the heart's
nor the mind's poem; it is the product of a fictionalized presence ushered in
by a single word that raises echoes across *The Church* and far out into its
canyoned sacred and secular sources. If that word were to come unconditionally, as God's saying it would imply, it would transcend the azimuth from
Adam to doomsday with a personal immediacy that abolished all distance.
Even distinctions between Hebrew and Christian epochs would no longer
matter. Delays, death, and judgment would virtually disappear. And so in
fact they do when love is not assisting the act of writing but coaxing a sinner
into communion and writing "loved" for the volume.

But like the phrase "my servant" of "The Odour" and the mended rhyme
of "Deniall," "loved" here I assume to be *not* given but merely taken from a
prepared store of readily available concepts. An integral part of the fable and
the doctrine is the assumption that the god of the new sacrifice may reenter
at any point. Equally integral to writing about it, in Scripture or in poems,
are his hypothetical entries and verbal openings. One way to prompt these is
to dramatize the faltering and cause mercy to replace judgment. The unusual
aspect of the openings that Herbert leaves for God's entry is that he has them
sized by metrical foot, placed in the line, and set up by rhyming mate: all
God need do is drop in one syllable. The sacrifice shows him willing to do
that, and more, for humankind generally; the question is whether he will do
so for this poet at just this moment.

Good Structure and Winding Stairs

Historicism for Herbert, whether local or global, is governed by a theological
vocabulary. It is the meaning of the abstractions that grows in the course of
the poem, often by reversal after movement in the wrong direction by self-
propelled and self-concerned speakers. Corrections are contained in the
recognition of basic doctrine. For instance, the speaker of "Redemption"
rushing headlong into the meaning of "redemption" is quite unprepared for
it by the episodic unfolding of his pursuit. The end of Christ's life, the final
phase of the sonnet, and the periodizing of the Law converge in one moment.
The meaning of "redemption," however personally delivered and immediately applied in this single story, can be applied to any willing person who
comes to the point of self-cancellation and the reception of grace. The power

of that single word provides a doctrinal foundation located in a visual figure at the end of one era and the beginning of another. I will consider the implications of this conversion for certain sonnet conventions later; here my interest is primarily in how Herbert works lexical expansion into a parabolic sonnet, much in the indirect, allegorical way he chastises in "Jordan 1." The winding-stair trope of the latter poem is appropriate for the structure of stanzaic evolution that Herbert often uses in building the units of a poem toward their cancellation. He also sometimes circles back by repetition, refrain, syllabic sound pattern, and thematic echo, but at a higher level exploiting multiple perspectives short of omniscience.

In "Redemption" other meanings of "redemption" pale beside the reversal that the saying of Christ brings into the poem, which is of course not new to Herbert or his readers. In ordinary usage, "redemption" means to ransom, buy back, recover, pay off, deliver, make amends or compensate for, and it applies to specific purchases. The Christian field of play is both narrower in diversity and larger in scope, and it is more or less given, although Herbert can approach it in his own way. The mere word brings virtually the entire scheme with it. It presupposes Adam; it presupposes the Law and its versions of sacrifice and thus the Hebrew Bible as reduced by Christian misprision. The sentence and the poem take a typical old-covenant expectation and bring it to the point of category change, maneuvering the speaker into position to be swept into it. He then presumably becomes a new person, a convert. This is as close to a conversion narrative as Herbert gets, since others who article with God do not come from quite so far away. A powerful trope and divine retort whirl into their orbit all ordinary language bound to them.

Both the sonnet rendering of the term "redemption" and the implied historical epochs that Herbert compresses into it have still another scaling task to perform, namely furthering the reader's progress in *The Church* at a place near the beginning when the reading contract is still being set. Again I want to set side most of that architectural concern as one too many complications for the present, but we need to keep in mind the intermediary units between the composite fable and the spiritual and psychological changes of single speakers. Individual poems intervene as do linked sequences such as that opening group, "potions" concocted of verses that lie many pages off, webbed metaphoric associations, and so on. It is clear that Herbert intends these groupings. As virtually all readers agree, his own verses are equivalent in that respect to those which "H. Scriptures 2" describes in the Bible. As a *biblia* or collection of writings, the latter provides a model for a loose-leaf binding of anecdotes, wisdom literature, myths, parables, and lyric materials, which makes repetition and metaphoric interweaving as important as linear development. All along, in any sort of connection we contrive, the segments are allocated to numbered chapters and verses, which manage enough autonomy to sustain individual interpretation and commentary.

It is also true that the Bible is not the only source of collaborations among discrete units, dramatic movement, and abstract pattern. Over a dozen poems of *The Church* specifically invoke the Renaissance sonnet, and Herbert often uses distinctive stanzaic forms based on Elizabethan lyric practice. If it is generally true of him, as Robert Alter says (thinking of the "contemplative and emotive inwardness" of Renaissance religious poetry), that he is the "most psalmodic of English poets" (*The Literary Guide* 259–60), it is no less true that he benefits as much as anyone from English tradition even if he has to correct it (Freer 7–8; Schleiner 46–71). The expenditure of craft raises no particular problems in most of his predecessors, but it can do so in a suppliant who from the outset puts the idea of "first fruits" under scrutiny and intermittently champions the plain style. A flagrant display of art molded into witty wordplay becomes one of the errors to be corrected. Rhyme has imprisoned the soul, which was captured by its own vanity and can only be released by self-examination. In Petrarchan courtship too such highly formal visible care can be an ostentatious display, but attitudes toward courtship and certain social conventions encourage it. It does not hinder courtship but is its very means. As a demonstration of capacity to play by the known rules, it vouches for the poet's credibility. It establishes his status even as it conventionalizes his praise.

Accordingly, among sonneteers the act of authoring is more prominent than writing ordinarily is in Psalms or for that matter in most biblical texts. Herbert finds his sources in serious conflict and the motives for writing dubious. It is as though he must move through the mined field of rhymed secular verse to get to the ironic twist of rediscovered and less fettered biblical meaning in such a phrase as "Your suit is granted." Christ obligingly plays the patron whom the speaker expects, uses his lesser word "suit" for what should have been a heart-searching plea for forgiveness and salvation, and then finds the clinching word "granted," which cuts off all discussion. Using sonnet vocabulary, Christ has managed to speak of things quite different from those of interest to aristocratic patrons and coy ladies. If we nonetheless have some idea of how much "is granted" does not say, it is thanks to the echoing context of *The Church* and the power of irony to say something other than what is intended and still convey a decipherable meaning.

Even where such expansion drives out the more ordinary language of pursuits with oxymoron, irony, and other figures of strain, it does not often ruffle the meter or the structure of stanzas. The complications are figural and thematic rather than formal. But Herbert's choice of the sonnet for themes that in biblical poetry would assume looser narrative and dialogue forms generates several of the more startling formal effects of *The Church*. Sonnets fall among companion poems obviously unlike those of Sidney, Spenser, and Shakespeare, or even of Donne, where they come with the assumption that each performance is relatively complete. Sonnets such as "Prayer 1," "The Holdfast," "Redemption," "The Answer," and the two on Scripture are quite otherwise, whether they approach the English form in their use of final couplets or the Petrarchan octave/sestet dialectic. (Herbert often blends the two, keeping the couplet pattern but staging a sestetlike reversal.) Much depends in them on the matching of voice to subject and on awareness that a sacred poem needs to question poetry's "enchanting language." Herbert is adept at allocating things of great representational scope to phrases of short compass; in sonnets he is virtually obligated to do.

One other facet of Herbert's formalism demands brief attention before we turn to further examples, namely the attraction of divine "beauty." In "Dulnesse," the beloved provides a stronger enticement for progress in courtship than a mistress does for wanton lovers who curl plain intention with "quaint metaphors." Herbert's attention there is on beauty as the force that draws the lover through phases and draws the poet through the structure of the poem and eventually its volume:

> Thou art my lovelinesse, my life, my light,
>   Beautie alone to me:
> Thy bloudy death and undeserv'd, makes thee
>   Pure red and white.
>
> When all perfections as but one appeare,
>   That those thy form doth show,
> The very dust, where thou dost tread and go,
>   Makes beauties here.

We hear echoes of the songs of Solomon, the psalms, and sonnet blazons, but a semi-theoretical comment on form rises above them. The first order of business, as it is with Herbert's early (1610) view of sonnets on love, is to capture the figures and forms of secular love for the expression of sacred love. One and all, the resources belong to the poet of *The Church*, who claims them as his own even while rejecting their former contexts. If he makes distinctions among his sources, it is only to use the lesser ones to gauge the more powerful ones. Here the abundance of paraphrases for the beloved quickens the rhythm of the run through loveliness, life, and light. The first draws primarily from the diction of feminine beauty and the second in part from Petrarchan hyperbole. But the third imposes a rereading on these forerunners by gathering the sequence into the precincts of the sacred, as does the "bloudy death," which makes "loveliness" paradoxical. "Life" and "light" already have the weight of devotional usage. "Life" is less exclusively devotional in its own right and has the mixed parentage of shared terms that look in both secular and sacred directions. The gathering power of the salvation scheme shows in the summary phrase "all perfections as but one appeare," which holds even particles of dust to be formally excellent.

Herbert establishes a doctrine of beauty here that he uses also in "The Forerunners" and implies in the rhetorical question of "Jordan 1," "Is there in truth no beautie?" But he does not cover all the bases, since extended "fictions," "false hair," puns, devices, and cleverness generally have very little to do with beauty as such and much to do with wit and strained decorum. The sonnet tradition takes in all of these, and his use of it raises more questions than "Jordan 1" asks, questions that he has not really answered in the 1610 sonnets.

Expanded or Exploded Form?

Formal units ideally reflect the harmony and proportion of the creation and of a tempered moral life whose trials improve the poet's music. The connection between such a contained life and sonnet formality is one of the earlier points *The Church* makes in "Sinne 1," a kind of miniature psalm. But Herbert allows only enough stability to set a norm and then departs from it, the formal equivalent to establishing a normal language level before relinquishing it to catachresis or oxymoron. The wreckage is all sin's doing:

> Lord, with what care hast thou begirt us round!
>   Parents first season us: then schoolmasters
>   Deliver us to laws; they send us bound
> To rules of reason, holy messengers,

Pulpits and Sundayes, sorrow dogging sinne,
   Afflictions sorted, anguish of all sizes,
   Fine nets and stratagems to catch us in,
Bibles laid open, millions of surprises,
Blessings beforehand, tyes of gratefulnesse,
   The sound of glorie ringing in our eares:
   Without, our shame; within, our consciences;
Angels and grace, eternall hopes and fears.
   Yet all these fences and their whole aray
   One cunning bossome-sinne blows quite away.

The life story is neither quite causal nor casual, thanks to cunning sin. No human institution provides a shelter; nothing regulatory suffices. The only thing immune to sin is the containing power of grace. The sonnet comes to a neat couplet summary that detonates its own amplified list and leaves a field of wreckage. We view that field detachedly, as from a great distance, but so polished a melodic couplet becomes ironic in this context. The noise of the detonation reverberates throughout *The Church* and sends various speakers scurrying for something safer and solider than the world provides.

In assuming a certain context for authorial self-estimation, "The Holdfast" works an even more inclusive wreckage under the universal force of sin, this time supplemented by the answering force of transcendence. It comments indirectly on the enterprise of writing by bringing forward the quarrel between one who must surrender and one who would serve. Behind it, as behind "Sinne 1," is the pressure to conform to the antitype that makes a mockery of other self-making enterprises. The added implication of "The Holdfast" is that by rights sonnets should also be included among the possessions surrendered for safekeeping:

I Threatned to observe the strict decree
   Of my deare God with all my power & might.
   But I was told by one, it could not be;
Yet I might trust in God to be my light.
Then will I trust, said I, in him alone.
   Nay, ev'n to trust in him, was also his:
   We must confesse that nothing is our own.
Then I confesse that he my succour is:
But to have nought is ours, not to confesse
   That we have nought. I stood amaz'd at this,
   Much troubled, till I heard a friend expresse,

> That all things were more ours by being his.
> What Adam had, and forfeited for all,
> Christ keepeth now, who cannot fail or fall.

This very puzzled inquiry in which each discovery cancels the effort that leads to it begins at the level of a more or less legalistic piety. Again some correspondence holds between the overall effort of humanity since Adam and the personal efforts summed up in "I Threatned," "I trust," "I confesse" (concluding what could stand as an octave), and "I stood amaz'd." The latter breaks into the third quatrain before "I heard" introduces the concluding wisdom. Putting his exhibitions one by one into the sonnet frame like this, the speaker only by stages finds that all accomplishment belongs to one who has definitive power over every part of the world's compiled record. After the first mistake, he resorts to "trust," a basic word also in "Temper 1" and one of the well-accepted abstractions, in the hope that such a small initiative might go uncanceled. He is by then well into a commonly accepted range of foundation words, each of which might have made a sonnet in itself were this patron like others to whom hopeful sonneteers bring their devotions. The entire sequence of increasingly less forward acts gives way to the paradox of seizing *only* by letting go, which arrives at oxymoron as the controlling trope of the wisdom statement. The riddling couplet establishes that principle as the pedestal of the sonnet. Taking over all mediating functions, the highest priest of Hebrews, history's only holdfast, leaves a narrative of error and passive conformity for the poet's portion. All the past compressed into the pattern of what Adam had and forfeited yields to a non-narrative present, the eternal now of Christ's unfaltering possession.

The answer to the question of "Jordan 1," "Is there in truth no beautie?" under these circumstances would have to be no, not if a human speaker utters it. Adam had all forms of speech and forfeited them. It is again ironic that a sonnet, an instrument of secular courtship, should be the vehicle of that realization. Even the timing of counterchecks is promising for conventional form-breaking, since listing the ways one might serve through three quatrains and being spurned only in the final couplet would mount a more crushing blow. As it is, unconventional placement of the reversals, at lines 3, 6, and 9, allow the speaker to work through his amazement with three-and-a-half lines remaining for the consolation. "I stood amaz'd" imitates the surprise of the midst, where experience misleads us and hopes are renewed only to be chastised by the rigorous discipline of the Fall and Redemption.

By comparison to the holdfast principle and the mistaken spiritual bustle that discloses it, poems to or about mistresses in Herbert's view insufficiently realize that futility of works. The very young Herbert had only partially realized that in the two sonnets to his mother, which conclude that such studied figures as flowers, clouds, and crystal eyes would find their best uses in praise of the Lord. On second thought, "The Holdfast" suggests, even a devotional sonnet runs certain risks unless it turns its industry against itself, risks that Marvell's "Coronet" finds inherent in the ambition of religious verse. Accumulated habits have fostered the illusion of sustained self-possession. What replaces them obliterates the distinction between better and worse, moral and immoral acts, excellence and mediocrity. The ending overpowers the preceding segments by replacing the "much troubled" loss of good intentions with a medieval-style moral. In summarizing the basic salvation story, it recasts as doctrinal formula the drama we have just witnessed. It concedes a sonnet's usual right to anchor itself in epigrammatic wisdom but adds the proviso that this one could not do so but for the marring-and-mending pattern.

The unquestionably hopeful couplet leaves open the question of what exactly the holdfast holds in these "things"? Do they readmit the principle of accumulated works in safekeeping? Presumably all avenues the speaker has tried are included in what he would want to see saved, but the leap to restoration is unimaginable in any available tropes. Whereas the compiling of misleading efforts makes strict decrees and trust seem momentarily necessary, the restored self will have no need for trust, which is a fine word in "Temper 1" but limited to the changeable conditions of soaring and plunging. Hence what is to be restored has to be something quite different from anything the world generates. Although all things are ours only through the holdfast, what "ours" means is precisely what is at issue where eschatology replaces a locatable Canaan as the place of promise. What is paternity? What is inheritance? What is the foretaste?

What a poet is to think who questions thus and still continues to write sonnets is unclear, since the friend renders the positive side of self-canceling in terms that should not allow the writing even of poems of praise. Whether the couplet is a continued indirect quotation that finishes the friend's statement or an affirmation from the primary speaker, what the sonnet knows is that if anything is to be ours it must first be his, and once anything is actually his, we cannot anticipate what it will look like when it returns. This is not strictly speaking a Calvinist or New Testament problem (Strier, *Love Known* 65–73; Fish, *Self-Consuming Artifacts* 176–77), because it is equally difficult to say who according to the Lord of Host is the victor—whether

YHWH Joshua, Gideon, Saul, David, and Samson. As John Goldingay observes, different books of the Hebrew Bible take different perspectives on that issue (48–55). The earlier writings express YHWH's presence through public miracles. From Joshua's halting of the sun onward, YHWH "deposits a quantum of power at the disposal of a chosen man or woman" (Friedman, *The Exile* 39). Even when heroes are called to arms and told that the enemy will be placed in their hands, the source of their victories proves to be highly ambiguous. YHWH must have champions, yet he personally chooses them, names the hour of battle, forms the plan of attack, and sometimes so terrifies the opposing host that it flees without an arrow being launched. Gideon's force is slimmed to a few hundred against thousands to make that very point. In the successive stages of the Hebrew epic, the land becomes "ours," then, but subsequent battle hymns then see the glory as not ours but God's. As warriors are to such victories, so works are to salvation, divinely guided lesser instruments used for ends quite beyond themselves.

The question of self-possession becomes even more critical in the salvation drama, because it is not credit for victory that is at stake but the status of the self, which is a product no longer of citizenship but of spiritual inwardness. Poems that address that inwardness may or may not salvage a function in their self-destruction. An altar made of the poet's heart is not a proper altar unless it is taken over by the "blessed sacrifice." Most sonnets as well as many psalms are poems of praise, but under the conditions of "The Holdfast" it is no wonder that Herbert's contain few equivalents to straightforward inventories, blazons, or clear steps toward their couplet summaries. Most of them are small dramas spoken by troubled voices that question the very laying out of conventional unit divisions and metrical patterns. In some cases where the suppliant threatens to become too prominent, Herbert reminds us that for the love that is the proper subject of a sequence, all that is defensible by way of diction and form is a simple "*My God, My King*," expressed in a minimal rhythmic doublet. It is very likely the friend of "The Holdfast" who also admonishes the speaker of "Jordan 2" (echoing Astrophel):

> *How wide is all this long pretence!*
> *There is in love a sweetnesse readie penn'd*:
> *Copie out onely that, and save expense.*

Other love poems nonetheless continue to sprout and swell and curl, "Decking the sense, as if it were to sell." Whereas Astrophel supposedly looks into his heart (even though he continues also to ransack volumes of poetry),

Herbert is advised to look into love itself, which as "Love 3" and the sonnets that prepare for it tell us, means *receiving* it under quite different terms than giving it or expressing it. To "copy" love's sweetness is to read the one book of love that makes one understood—understood not in one's own language but in received types of the forfeited and the saved.

This erosion of authorial autonomy results in a different concept of a book than either Herbert's Elizabethan predecessors or the psalms pursue, the latter of course from within a Chosen People's precepts of service. For Herbert love poetry cannot fall into courtship sequences if it disdains the usual beauties and idealizations of erotic love that guide many if not all of them; but it cannot be quite like the psalmists' collection either, because it has little application to choral occasions and no concern for national triumphs. Yet each of these provides a reserve of forms, and in combining them Herbert uses a double-edged irony: the shift to psalmic subjects exposes the hyperbolic waste of sonnet language; the new covenant exposes the presumptuousness of petitionary psalms. Either together or apart, both models advise the utmost craft, devoted to the best of subjects; yet the sacrificial principle of "The Holdfast" and the plain-style declarations undercut the entire idea of a display form. It is the greater echoic structure of *The Church* and the thematic pointing of its repeated vocabulary that finally give us the needed perspective on this apparent contradiction and teach us to draw no conclusions without the entire fable in sight and "Love" at hand.

Sonnet Containment

Fulke Greville's midstream switch from secular to sacred lyrics in *Caelica* parallels a number of cases heralded by Sidney, in which poets express dissatisfaction with the secular roots of poetics and rhetoric. Like Milton in *The Reason of Church Government* and *Paradise Regained*, Sidney finds biblical models able to hold their own with classical literature, especially the psalms of "holy David," which are notable expressions of the *vates* in lyric and a "heavenly poesy" of passionate love. Milton enlarges the list of genres well exemplified in Scripture with "divine pastoral drama in the Song of Solomon," tragedy in the apocalypse, brief epic, magnific odes and hymns, and "all kinds of [incomparable] lyric poesy." Christ in *Paradise Regained* finds Hebrew arts unexcelled:

> All our Law and Story strew'd
> With Hymns, our Psalms with artful terms inscrib'd
> Our Hebrew Songs and Harps in *Babylon*,
> That pleas'd so well our Victors' ear, declare
> That rather *Greece* from us these Arts deriv'd;
> Ill imitated, while they loudest sing
> The vices of their Deities, and thir own
> In Fable, Hymn, or Son, so personating
> Thir Gods ridiculous, and themselves past shame.
>
> (4.334–42)

Oratory and rhetoric are not excluded from the list despite their preeminence in Greece. John Smith's adding of sacred examples of schemes and tropes to the usual classical ones in *Mysteries of Rhetoric Unveiled* demonstrates that he concurs with that judgment. Although the latter work was not published until 1657, it reflects a tendency already prominent in Thomas Wilson's *Arte of Rhetorique* a century earlier.

Despite this intermittent effort to resituate letters in a biblical context, no theorist or poet goes as far as Herbert does into the problems raised by putting rhetorical conventions to sacred service or for that matter as far as he does into the quite-different formal implications of the two testaments. Taking sonnets as a prime example, he pushes the idea of a Christian poetry to an acute pitch of self-awareness. Rather than smoothly voyaging through one level of metaphor to another or from old heroic stories to the holdfast, he finds gaps between deed and outcome and (in love poetry) between speaker and beloved. The difficulty of making connections is compounded by the forms of address he has to adopt from both the psalms and the secular tradition. That the inimitable sacrifice discredits human offerings raises the question, why write any elaborately shaped form at all? No single answer to the question of what constitutes a proper divine language fits all cases, and the same goes for the syntactical figures and sound patterns that accompany the "Lovely enchanting language" that "The Forerunners" regrets losing. As I suggested, the idea of a decorum that puts true beauty and beauteous words together is not adequate to account for the extent of Herbert's psalmic echoes, literary allusions, punning, intricate stanza forms, wordshape diagrams, and anagrams—overall, as full a bag of tricks as any Renaissance poet could boast.

It is sometimes the confessional potential of a complex form that justifies the poetic undertaking. In "The Sinner," the first sonnet of *The Church*, the speaker is desperate to exchange his vanity-laden heart for a purer one, but even as he says this he piles up metaphors for the corrupted heart, making the poem into its image:

> Lord, how I am all ague, when I seek
>   What I have treasur'd in my memorie!
>   Since, if my soul make even with the week,
> Each seventh note by right is due to thee.
> I finde there quarries of pil'd vanities,
>   But shreds of holinesse, that dare not venture
>   To shew their face, since crosse to thy decrees:
> There the circumference earth is, heav'n the centre.
> In so much dregs the quintessence is small:
>   The spirit and good extract of my heart
>   Comes to about the many hundred part.
> Yet Lord restore thine image, heare my call:
>   And though my hard heart scarce to thee can grone,
>   Remember that thou once didst write in stone.

A confessional meditation on mediation and a piece of writing about an ultimate inscription, this sonnet is alert to both the rewards and the perils of self-examination. The speaker works in agitation over what memory and heart yield under inspection, but he would have no poem if they did not yield so much. Recollection does not return all the way to Adam and bring into play the marring/mending therapy of *The Church*, yet without a reinscription of the Lord's image, the poet could not look in the heart and write. Finding any commanding voice depends largely on the result of the appeal, "Yet Lord restore" and "heare my call," standard appeals in what sounds like a common voice, not particularly personal. One act of apt remembrance, the right one, could drive away the profusion of images, but the couplet, set up by a line borrowed from the third quatrain (as though to augment the Lord's portion by at least a little), only transfers remembrance to the Lord and suggests that what he once did he might do again.

The problem lies in the infected will. The heart has grown great not with a foreign invader but with its own accomplishments. The speaker's recollection is not a session of sweet silent thought despite a distant likeness to Shakespeare's sonnet 30; it is rather the onset of a feverish bout with personal memorabilia, which now seem no more than empty images. Mixing musical, chemical, and geometrical figures, the speaker finds a very squeezed center amid a large pile of vanities (or "circumference" or "dregs"). Despite this proliferation of tropes, the poem makes a fairly typical sonnet pattern of what it describes as recurrent self-searching. It marks the quatrains, fills each to the brim, and—appropriate to so closely numbered a form—sets up quantitative measures for the state of the soul. It allows for the survival of a quintessence, which defies measured portions by harboring in all of them and controlling them, as a powerful abstraction can overcome the dispersal of many a concrete part and as one name can control all names. Such a word the Lord can and has written in stone.

Earlier I considered perhaps Herbert's best sonnet, "Redemption," from another angle. I want to return to it for a moment here, primarily for the implications of its variation on sonnet form, and rise from the circumstances of its narrative to Christ's ironic turn on "suit." The speaker's assumption that sonnets travel in elite company reflects the Renaissance love sonnets's establishing of its credentials. He begins in the quatrain fashion of his usual English form:

> Having been tenant long to a rich Lord,
> Not thriving, I resolved to be bold,
> And make a suit unto him, to afford
> A new small-rented lease, and cancell th' old.

The suspended temporality of that opening, which reaches as far back as the Law goes, could be paraphrased "having been Jewish a long time," or more elaborately, "having operated within the economy of works and rewards, in a world of devotions, tithes, monarchs, taxes, and wars against misdevotion." The "not thriving" puts the speaker in league with all those in the condition of "The Bunch of Grapes" and other affliction poems who have learned to mistrust a supposedly providential world. Christ's words preempt the request itself and are typical of exchanges between Jesus and those who question him. At whatever level they enter, it is never high enough. Nor do they realize that their every word participates in an epochal making of parabolic form.

It is that form, with an ironic twist, that controls and justifies the sonnet here. Having stumbled on the Crucifixion, picking up momentum as he plunges into confusion, the speaker leaves just one line for the reversal, which as it turns out is adequate. The pivot comes late for the same reason that turns in "The Collar," "Affliction 1," "Temper 1," and "Love 3" do: it breaks down elaborate worldly motives and their conventional handling without bringing a replacement, which awaits further dialogue. Seizing upon the figure of the cross, the reversal brings salvation into a history that has not seemed at all promising for it. A change in pace finishes the narrative buildup and settles into an aftermath that leaves a need for adjustment in the suppliant, who could be either devastated or remade by this. He has discovered a compassionate and willing Lord; but he has discovered too that the new lease refers to some level beyond any he recognizes. The answer parallels the "losse of rime" that comes to those who plainly say, *"My God, My King"* in that it prevents any further commentary for the time being, even as it makes the finishing of the story all the more necessary. Whatever the allegorical covering of the search, the offer of grace is unequivocal. In retrospect, that makes the preceding lines seem so much useless bustle. They are mere preparation for the encounter of the one who works redemption by surrendering the very power the speaker assumes he has.

As it traces the suit from one reminder of empire and dynasty to another, "Redemption" calls into question other sonnet assumptions as well as the decorum of courtly circles. The "ragged" noise suggests a speaker who turns up his nose at those who would not be allowed in a sestet were it not for the Redeemer's presence among them. Some aloofness persists in the word "espied," before the visible bearers of cultural idiom come up against an unexpected rudeness. Everything that sonnet practitioners and the speaker stand for comes tumbling down along with the idea of a powerful lord. Herbert thereby plants another gesture toward "Love 3" and its revised wooing. Where the love poems project the union of human and divine natures, "Redemption" stops at the edge. Like "Justice 1" it maintains enough prominence in its abstract title that *The Church* can draw upon it and upon redemption's break in human expectation numerous times.

Together with "H. Scriptures 2," these poems are perhaps sufficient examples of Herbert at sonnets to make the main formal and structural points: that he takes good care of standard measures, often using them ironically to correct his predecessors or the speakers themselves and either by concept or by some irregularity or aberration introduced into them stretches or explodes them; in the progress toward "Love 3" he prevents any conceptual closure to match their neat formal closures; and through such typological figures as the holdfast and such abstractions as "sin" and "redemption" and through interwoven figures and images, he augments the echo system with formal reduplications that make an enlarged system of assembled independent verses in the biblical manner.

A few other useful comments on the interplay of form, historical narrative, self-making, and style can be extracted from "Prayer 1," the two sonnets on love, the sonnets on the Scriptures, and "The Sonne." Let me conclude with these somewhat generally without trying to package any complete sampling of the formal and structural devices and links that I listed initially or going into unnecessary detail. In its denial of prayer's definability, "Prayer 1" resembles the abruptness of "Redemption." An assortment of metaphors reaches toward the mystery of divine/human communication without resolving that mystery in an entirely satisfactory manner. The opening quatrain finds prayer summing up the self and sending it on its way. In its efficacy as petition in the second quatrain, prayer is a force to be reckoned with and requires powerful verbal weapons to match the world-making Word. At the beginning of the sestet, foretastes of Paradise transcend that list of functions, as prayer shuttles between the world of striving and the place of delivery. The abstractions that mark the sestet's quieting of the octave's furor forecast the calm of heaven. In denying figure and description altogether, the concluding "something understood" suggests a pentecostal ideal, a miraculous return to adamic language. It passes beyond calculation, overleaping all times from the first issuance of breath to the closed communion. Like other lyric moments at their most compressed, prayer's moment can contain creation and can gesture toward eternity, but it also abandons specific requests and is felt as the instrument of mutual presence. It calls silently upon love and contributes to the finality of its eventual fuller presence. Planting any such suggestion along the line in *The Church* inserts useful stability that personas can call upon to overcome the uncertainty of their complaint-filled stories. Much like the sacraments, prayer is recurrent; it restores confidence in language and decorum, despite the unfitness of even the best-dressed human vocabulary.

It is evident from this example too, however, that the increment-and-arrival implications of form, whether in narrative, confession, or prayer, is likely to be canceled at last by the leap of abstract formulas, as they are by the equivalent insights of "Sinne 1," "The Holdfast," and "Redemption" and perhaps even "H. Scriptures 2." The reason again is basically that the very concept of a last phase undoes the articulation of parts preceding. In moving closer to inspect secular sonnets in "Love 1" and "Love 2," Herbert repeats the call for assistance in the special affair of heart that in divine love forces the rethinking of the petitioning and complaint basic to secular poetry. If one form of prayer is poetic invocation, these poems should locate the something understood in terms specifically applicable to the strongest of intuitional and heartfelt bonds between suppliant and master. The difficulty is that a sonneteer uses a fixed form, usually with certain assumptions. In "Love 1" he finds conventional beauty and wit the products of mere fancy. In the answering sonnet, the cure for that is less a disciplining of feeling than the discovery of a still-more consuming passion, the presence of the Lord in the sonneteer's heart. The foreshadowing of the final "fire" is both a metaphor and a heralded actuality:

> let those fires,
> Which shall consume the world, first make it tame;
> And kindle in our hearts such true desires
> As may consume our lusts, and make thee way.
> Then shall our hearts pant thee; then shall our brain
> All her invention on thine Altar lay,
> And there in hymnes send back thy fire again.

To put the brain's clever inventions on the altar and burn them means not to forebear using them but to incorporate them into poems dedicated as first fruits. Such fire must turn sonnets into inflaming psalms.

However—to harp on this much-repeated feature of Herbert's concern with answerable form—the actual statement the sonnet makes is not itself a hymn, merely an appeal to become one. The sonnet cannot be expanded into a true love poem; it is preliminary to one. A heart so thoroughly given to divine passion would presumably purge its vanities and replace other motives for writing poetry with a consuming reach toward the apocalypse. If that were to happen, memory and anticipation would give way to a totality mastered by the Pauline fable. To lay invention on the altar would apparently not be much different from making an altar-shaped heart of it, as "The Altar" does. In any case, tribute is always to some extent ceremonial in the preliminary stages that one can reach on one's own: "All knees shall bow to thee; all wits shall rise, / And praise him who did make and mend our eies." Thus Herbert completes the sonnet without proceeding much beyond laying out a permissible subject and setting up the third love poem.

Sonnet units themselves are the implicit subject of the sonnets on the Scriptures, where the amalgamation of parts suggests the analogy to book construction that I explored earlier. One could argue that as form is stretched by these sonnet-breaking endings, so the temporal phases of the speakers' various stories and of the church generally are to be superseded by "Love 3." "H. Scriptures 1" puts the quantifying of scriptural evidence in terms of containers loaded with nourishment. As the reader sucks each sweet letter, one particle of good health added to others reaches toward "a full eternity."

Some form of analogy must obtain between historical life and its anagogical level or there could be no such accommodation. Just as nature's objects in "Vertue" have mass and volume—the world is a box compacted of sweets analogous to paradise—Scripture here is a "masse / Of strange delights' permeated with divine honey. Yet in "Vertue" it is not through metaphor or the language of the seasons finally but through the burning of the world that the soul comes to its "chief" life. And in "H. Scriptures 2" crowding the whole into each verse in a sense undoes the parts. Once the greater story is invoked, sonnet parts have a limited access to it, as do synecdoche and metonymy. "H. Scriptures 2" overruns lines even as it observes the quatrain divisions. It concludes in the usual couplet and in that regard counterbalances the first sonnet, but by directing the reader's gaze toward eternity it too challenges limits in ways that occasional overruns of limits in Shakespearean and Petrarchan sonnets do not match. Presumably at the far end of Herbert's "read" lies the abandonment of Scripture itself as a set of interim verses and strategies for dealing with God's historical absences and mysteries. Once judgment is past and heaven is entered, no more written verses need be scrutinized in the way "H. Scriptures 2" advises.

This hypothetical or wished-for principle of holistic reading parallels the turning inside out of ordinary metaphors. "The Bunch of Grapes," for instance, traces apparently logical parallels as though following the instructions of "H. Scriptures 2," until the incongruity of the wine-pressing figure puts the "delivery" of God in the sacrifice and in the Eucharist. And in that new sacrifice, "grapes" become a serious misnomer. As I suggested earlier, we have no success in trying to visualize an incarnate god pressed and trampled until the blood runs, blood which is wine and which when taken in Holy Communion is symbolically converted back into blood. To go from the actual Crucifixion to the Eucharist both uses and abandons the grapes/wine image. Similarly, one cannot actually place an anagogical level in the old Jerusalem or other exemplary pre-Christian types. Herbert accordingly tells us in "The Thanksgiving" that nothing is more difficult than applying conventional poetic habits and forms to the sacrifice when such titles as "king of grief," which applies a dynastic epic term to a different sort of king, are so obviously inadequate. The usual flowers of rhetoric, as "Life" suggests, are fit to be emblems only of time; objects tell most eloquently of their own limits, as do the sweet days and springs of "Vertue," where heaven is veiled by the smoke of apocalypse.

The rules of reading are radically changed by that translation of "victory" terms into nonequivalents, which follow a genre-belittlement tendency that

Harold Fisch finds in numerous places in the Hebrew Bible. As a sample reading, "The Bunch of Grapes" puts the hermeneutic principle of "H. Scriptures 2" to a drastic test and shows not only the speaker discovered in the parallels but the principle of similitude itself cracking under the strain. The problem is always the same: figures drawn from material images and known landscapes bear no real resemblance to what the fable implies and states as abstract doctrine. Looking for tropes to describe the reading process itself, "H. Scriptures 2" comes to the end of its quatrain parallels and gestures into space for the uncontained remainder. Form is so fretted by the enormity of the new covenant in "Redemption" and by the unrepresentable whole in "H. Scriptures 1 & 2" that as Terry G. Sherwood remarks, minutely crafted lyric frames are broken, then completed ten pages later, only to be broken again to build the architecture of *The Temple* (Sherwood 144). Herbert slips sonnets into place as pieces of that larger book, which is surely his main point in proceeding from two largely invocational love sonnets to "Love 3" and from readings of particular scriptural passages to end things and sacramental reenactments.

An apparent exception to the fruitless search for metaphors that do not lead to their own undoing is one of the later sonnets (later both in placement and in composition), "The Sonne," which sets a more modest task for itself and does not try to point to the end, where the enigmas and paradoxes come to a head. It works instead upon the conventional interplay of *sun* and *son* and uses the conversion of the natural light-giving body into supernatural light as an example of the resourcefulness of English. A delight similar to the one Herbert takes in the special properties of the words "tent" and "host" in "Anagram" governs the burst of enthusiasm in the poet's rediscovery of this trope: "How neatly doe we give one onely name / To parents issue and the sunnes bright starre!" One only name is the point: one thing to the ear but two or more to the eye and brain. Like all metaphor, the pun also contains an element of deviance, doubled by the service that "son" by itself performs. This Son is unlike any of human fathers, and his likeness to the sun marks some of the differences—his transcendence, his "showing" to all viewers, his incorruptibility, his remoteness, and his great magnitude.

As God's issue, he nonetheless makes for a comparatively easy exchange between things patrilineal and things spiritual. The qualities of one term double with the addition of the other, and for once Herbert is not greatly troubled by the incongruity. The sun is a mirror in which we see the Son, not duplicated but recontextualized. The sun gains the added force of divine illumination, which (as in "Coloss. 3.3") greatly increases its native light; the

Son gains an evangelical movement from east to west in his manifestation phase. Both are multiplied by refracted images throughout *The Church*, as by this late stage the sonnet itself is an elaborate repetend, carrying a full cargo of commentary on naming, authoring, praising, and love. The language of genealogy gains dimension by the "light and fruit" of the Son's productivity as he himself describes it in John 15. The pun hangs on the Incarnation's raising of humbleness to glory in a conventional paradox. The Son's humility is greater than the sun's resplendence, and despite the lexical expansion the great does not erase the small. The sonnet places before us, removes, and replaces a recognizable object and by this means expands into a psalmic hymn of praise. The final naming, "We him in glorie call, *The Sonne of Man*," allows a modest rise without the poet's feeling that he is making all structure into a winding stair or crushing real flesh to produce eucharistic wine. He mounts to that praise without apparent stumbling and self-doubt, as though the sonnet had at last located its true subject and could contain in a word what "Love 3" enacts as a single, intact drama of submission.

Yet even this poem hints at a very unusual decorum, which crowds much into little. It assigns a celebrational role to Herbert's usually complex manipulations of discrepant language. "The Answer," two poems later and the final sonnet of *The Church* (it is appropriately "A true Hymne" that intervenes), does just the opposite. It suggests in retrospect how much is suppressed in "The Sonne," and why more typically in the other sonnets Herbert ascends to the holdfast or the "something understood"—sonnet equivalents to the trope-defying riddle of "Temper 1," "makes one place ev'ry where." Also more typically, he crosses out the sun in inscribing the Son in "Coloss. 3.3." At one and the same time, the poet's small measure is adjusted to the greater matter and the Pauline text, causes a brief moment to compress the chronicles of Providence, and then has the poet linger on the moment, perhaps requesting a fuller delivery that requires divine intervention. In the language of "The Flower," all episodes ("this or that") give way before the realization of the word that is all. These are parallel acts of transfigurative violence in Herbert's more searching poems. The other sonnets confirm the constant wrenching-and-fulfilling, making-and-unmaking of the central fable when its full impact is allowed to register on forms rescued from "brothel" usage, as "The Forerunners" says, rescued but then more often than not undone by the impropriety of even a "broider'd coat" for divine beauty.

6
THE VISIBLE CHURCH AND ITS CALENDAR

> I cannot ope mine eyes,
> But thou art ready there to catch
> My morning-soul and sacrifice:
> Then we must needs for that day make a match.
> —George Herbert, "Mattens"

Greater and Lesser Periodicities

Incorporating segments of the fable or implying that its entirety strains the elements of lyric—containment and structural relation of parts, sound system *(melos)*, imagery and metaphor *(opsis)*, and argument *(logos)*. Concepts of a pretemporal reality or post-apocalyptic destination, once admitted, devalue ingenuity and wit, shrink to virtual toying the intricacies of craft, erode the motives for lesser historical acts and pragmatic social or political goals, discredit secular learning, and at a psychological level define the heart's personal achievements as sin and vanity. Given a Calvinist or Lutheran twist, they make suspect even the rendering of divine service and praise. Guilt and capitulation are the common narrative accompaniments of that temporal erosion in Herbert; the British church and its liturgy become all the more important in providing a framework within which the human and the divine can be accommodated and temporal spans can be periodized and measured. In the previous chapter I explored some of the echoing and mirroring devices by which Herbert constructs poetic supplements for that churchly mediation; in this chapter I want to turn to other kinds of periodicity, some of them with similar refrain-like effects, namely the church's formal rites and holiday observances.

These liturgical matters must stand against the extended historicity of the church and its encounter with cultural diversity and diachronic change. "The Church Militant" is well aware of the far-reaching consequences of dispersal that follow the separation of the new covenant from a single people. Since the Incarnation, history has been more difficult to read, because no one locality is singled out as God's visible theater of operations. The state of the world, all its weather, harvests, societies, and churches, becomes an index to divine intent and to the progress of prophecy. But any particular alliance of civil power and Church is quite fragile and temporary in the westward movement that Herbert chronicles. Just as "Israel" had proved to be not its kings or even its homeland but a system of laws, customs, and beliefs, so the universal church should be not what this or that magistrate makes of it but a capacity to teach and to reenact the focal events of history as sacrament and liturgy. The best national location of the civil/religious alliance to Herbert is England, but England has not always been a haven of faith and is not now its exclusive home. It is divided by schism; and if "The Church Militant" foresees accurately, it may soon cease to be such a haven at all.

When it comes to proposing a relationship between Providence and nation, Herbert has the Hebrew model to apply, and when he turns from the individual concerns of *The Church* to the collective evangelized body, politics might seem necessarily to enlarge its role in a manner reminiscent of the state/temple alliance of monarchical Jerusalem. YHWH's engagement with his people depends on the behavior of judges and kings, sometimes on the devotional practices of the entire people, and on the joint governance of nation and temple. In repetitive narrative formulas, Judges converts the apparently haphazard fortunes of the Chosen People into tests of their relation to a Lord of Hosts who supports or abandons them according to their relations to foreign cults. Whether bondage lasts seven years to the Midianites or forty years to the Philistines, the effect of the narrative formulas is to forge a cyclical rhythm out of history's apparent irregularity. Such cycles go some way toward incorporating particular reigns into a connecting thread by way not of abstract doctrine and policy but of narrative typology. Emphasis falls on doing—the conversion of belief into devotional and especially sacrificial practices under a watchful priesthood. The struggle is both to maintain the Law and to gain (or regain) control of a homeland for the Law's better observance. These cycles are eventually discarded in long-term, goal-oriented prophecies and retrospects that make them linear and anticipate a permanent settling, usually in recapitulative lyrics and songs such as those of Deborah and Moses.

In New Testament perspectives, the older periods are drawn together under prefigurations of a Messiah who will not be defeated, but after that Messiah has turned his ministry over to apostles, new cycles begin under the militant church. More necessary to the Church at a given moment than any regularity of pattern is the Spirit/Comforter, which alone validates a church in Pauline thought. As Herbert realizes, belief may reside anywhere, supported by the magistrates or not. Even dispersals leave behind pockets of the faithful. Despite the travels of the Church and the obvious ups and downs of Christian monarchs, the cyclical coming and going of God's favor is more firmly teleological after Christ than in even the most eschatological of the late Judaic prophets. Although Herbert's visible church heads westward and returns to its origins in the contest between linear and cyclical patterns, the linear one eventually wins out. While expecting a returning Messiah to bring about an apocalyptic end, those who dwell in the interim must settle for the Church and its Christian princes.

It is impossible not to be troubled by the dislocation of the Church if like Herbert one's own nation is at issue. In "Peace" the seeker of repose tries three times before finding it, and when he does, it has no specific location. Building upon the idea of a transcended homeland, Herbert finds peace in a combination of the church founded at Jerusalem, a recurrent eucharistic ritual that can be enacted anywhere, and a psychological regimen that builds up the interior spirit to a strength that can resist the disturbances of the temporal world. The right place seemingly disqualifies any specific alliance between ordinary princes and the prince of Jerusalem. The last wrong place bears a resemblance to the right one but is no more to be equated with it finally than Solomon's temple is:

> Then went I to a garden, and did spy
> A gallant flower,

> The Crown Imperiall: Sure, said I,
> Peace at the root must dwell.
> But when I digg'd, I saw a worm devoure
> What show'd so well.

Sidney Gottlieb's argument that the phrase "Crown Imperiall" has a special Caroline twist (in view of Herbert's championing of a peace policy and the occurrence of the word in such places as *Love's triumph through Callipolis*) is suggestive but not totally compelling ("Social and Political Backgrounds"). That the phrase is universal seems to be Herbert's point: in the Hebrew Bible, political and religious establishments are supposedly inseparable—until they in fact separate in the Exile and the cult survives. As "The Church Militant" makes clear, the Church survives but it also travels, and if it must leave its local habitations, it cannot be very stable politically. Peace resides foremost in the Gospels and only secondarily in institutions. The descent is from *the* prince to his disciples to Gospel, and only through these to ecclesiastical orders seeking harbor in political orders. Peace of mind and perhaps civil peace depend finally not on this or that civil or foreign policy but on the test read correctly. The yielding grave of the Salem prince germinates the wheat of a communal feast; one prince and one only truly sets the table, whatever administrative hands assist it. Being universal, that feast is not unduly affected by the local ups and downs of the militant church.

In terms of narrative technique, not until the speaker discovers biblical allegory does he escape specific place-oriented symbols and the rise and fall of crown imperials. In this history of the one true prince, Herbert goes beyond psalmic recapitulation. The cave and the gallant flower are part of the winnowing process. If it is not the showy blossoms of the gallant flower that bring peace, neither is it the contemplative retreat of Plato or hermits. Where the truths of caves are intangible, the prince of Salem was incarnate and taught in simple parables, like "Peace" itself. "Peace" thus retreats to an origin locked into place in the text of the fable and the rites of the Church. Those who subsequently taste the apostle's wheat can "rehearse" its virtue anywhere. One can go to all countries and miss the wheat, or one can stay at home and find it. It is transportable by the word in a way that the ark and the tabernacle of old never were, and it evangelizes as Jews in Egypt and Babylonia never managed. Whereas the latter barely maintained themselves in makeshift tabernacles, Christian doctrine is designed to be exported—such basic doctrine in "Peace" that it encourages no sectarian dispute.

But this abstracting and universalizing of peace also makes the Church somewhat elusive. It consists of more than the apparatus of devotion such as altars, monuments, and windows, and it must be more too than its human membership. Although Herbert reserves consideration of that membership for "The Church Militant" and *A Priest to the Temple*, he is aware in *The Church* that anything having to do with architecture, devotional practice, and the observance of holy days is relevant to the relocating of peace—so important to the spiritual well-being of both the heart and the Church in "The Familie" and elsewhere. In this respect even a poem like "Peace," with its "revrend good old man" and his garden, carries a residue of location despite the dispersal of doctrine "through all the earth." This is not a matter that unpacks easily, however, partly because of the fatally afflicted crown imperial and partly because nowhere in *The Church* does Herbert mark the national thanksgivings that some of his Anglican contemporaries used to tie the church to the court and to link local with universal history. He does not commemorate the escape from the Gunpowder plot, for instance, or James's deliverance from the earl of Gowrie's conspiracy or any equivalent to "A Fourme of Prayer with Thanksgiving, to be used of all the King's Majesties loving subjects every yeere." Whatever it may have meant to Herbert the citizen, secular hierarchy is incidental to Herbert the poet, and as his biographers usually surmise, it meant less to him after the mid 1620s than it had previously.

Yet by custom and ideology, the calendar and the visible British church were inseparable from the national body and its secular offices. We can find enough connection between church and court in *The Temple* to suggest why Izaak Walton and Christopher Harvey felt justified in appropriating Herbert for partisan causes in the 1630s and 40s. Of late, critics have more and more associated him with causes; and indeed, once the court and the church become closely linked it is difficult to disengage them—just the problem the Brownists raised with an Elizabethan establishment that felt it must hang three of them for sedition despite their insistence that their disagreements were strictly ecclesiastical. Separatists raised similar issues with King James, and they were still raising them with his son forty years later. No interval between the rise of Puritanism and the Glorious Revolution was totally free of agitation over the magistrate's role in church administration. That role was not so person-oriented that it could be settled by the removal of Charles, since Parliament also legislated religious observances. High-church ritual of the kind that Herbert hints at in "Peace" and returns to in the sacramental poems tends to solidify the alliance between the sacerdotal institution and magistrates, even if questions of surplices and ornate church architecture are not explicitly raised. As Horton Davies puts it, though divinely supported privilege is only one aspect of a regulated state religion, *socially* "the Anglican calendar led to the sanctification of stratification" (*Worship and Theology* 239). That is perhaps partly what John Wall means by linking Herbert to Spenser and Vaughan as a poet who promotes the social agenda of the English church (6) and a justification for Stanley Stewart's developing of Herbert's Little Gidding connection, with its rosaries, primers, breviaries, missals, and Books of Hours (*George Herbert* 58). Even Bacon's six-page history of the world takes time to work in a description of the universal or catholic church that includes anointed and ordained priests in the apostolic succession (*Works* 7.225), which constitutes an endorsement of the British church as it stands.

After Robert Browne in "A Treatise of reformation without tarying" (1582) had condemned solemn feasts, Christmas, Easter, Whitsuntide—all traditions "received of Baal" (168)—the observance of such moments was usually taken by separatists as evidence of romanist practice. A good deal of Laudian rhetoric went into proving that they were not, that a distinct line could be drawn. Three decades before Prynne and his group resisted Laudian festivals, Henry Ainsworth in *An Apologie or Defence of Brownists* (1604) urged the church not to observe such "Jewish and Popish" days, since what they once stood for is now accomplished "in Christ" or in the spirit's inhabiting of the soul, regardless of what nation or what ecclesiology stands nearby. To those who put their confidence solely in the living spirit and the written word, the special holy days defined by law and ceremony are mere human inventions and should be dropped "for the avoiding of superstition and corruption." To this point of view, a periodized holy calendar, civil and economic repression, and a national church go together. Their unholy alliance explains the cyclical ups and downs of Church Militant, which, if once it could be freed from magistrates and priesthoods who bind the universal spirit to restrictive forms that insure their own power, might actually proceed toward a global Christianity. So the Brownists argued, and their Anabaptists successors continued to do so.

Contrary to appearances, perhaps, the universal scope of the Gospels and the separating of individual spiritual welfare from that of a collective body— and of the Church Militant from any particular nation—is consonant with Herbert's view of a traveling militant church and Augustinian view of end things, which makes individual death rather than collective reform the gateway to lasting peace. But Herbert is also clear about the valuable mediation of the British church and its prefiguring of apocalypse as the bride of Christ (Claude J. Summers, "The Bride" 84). Although he apparently did not share the annual parliamentary anxiety over popery when he sat in the House of Commons and listened to alarm after alarm (see *Debates* 1625, for instance), he has no difficulty in "The British Church" explicitly, and in several places implicitly, finding a middle way between Roman lavishness and Genevan plainness (Marcus 191). Nor did he share many of the Arminian views growing prominent in church, court, and Parliament in the late 1620s, or seem particularly convinced that where Arminians came in, Roman Catholicism was likely to follow—the view not only of Dissenters but of many conforming church members (Lockyer 117–19; Smuts 38; Finlayson 95). That peace does not depend on victory over the antichrist and the Turk or on a gathered sainthood keeps him a healthy distance from the more militant Dissenters as well, whom he chastises in "The Familie" as wranglers and disturbers of the peace, both of the spirit and of the church (Summers and Pebworth, "Politics").

That the soul in search of peace may not need the ministrations of a specific church at all is at least arguable in some poems. In the squence of poems "Death," "Dooms-day," "Judgement," and "Heaven," he imagines a gathering of saints at time's end that brings nothing like the vengeance of Revelation and the psalms or any sense of having been triggered by prophets. The "we" of "Death" seems to be the entire interpretive body whom Herbert imagines before and after "our Saviors death." In this kind of nonsectarian poem "we" obviously means "we Christians," not merely "we British." The difference governs not only the move from before to after the time of Christ— the truly encompassing rhythm for any Christian view of history—but also the movement from a restored Jewish nation to the king of heaven. Before, we looked at death only six or ten years hence; now we behold death "gay and glad, / As at dooms-day." This enlarged church body regulates death and makes it too, like "peace," an abstraction. Or rather it is both very personal and very general. Death is specific for individuals, yet fixed in the pattern of the antitype as completed by the Resurrection and in that pattern given regular liturgical representation. A personified servant-death is a very useful trope for the conversion from worldly to heavenly language.

Similarly in "Dooms-day," the "flock" that threatens to stray if the final trumpet does not sound soon is the dispersed body of humankind. The trumpet makes another useful conversion trope, since it sounds one series of notes in history, heralding an event, and another series as a setting of the key for the saintly consort. Not one or another person or nation but "man" will be hurled out of order if that heralding does not get underway, and it is a group of singers that the Lord will raise when it does—a Christian society gathering at the point when epochs, magistrates, and geography no longer matter. Again in "Judgement," when the "Almighty Judge" calls for "ev'ry mans peculiar book," the speaker, now acutely aware of his singularity and its incriminating history, will distract attention from it by thrusting forward "a Testament" in its place. This gesture composes still another pageantry that substitutes a paradigm-setting text for an anecdotal one. The Christian, at least in meeting his end, needs no other advocate than that. No priesthood stands by him; he has gone well beyond the teaching and liturgical phases of mediation. The grounding of peace in the prince of Jerusalem is never more evident than in that Bible-wielding gesture and in the removal of all "peculiar" books. As the "reve'rend good old man" of "Peace" describes it, peace of mind comes only from the sufficient grace of the sacrifice through the savior of "Redemption," whose words "Your suit is granted" mean that a freehold in heaven is now guaranteed. Protected by the end sealed at that instant, the individual can safely say, "My faults are thine," pushing the testament out in front of him. No civil order however well ruled, however reformed and properly Christian, puts anything comparable into its version of peace. No church has a monopoly on the printing of testaments, the dissemination of which makes every press potentially an apostles' helper.

We will need to look at this group of end poems again in the next chapter to gauge the impact of the fable's culmination on the whole of *The Church*. Suffice it to say here that one effect of the fable's beginning-and-ending emphasis in Herbert's anti-millennial historicity is a limiting of institutions and their ceremonies to a sustaining and prefiguring role. In "The Church Militant" more than in *The Church* proper, they appear to be at best imperfect—not much more answerable to the end than poetry's finite tropes. Even sacraments that mystically offer a substantial god do so as recollective and prefigurative moments. Some Dissenters would go even further than that in discarding civil and cultic prospects and any more refined periodicity than the simple before-and-after of the Hebrew/Christian epochs. Herbert himself often stresses that basic division almost to the exclusion of other dates or the places that the dates reflect (Bloch 133).

As against the militant view, however, he is as scrupulous as Sir Thomas Browne in *Religio Medici* in expunging from his view of cycles and sequences any stages that might encourage the more violent reforms that Revelation seems to some to justify. For Herbert, Revelation offers a set of prefigurative symbols, not an agenda for action, and this is a fairly typical Anglican use of apocalyptic imagery. In *A Priest to the Temple* he talks of alternating peaceful and "military" periods, but he makes clear that these are not national or local; they are parishioner-specific and require that the country parson read each case separately and offer "dexterous" spiritual guidance (280). As Kenneth Hovey suggests ("Holy War"), we must distinguish between civil militancy and holy war in that regard. To Herbert a war of words helps spread both the Gospels and the good abstractions (bliss, hope, peace, love); a war of swords is more likely to destroy them, as wrangling within the church destroys the repose that the spirit requires if it is to listen quietly to God's words.

By timely applications of those words, the country parson helps individual parishioners over their spiritual crises. The accomplished spiritual goals are uniform, but the timing and the ways to them differ with each biography. In *A Priest to the Temple* they also depend on the unpredictable coming and going of "the Divell" and are modeled on one of the two states of the Savior, his rejoicing in spirit or his struggle against Satan. Similarly in "The Flower" and "Temper 1," the poet finds himself helpless before arhythmic and seemingly unresponsive visitations of the Lord of Power, visitations that govern his personal narrative but do not answer to it in an interpretable way. Since the chief power against the devil is the comforting spirit, the country parson's flock can only ask with "Whitsunday," "Where is that fire which once descended / On thy Apostles?" One's spiritual condition may or may not coincide with church celebrations of the spirit's open house; the calendar remembers the occasions, but it cannot automate inner renewal.

Secular historiography is clearly not an acceptable alternative to this grappling with the spirit's abrupt comings and goings in any of the parties who dispute the role of the visible church. Both bibles issue warnings against diversions from providential interpretation, and Herbert's country parson takes these warnings seriously. He applies them to farmers, for instance, who mistakenly think that weather and sound agronomy produce their crops. Combatting the "great aptnesse Countrey people have to think that all things come by a kind of naturall course" (270), the parson must convince them that God alone sustains and governs, that no moment drops out of the schemata. If the corn does not grow and a fountain dries up, if fire destroys, ships sink, and houses burn, it is because God decrees each individual instance. A farmer that has put hand to sickle and thinks all is sure may find his full barn consumed by fire. This is the same Lord of Power that strikes down the presumptuous poet in "The Flower" and overpowers the speaker of "Temper 1." He has not really changed from the jealous YHWH of the psalms and the various chronicles they digest, where war or drought inerrantly reflect his anger. Allowing human and natural causes to intrude destroys the articulated purpose that the Church exists to enforce. Thus, as a mythopoeic translator, God applies motives from one realm (devotional practice and obedience to the Law) to another (how locusts multiply, wheat grows, or enemy armies fare against Jerusalem).

But as I said, this issue does not unpack easily in Herbert, because the usefulness of the mediation of the church depends on the spiritual problem of the moment, not on invariable policy. The historical individual, the citizen, is always part of a collective church even though his or her fate at judgment may not be determined by it. Holy days do not merely recapitulate the ancient victories of the Lord of Battles, as the psalms might suggest; they reformulate what threatens to escape the precincts of the holy. A church holiday is an instrument of rule as well as a periodic renewal of the covenant. State and church, joined in common holidays, enforce conformity in Herbert's church, whether or not his country parson takes a very active part. Schism means to Herbert, both the poet and the parson, approximately what it meant to Josiah, David, and Solomon: God is not merely universal but also in some way jealous and local. He must be worshiped in ways defined by the Book of Common Prayer and the catechism.

A troubling dialectic is inherent in that claim for a church in an evangelical phase. If the doctrines of Geneva, Rome, and Edinburgh that it collects in its travels cannot be reconciled and if only one universal church exists, each party will naturally construe the apostolic mission as its own, a problem that disturbs Donne more than it does Herbert outside of "The Church Militant." Fervor is impossible to keep entirely free of national chauvinism. Certainly the Hebrew Bible provides no incentive to do so. It is basically the Hebrew "ban" that gets reissued under a Christian banner in the European holy wars that Herbert so much disliked. That is one of the problems that Herbert confronts when he considers church rents and schisms. It is no doubt the source of some of his uncertainty concerning whether the universals and abstractions (peace, faith, hope) find better harbor in institutions or in individual hearts. Even tolerance and pacifism can be implicitly militant if one's preferred church happens to be already in power; the god assumed to be present in regularized rites and holidays need not be championed on the battlefield or reinstated in a reformed ministry if he has already appointed and ordained mediators. In that regard, the serving of something so apparently neutral as a communion supper can make a political statement, specifically, in Herbert's case, against those who wish a purified communion and a visible church that baptizes only adults.

Another difficulty arises in gauging Herbert's loyalty to the British church when we consider that his appreciation (in "The British Church") of perfect "lineaments and hue," trampled underfoot lately by "rude unhallow'd steps" ("Church-rents and schismes"), does not square perfectly with his recurrent awareness that self-denial and plain style befit human powerlessness more than well-clad language. True, as Leah Marcus argues, Anglicanism had its plain style as well, and Herbert did not need not look outside the church to find it in preaching, catechism, and devotions. But what he defends in "The British Church" is not the devotional simplicity he advocates in the Jordan poems; it is closer to his own witty and elaborate metaphoric practice in *The Church* at large. That he is not consistent in choosing one way or another helps explain why critics as far apart as Tuve, Summers, and Stewart on one side and Strier and Lewalski on the other can make well-documented claims for both Roman and Genevan leanings. Anglicanism and *The Church* both occupy a broad middle way between extremes, wide enough to allow their own pendulum swings. That many others besides Herbert could be Anglican in liturgical preference and Genevan in doctrine shows how little the tension between devotional splendor and individualized spiritual conflict depended in the 1620s on doctrinal support. Nor did Herbert expect to find anywhere outside the individual heart spiritual stays and supports of adequate strength against the cunning "bosome-sinne" that so easily overcomes all such stays and supports provided by a church or the Bible. Praise of God's abundance in his somewhat lavish "Providence" quickly gives way to hardship and a dismissal of corporeal life; the tranquillity of "Peace" is promptly lost in "The Discharge" and "Longing"; the frailty of "Giddinesse" and the grievances of the affliction poems deny the speakers of those poems even deferred assurance. These changes of state amid periodic devotion point up the difficulty of reconciling the synoptic story with any detailed chronicle. However, that is not to discredit the genuine comfort of such periodic rituals and the contribution they make to the echoing patterns of *The Church*, which conclude in the rite of "Love 3" and its sacramental reinforcement of preceding poems.

Church Ceremony

Many of Herbert's lyrics are occasioned by a calendar based on the repeatable events of Christ's life, and the reinsertion of those events by recitation or reenactment is one way to respecify them; but they are like repetends or refrains in that with each reinsertion they are newly contextualized and mean something slightly different: they meet different living occasions and therefore become a different rhetoric. "Easter-wings," for instance, puts the history of humanity, a church holiday, and the poet's moment into a single model of waning and waxing and brings it to a current implication that redefines Easter as part of the church's opening sequence. In one sense the poem could be Everyone's request to soar with the ascension; in another, it is very specifically Herbert's, as interpreted by "The Altar," "The Sacrifice," "Redemption," and the rest of *The Church*. It is a paradigm of human shrinkage, a recovery in the Adam-to-Christ story, and an application of the pattern to a situation—both a church calendar event, a biographical event by implication, and an event in the writing of a book.

Following a different method and using a more hypothetical speaker, "Redemption" suppresses the poet as an individual and stations its representative seeker at the juncture of the old adamic heritage and the new Adam's restitution. One method of integrating the self with this progress transports the events of Easter week into the now of *The Church*; the other collapses the distance between now and then by going backward in time via parabolic fiction. "The Sacrifice," also a poem of collapsed distance, shows sacramental rites emerging from Christ's progress toward the cross, in very specifically historic moments to be reenacted later, now being voiced by Christ as part of his dramatic agony. In approaching the pattern of the divine birth and death, each subject discovers it only once, since such knowledge is irreversible, but the main patterns and the abstractions of the lexical field that accompany them can be renewed innumerable times as reaffirmation and encouragement.

Unfortunately, those patterns can also weaken in their command over new trials and in confrontation with historical confusion. The communion supper, approaches to the altar, and the church floors and windows of *The Church* assist Herbert's resituating of such moments in current time, but like individual flourishing, the calendar contains a reverse side, turning or troping of the pattern in the company of speakers getting to know their inadequacies. The experience of a given person moves *toward* the reenactment, but no speaker in *The Church* actually arrives as a participant until the last line of "Love 3." What returns most often in holy-day recollections is the sacrifice that replaces previous sacrifices and redefines the devotions focused in them. Yet the Easter holiday that features it constitutes only one episode in the life of the temple, and as powerful as it is, it is constantly being forgotten. "Easter-wings" is as compressed as a sacred story can get and yet is suspended between the requests of "now" and the pattern of the wasted past.

"The Holdfast" is even less sanguine about its speaker adding something: "What Adam had, and forfeited for all, / Christ keepeth now" means that all the circumstances of all the stories are put away in Christ's current residence, which is no longer historical. As I suggested earlier, we cannot tell what shape what is "ours" will take when it returns. "Easter-wings" would change the holdfast's *keeping* to a prospective *sharing*, but Herbert's emphasis is often on the former, and the sharing is vicarious only.

But let us concede the comparative joyousness of the Easter sequence and return to the matter of high-church ceremony. In some readings, *The Temple* attempts to resolve the differences between reform elements within the church and the embellished worship they find there. As Heather Asals and Graham Parry point out, Herbert is close to Lancelot Andrewes's position on ceremonies (Asals 68; Parry 75–94). Gene Veith holds that his biblicism is "not at all inconsistent with a love for traditional symbols and ceremonies" ("The Religious Wars" 30). "Love 3" eventually psychologizes the communion ritual and ritualizes the psychology, thus reconciling two pathways to the divine/human juncture, one regulated by the church and the other self-searching. Whatever the incompatibilities between a devotional and a narrative-dramative sequence at other points, Herbert has them converge there. Certainly participation in the church is desirable, if only at times a goal. Herbert fills the lesser holy days with an examination of doctrines that have to be reaffirmed intellectually before the heart can soften (perhaps a trademark of an orthodoxy made sensitive to a oriented toward preaching clergy). The days that show the church and its ministry most effectively, especially Good Friday, Easter, Christmas, Lent, and Sundays, are simultaneously reenactments and reminders of personal unworthiness. Yet dissatisfaction with the devotional development of the church is no doubt partly what prompted Herbert's immediate imitators to finish his work for him, and in doing so to distort him.

It is instructive in this regard to read the seventeenth-century reaction to him as a favorite poet, certainly accessible but also one who resists the more elaborate devotional calendar they would impose on him. In place of Herbert's sequence of personal trials, Christopher Harvey's *Synagogue*, like John Cosin's devotions, offers verse equivalents to an extensive list of church fixtures and occasions. Other seventeenth-century Anglicans as well sought to nudge Herbert further than *The Church* warrants, not only Izaak Walton in his biography of Herbert but also Henry Coleman, Richard Crashaw, and Henry Vaughan. In assigning its first three-dozen poems to the church (history, architecture, grounds, furniture, and holidays) before turning to topics of the sexton, the clerk, the overseer of the poor, the churchwarden, the deacon, the priest, and the bishop, *Synagogue* suggests what a typical Anglican expectation might have been. Cosin's *Collection of Private Devotions*, a contemporary supplement to the *Book of Common Prayer* favored by Lancelot Andrewes and despised by William Prynne and Henry Burton, contains a good deal that even the industrious Harvey leaves out. In includes vigils before nativity, purification, annunciation, saints' days, prayers, collects not only for matins and evensong but for the ninth hour, noon, and afternoon, plus poems for twenty-five Sundays after Trinity Sunday, thanksgivings and confessions for special occasions (weddings, births, and funerals), and the usual special prayers for the king. So thoroughly are the originating moments of Christ's life reinscribed in such turns of the year that scarcely a week passes without its special occasion, or an hour without its marked devotional use.

Harvey finds his opening in both Herbert's devotional sequences and his omissions, and—more in silent correction than in reproach, but scarcely innocently, as Ilona Bell argues—in his exploitations of the anti-separatist possibilities ("Herbert and Harvey" 265). If the Laudian church wished to claim Herbert as a supporter of its ceremonies and festivals, it needed first a spokesman who could supplement a rather sparsely furnished place of worship and almost total lack of acknowledgment of its officers and administrators. In marking how sacraments flow from the passion, Herbert's opening sequence uses the Easter week to establish Harvey's calendar for him. But it also initiates the spiritual conflicts, and even with that week his concern is less ecclesiastical policy than how the events with that week his concern is less ecclesiastical policy than how the events register personally (not necessarily on Herbert personally but on first-person speakers). John Hollander finds an appropriately conflated term for this "hymnody of the rectory, the liturgical year of private devotions" (233), which concedes both the parish context, the nationally established events of the year, and the inner absorption of them.

Harvey no doubt knows as well as Herbert that liturgical days and hours are sensitive matters, but he chooses to flaunt them; Herbert picks and chooses his moments of contention and situates them strategically amid portraits of spiritual conflict. "The British Church," for instance, follows "Conscience," which commands "Peace pratler" to noisy thoughts within; "Sion," which finds "all this pomp and state" of great churches superfluous for a lord whose "frame and fabrick is within," whose struggles are with a "peevish heart"; and "Home," an anguished personal statement that locates the soul's home not in the church but in heaven where "The most of me" is already fled. It is followed by "The Quip," which looks forward to an ultimate answer to the world when God destroys it, and by "Vanitie," whose focus is again on the "Poore silly soul." The church is both a comforting stay in these struggles and only one of several instruments the Lord uses in meeting sin and pointing toward the church triumphant.

Rising to the Occasion

Much of what Herbert observes in the opening sequence and again in the matins sequence goes against the separatist complaints about the coercion of conscience. But as I suggested, it is also true that he devotes only a handful of poems, and arguably none of them his best, directly to devotional hours and occasions (including "Lent," "Trinity Sunday," "Whitsunday," "Christmas," "Mattens," "Evensong," and two to church history)—a little better than a tenth of *The Church* all told. The playing down of formal observances perhaps explains why (to Basil de Selincourt's satisfaction) Herbert aborts the reader's progress through *The Church*. He may be avoiding controversy or he may be entertaining two quite different kinds of poetic sequence, one governed by the calendar, the other by personal conflict. These two orders cannot easily be coordinated, as the dropping of "The British Church" into the "Conscience," "Sion," "Home," "The Quip," "Vanity" sequence suggests. (That poem is usually read quite apart from any function it may have in this context, as though it were immune to the principles of dramatic technique that Herbert uses nearly everywhere else in *The Church*.) But neither can the calendar and spiritual life be kept neatly apart, since the speaker's resistance to submission is gauged partly by what the calendar brings before him in given devotional settings.

In much the way he absorbs love poetry, Herbert refashions occasional poetry in marking the passage of the year and the day. As the introductory sequence of *The Church* sets the task of writing, it must strive to conform to devotion, which would be less troubling if Herbert were the thoroughgoing church ritualist that Harvey implies. How the poet is to join the occasion is always a question of that narrative moment and the levels of language applied to it. Does competition between public devotion and inwardness bring confusion to the architectural order of *The Temple*? Or is that order a product of a configured inwardness and calendar typology?

Easter provides the first tentative answers. In a certain mood the poet can greet that day of all days expectantly, since it is the brightest hour of both the yearly cycle and the epochal transition, a time when a Christian poet must awaken and come forth if he is to make a contribution. And so the speaker in "Easter," a poet, as so many speakers are in *The Church*, rouses himself:

> Awake, my lute, and struggle for thy part
> > With all thy art.
> The crosse taught all wood to resound his name,
> > Who bore the same.
> His stretched sinews taught all strings, what key
> Is best to celebrate this most high day.
>
> Consort both heart and lute, and twist a song
> > Pleasant and long:
> Or, since all musick is but three parts vied
> > And multiplied,
> O let thy blessed Spirit bear a part,
> And make up our defects with his sweet art.

Instead of immediate and self-evident glory, this day brought stretched sinews and the dilemma of those who would celebrate such an event by a pleasant, lengthy song. This would-be participant is well aware of the physical nature of the song and its subject, as its connecting of the body of the lute to the cross and the strings of the lute to sinews indicates. The components of the woven song are self, instrument, and inspiration, but others (the tradition of poets such as Thomas Wyatt, in "My lute awake!") are left unnamed and compose one of several subtexts. Such performances obviously come in layers: the gaiety of the rousing, the almost grotesque wit of the tuned sinews, and the underlying urgency of the appeal on which the poet's rising depends. The roughened metrical course of the final line forces a slower pace before the switch to a second phase. The balancing contrast is "our" and "his," but "defects" claims its own stress and rises to prominence together with the double stress of "sweét art." Played off against the Savior's "sweet heart," the defect is located not in the lute or the fingers but in the human character. The "making up" must therefore in some way be similar to the sacrifice itself, a purging of the hymnist, and in any case the heart is virtually broken on the cross before it is converted into the music of wood, string, and spirit. The result is anything but an ordinary song, not even in its secondary function as a parody of the troubador tradition. The distant echo in "Love 3," "who bore the blame," restores the historicity of the cross in shadowy form in the otherwise unmetaphoric "bore." It thereby carries Easter-song "strain" into a dialogue poem and provides the closure that defects of art and the nature of the occasion prevent here.

"Easter" uses a number of devices to close the distance between the current celebration and the original event. One is the odd personification of the teaching cross and sinews and the instruction they offer, not to this or that chosen instrument but to "all wood" and "all strings." This in effect virtually insures not only the universality of the Church but the performative excellence of anyone who capitalizes on the oxymoronic "sweet art" of dying. "Resounding" would revocalize the name and convert it too to a musical equivalent. Immediacy is the common factor in all these connections: these are very personal wood and sinews and very heartfelt music that the poet would contribute. The teaching is also personal, as is the address to *my* lute. The sacrificial victim himself becomes addressable in "O let thy blessed Spirit bear a part." If the other personifications are miscategorizations of the inanimate as living presences, this one closes the distance between the victim and the singer in the manner of prayer.

Although the chief figures that bridge the temporal distance are based on personification, paradox is also prominent on Easter day. Everything becomes the opposite of what it seems. The first step is to acknowledge that weakness now becomes strength, wood and agonized sinews sing with the harmony of angels, and what have been cultic demands for sacrifices and burned offerings now become the Son's universal sacrifice and teaching. If we ask how all these transformations can be accommodated by the would-be hymnist, the answer he encourages is that without the Spirit as an active participant they cannot be. In the second song (as in "The Thanksgiving" and in a different way in "A true Hymne"), Christ has already anticipated every conceivable offering:

> I Got me flowers to straw thy way;
> I got me boughs off many a tree:
> But thou wast up by break of day,
> And brought'st thy sweets along with thee.

Reflecting old ceremonies and Laudian-sanctioned festivities in a common idiom ("I Got me"), the poet's culling of rhetorical flowers has been precluded by another lexical realm altogether in which the cross is all the "sweets" the Lord has carried. The incongruity between the redemption

story with its bitter suffering and Mayday games is compressed into the
rousing spirit of one who did not get *himself* "up by break of day" but was
rudely forced out on a day to break him, taking his "boughs" off just one
"tree." The poet nearly misses the occasion, lagging behind in his sense of
its preeminence, which he realizes renders other days null and void. The
materials of traditional Mayday celebrations are redefined by the new emblems of this day: "We count three hundred, but we misse: / There is but
one, and that one ever." The very word "day" becomes a mysterious
misnomer, since it is meant to measure twenty-four hours or a seasonal
passage, but as a Christian philosopheme now means "eternal day," without
night or season. This eclipse of the ordinary is in small the eclipse of epochs
and their accompanying measurements and definitions. As we have seen,
such cancellations are typical of the fable's overhauling of conventional
terminology; in addition they are the return of holiday to holy day.

If one supreme day does overshadow the rest of the year, it also lays waste
to such works as flower gathering, or the poet's going a-troping. Yet to stay
within the new meanings of the Easter vocabulary is impossible for one
whose life counts the other days. A flood of parallel difficulties comes with
this realization. Whereas in the old cultic system of sacrifices, apostasy was
relatively easy to identify—it was marked by sacrifices in forbidden places to
rival gods—in this one, any attention to the other three-hundred days, any
naming of "this or that" as though the old values still held, can be construed
as a betrayal. Guilt is thus multiplied by the replacement of worldly similitudes with that catachretic "day." Holding the Easter note is as impossible as
realizing these implications of the event over and over until consciousness is
filled only with them. Easter week events can be portrayed, narrated, and
ritualized, even analyzed; they can be made into icons and pageantry. But
can they also be internalized to the extent the opening sequence demands of
the poet? Herbert's inclusion of "Thanksgiving" and "The Sinner" in the
sequence and coming to "Easter-wings" as its most comprehensive pattern
(with its concluding provisional "if") suggest not. Love's courtship in "Love
3" and its replacement of Easter chronicle and song with a paradigmatic
easing of guilt reinforce that impression.

The church itself singles out particular feast and fast days that recall divine
interventions, especially at the nativity and the sacrifice. To see what conformity involves, we must think not only of what the ecclesiastical calendar
requires but of sequences that interweave the spiritual condition of various
speakers, church architecture and furniture, and fixed forms of devotion.
These attempt to do for other occasions and hours of the new "day" what

Easter does for the year. Although not as prominent as the opening sequence or the concluding groups, the series beginning with "Mattens" and running through "Trinitie Sunday" reminds us of the solace of patterned repetition and correspondences between hours of the day and episodes of the fable. Not required to confront the sacrifice directly, this nine-poem group finds satisfaction in recollective returns to origins. It salvages some hours of some days that Easter overpowers. It contains one superb contribution to the anatomy of inner conflict in "Church-monuments" and several functional ones that are more than formal exercises. "The Windows" develops the notion that a visible virtue (as opposed to words alone) combats laxity of conscience by showing biblical chronicles both in stained glass and in the exemplary life of the preacher. That Herbert omits any mention of saints' lives distinguishes it from forerunners that increase lower-level mediaries and proliferate exemplary stories, weaving scattered moments into the fable; that it is illustrated at all separates it from Puritan plainness and strict reliance on the Bible and on preaching, which tend to be skeptical of nonbiblical stories.

In "Trinitie Sunday," the last of the sequence, Herbert establishes several links between the justified Christian and the Father, Son, and Spirit. One parallel derives from the line stemming from Adam as repeated in the speaker, whom the Father has formed, the Son redeemed, and the Spirit sanctified. A strongly accented meter suggests a recitation prayer, or a book of devotions to be repeated. Certainly this is one poem (an earlier Williams manuscript poem) that does not pretend to follow the curve of extemporized feeling:

> Lord, who hast form'd me out of mud,
>   And hast redeem'd me through thy bloud,
>   And sanctifi'd me to do good;
>
> Purge all my sinnes done heretofore:
>   For I confesse my heavie score,
>   And I will strive to sinne no more.
>
> Enrich my heart, mouth, hands in me,
>   With faith, with hope, with charitie;
>   That I may runne, rise, rest with thee.

The second and third stanzas equate the speaker's purged past, confessed present, and anticipated future with the heart, mouth, and hands—the heart being purged, the mouth confessing, and the hands performing charity. The past episodes of sin that constitute one's personal history are gathered into the current instruments of one's working reclamation, thus answering for the littered trail of spiritual offenses. These instruments in turn become vessels of divine enrichment and thus receive some of the treasure that Herbert's pearl cluster reinstates at intervals in *The Church*. That amounts to a transfusing of new blood in the adamic body equivalent to the annealing "in glass thy story" in "The Windows." So enlivened, the speaker may spring into action like the original Adam free of sin.

The climax of this renewal is active participation in the source and the end of the marring/mending story, incorporation of his running, rising, resting "with" God. To run presumably would be to finish the movement through time; to rise would be to make the transumptive leap; to rest would signal the completion of days, the total translation of earthly terms into heavenly ones, the goal of a hymnody of the rectory making the liturgical year a not-so-private devotion. All this, however, is now to be accomplished in virtual rather than actual terms, as a proleptic ritual devotion. The running, rising, and resting derive from the heart as the motive power, the mind enlightened by the word, and a sanctification that issues in beatitude. Perhaps too the actual doing of charity would put to rest the motion generated in the other two as the deeds of spiritual life. These are all geometrical triads of a kind that Herbert does not usually construct in so ritualized a form, yet despite them, the poem addresses the Lord as one and makes the self also arguably one once it gets past its struggle with inherited and personally augmented sin.

Sunday

Despite the "Mattens" sequence, I think it fair to say that in general Herbert is not often interested in a topicality that cannot be made to bear upon spiritual struggles. Another poem in the Dissenters' hymn collection, "Whitsunday," does exactly that in commemorating the spirit's descent to the apostles and reiterating its descent to the Church. It gives another occasion for the speaker's coming forth to devotion. The first day of its kind linked many biographies to one, not as ritual but as startling new realization; the many succeeding pentecostal days present a reiterated challenge to the ordinary. At stake in such presences of the Spirit is the compromise between Peter's and Paul's opinions of the patriarchs and the exchange of tangible victories for spiritual triumphs. Needless to say, the Puritan erasing of festival days altogether—which of course goes far beyond Herbert's limiting of them—is rooted in justifications by faith that stress the Spirit rather than sacraments and ceremonies.

Construed as an equalizing belief, that reduction of mediaries undermines not only ceremony and church hierarchy but Easter, Trinity Sunday, and other holidays, all focal points in the radical attempt to free the church of set forms of worship. The Puritan sabbath was devoted to self-examination and Bible study unattached to any ordained ecclesiology. Among the Shakers, Levellers, and Quakers, it tended to become pentecostal. Henry Ainsworth (*An Apologie* 74) is typical of more-moderate earlier groups in agreeing to Sunday's special nature and yet suggesting that Christ and the spirit nullify specified holy days and equalize Sundays with the remainder of the calendar. In contrast, in "Trinitie Sunday" it is partly the sabbath that guides the speaker toward the elaborate conformity to the Trinity, which is imprinted on the creation, on the weekly structuring of history since time began, and on all those who take their patterns from the church. That both "Easter" and "Trinitie Sunday" (the latter as "Dominica Trinitatis") were popular among later seventeenth-century Dissenters suggests that they were not found to be overly contaminated by ritual. Although rewritten for inclusion in the anonymous *Select Hymns Taken out of Mr. Herbert's Temple*, the changes were not designed to keep popish elements out of an emerging hymnody but were in the interest of regularized meter and conformity to preexisting tunes (for Psalms 100 and 67 respectively).

For Herbert, an ordinary Sunday is the least specifically appointed of the holy days, but it is sufficiently set apart to offer a special peace of its own. That it promises more than it actually delivers does not make its gifts sparing but suggests greater and lesser divine presences and more or less pronounced anticipations of the "rest" that one runs and rises to meet. Keeping contact with ordinary similitude, it represents both bud and fruit—fruit because the world provides nothing better, bud because Sunday too is only anticipatory:

> O Day most calm, most bright,
> The fruit of this, the next worlds bud,
> Th' indorsement of supreme delight,
> Writ by a friend, and with his bloud;
> The couch of time; cares balm and bay:
> The week were dark, but for thy light:
> Thy torch doth show the say.

Herbert proliferates metaphors, each in itself inadequate. Sunday is an
"indorsement" because it carries the sacred voucher of the sacrifice given by
a "friend." The latter is a reiterated trope that Herbert adapts from literature
based on classical concepts, given a prominent place in Spenser's relations of
two in *The Faerie Queene*. But this friend underwrites the peace of Sundays
with the violence of sacrifice, which plunges even a peaceful day into paradox.
The creation's day of rest and the Hebrew sabbath precede and prepare for it
but are then eclipsed by it.

The usual paradoxes show in these tropes. Sunday is a couch because the
only regular place of rest, yet a torch because even on that day one must be
searching a lighted way. Standing between the typical and the eventful, it
belongs jointly to God and to people who wish for peace's "supreme delight."
It applies doctrine to life with a force and vigor that weekdays lack and
endorses heaven in the manner of the new lease written on the back of the
week, which brings Herbert to his most "abusive" tropes:

> The other dayes and thou
> Make up one man; whose face thou art,
> Knocking at heaven with thy brow:
> The worky-daies are the back-part;
> The burden of the week lies there,
> Making the whole to stoup and bow,
> Till thy release appeare.

Along with an itemizing akin to classical celebrations (as again in Vaughan's
"Sonday" and Harvey's "Church Festivals"), a certain lightheadedness in
ingenious metaphors reinforces that release from labor. Personifying Sunday
as an addressable party and giving it a face reaches the catachretic phase
when its brow knocks at heaven's gate. It has run and risen but not yet found
rest. Indeed, carrying the "worky-daies" on its back, this Sunday man is
bent and stooped in the posture of an aged beggar at the door, as the language
becomes liminal. "Worky-daies" and "back-parts" are concrete terms out of
the poorhouse diction of an unredeemable world. Across the threshold is the
unimaginable glory that has no such descriptive gauge. Just now—in the
poem on this side of the portal and in the precincts of Sundays—the
perspective is historical and anticipatory, and the mediating figure is the
pilgrim week putting its best face forward.

The instituting of Sunday, like that of communion, presupposes a contin-
ually lapsing soul that needs recurrent prompts and reminders. In "The

Discharge" the speaker admonishes his busy "enquiring heart" to make all days the same, because to God the time to come is already gone, and "Onely the present is thy part." Yet the sacraments would have been unnecessary if every day were in fact the same, and so once again Herbert lands somewhere between the more radical cancelings of ceremony's mediation and the language of transition and liminal expectation:

> Man had straight forward gone
> To endlesse death: but thou dost pull
> And turn us round to look on one,
> Whom, if were not very dull,
> We could not choose but look on still;
> Since there is no place so alone,
> The which he doth not fill.

That nearly all times God does *not* fill is the perplexity of a periodicity that should not be necessary after the first Easter and Pentecost but recurrently is. What Sunday makes Herbert realize in part is that the other six days are not as they should be and that foretastes of the end must therefore come as displacements. If the Lord's day *is* different, as even Ainsworth concedes that it can be, it argues that "although the ceremonial rest and prescript day thereof according to the law be now abrogated by the death of Christ," it can be marked in good conscience, especially if it includes not chiefly sacraments but the instruction and edification of the verbal ministry: hence six days for the body and for work, the seventh for the well-taught and disciplined soul (*An Apologie* 74–75). Such a weekly rhythm resembles the twofold regimen that Luther too concedes, one devoted to salvation and the other to the worldly body—to property, wife, and children, and subject to reason and civil law (Headley 5).

Searching for responses to special days and pursuing the spiritual welfare of individuals and nations through their cycles go against the side of *The Church* that wants an end to temporality altogether. It is that side that takes up the psalmists' acknowledgment of the God who alone can grant eternal peace and acknowledgment of the spiritual conflicts that resume virtually every day of the year. If one cannot have that end, then perhaps a more controlled eventfulness, less subject to peaks and valleys, will suffice. Baptism, the most important and most controversial rite next to communion in contemporary disputes over church authority, Herbert sees as useful to some extent for such a stability. Although not a regular calendar event, it warrants brief concern here for its place in the individual's private date book and the soul's itinerary. Offering mainly a recollective mainstay, it heads off occasions of sin and theoretically should be adequate to everything sin invents: "In you Redemption measures all my time, / And spreads the plaister equall to the crime," the speaker of "H. Baptisme 1" remarks. That thought is reassuring, but it does little to relieve actual tribulations or prepare for them. That it is the sacrament rather than belief or election that atones for sin does not quiet one's personal uneasiness, nor does it necessarily challenge election, although any automating of rites goes against the "rebaptizers," who made confessed belief the crucial test.

Taking sides on that issue was nearly unavoidable in the 1620s, since for some decades, to those who wanted to purify the church, adult baptism was more than a sign or a sacrament; it was the heart and soul of the universal church founded on consent and belief. A church body that includes those who have not so consented is necessarily compromised. Thus against arguments such as Robert Some's that a true sacrament cannot be undermined by a hypocritical membership, Dissenters held that a rite applied to infants is a mockery. However many priests it has and sacraments it administers, Robert Browne tells Thomas Cartwright, a "denne of thieves" is not a church (Browne and Harrison 437). By stressing belief alone and reducing priestly functions, the reformers painted themselves in a corner with respect to baptism, as they did with Sundays. They made it difficult to save infants either by belief or by innocence, for instance, because if by election alone, not only they but no one needs baptism; if by innocence, the condemnation of humanity through Adam would be removed without Christ's intervention. Yet the undeclared souls of infants could be grouped in baptism with professed believers only if one granted the priesthood virtual powers of salvation. Yet again, infant souls could not be damned without a wrenching of humane affection. The compromise that both Dissenters and Anglicans sometimes settled for was to exclude the infants of known evil-doers but consider the infants of professed believers as probably predestined, hence baptizable (Ainsworth, *An Apologie* 72)—with the curious result that salvation is connected neither to belief nor to church power but to family and genealogy. Cartwright's option in *A Christian Letter of Certaine English Protestants* (1599) is to make the word the exclusive instrument of the remission of sins and the sacraments merely the seals affixed thereto. The baptismal "sealing" date could thus be delayed until long after the rite itself, until adulthood brought with it the capacity to receive the evangelized word.

Herbert is agile enough in the Sunday and baptism poems to avoid some of the pitfalls of the question, which is effective, belief or sacrament? What signifies salvation and peace of spirit for him is a successful struggle against sin, which leaves baptism less to do once it marks the beginning of individual wayfaring. It is ordinarily through baptism that the Christian passage takes "A narrow way and little gate." Herbert's setting of a time for conviction to take root requires him to synchronize the personal clock with evidence of predestination, which it is impossible to do with the infant. He thus bends chronological priority by having early baptism merely anticipate what is to come, to be confirmed by a timely retrieval. The idea is to reconcile the inner condition of the spirit with institutional practice, ignoring the interim and the question of true priority. He is not in doubt (in "H. Baptisme 2") that he himself has been chosen, or that the doctrine of grace alone can be applied to infants as well as to adults:

> on my infancie
> Thou didst lay hold, and antedate
> My faith in me.

This is not only a way around the quarrel with Anabaptists but a pattern-setting surrender to "the master" and an avoidance of antinomian controversy. It is also in keeping with the fable's capacity to circumvent chronology by using omniscience and foreknowledge to implant the whole in any part. Last days are already present in first days, as beginnings touch their ends. And so on the biographical level adult days are already present in infant days. As "Easter-wings" makes graphically clear, the story of individuals and the story of humanity follow the same principles. Knowing that, however, never seems to relieve the pressure of the moment, which comes bearing all the renewed troubles of the vanity-filled heart and unmastered spirit.

That Herbert's request for a return to innocence—however innocence may be said to exist in infants—is not to be granted is suggested by the surrounding poems, in their plunge back into experience, by the poet's current appeal "O let me still / Write thee great God, and me a childe," and by his reiterated need for a softened heart and will. These have a dramatizing effect on doctrinal statement similar to Herbert's problematizing of the speaker's confidence in "The British Church" with the qualifications planted in the surrounding poems. The sequence that follows "H. Baptisme 2" includes "Nature," "Sinne," and "Affliction 1," in which neither faith nor baptism can hold back an accumulating contamination. The power of baptism and the binding power of election are not necessarily challenged by the sinner's worthlessness; they simply reveal the dilemma of the elect living as though they were not elect and the non-elect living as though they were, a problem parallel to the chastisement of a chosen people by divine wrath while wicked neighbors prosper, even within their borders. Again the broader parallel is that the church too is subject to historical crosscurrents despite a legitimate founding—the collective equivalent to individual baptism. As the poet moving toward these occasions realizes, it is the riddling purpose and extent of history since the Incarnation that has put psalmic recapitulation and other lyric moments under duress amid the strong reassurances of church ritual and personal election. The comfort of daily devotions will turn out to be illusory if the appeal to "purge all my sins" and "enrich my heart" that "I may run, rise, rest" is not answered. The comfort lies in the statement of a program and the anticipated joining of the individual to the redemptive pattern. It is posited on the speaking of the appeal itself and (in context) is as much a poetic or verbal event, intersecting the spiritual conflicts, as it is a cyclical or calendar event.

Concern for the administration of holidays and sacraments Herbert generally omits from *The Church* except for "The Priesthood," "Sion," and "Aaron," and even in "The Priesthood" he subordinates to the teaching of holy writ the troubling question of vestments and the relationship between the ministry and laymen. "Aaron" I read (as the end-of-the-century Dissenters possibly did as well) as a point-by-point substitution of inner light, holiness, profaneness, defects, and Christ's redemptive presence for the vestments of priesthood. To say that "Christ is *my* head" is to deny both one's personal will and a mediating church head. It is "my" doctrine that is "tun'd by Christ." At the same time, by comparison to the inspired word, Herbert devalues not only vestments and ceremonies but poems. He marks his greatest difficulties in meeting the divine occasion not as a man who wishes to be a worthy priest but as a poet who would write new psalms in the light of a new covenant. Whereas one may preach as an officer of the church, one writes as a layman in another kind of service less under institutional directives. One is more end-oriented than cyclically renewed. If spiritual conflict is crucial despite election and despite liturgical reassurances, the point could also be made that poems, by their self-scrutinizing and verbal nature, are able to articulate further what the conflict is and, as drama, to plunge into it. If they succeed in carrying it forward toward one of the periodized rest stops, so much the better. Obviously Bunyan would not have been the same without *The Holy War* and *The Pilgrim's Progress*, authorial supplements to "Bishop Bunyan" the preacher. That the poetic calling may have such a purpose, not exactly parallel to any of the church functions but in support of them, and that in a sense it allows every day of writing to be a new holy day, depends on the idea that just as God must make sacred vessels of clay if priests are to convey his substance (in "H. Communion"), so he *might* make sacred poets of "mean stuff." He has done so in Hebrew poetry in the spectacular songs of Deborah, David, Moses, and the psalmists. His doing so as requested in "Easter-wings" and "Trinitie Sunday" and other marked creative occasions would make the poet one of an impressive line of spokesmen, imping his wing not only on the Easter ascension but on effective Hebrew imprecation generally.

However, to say just that and nothing more does not explain the relationship between liturgy and poetry or find a solution to the eclipsing of poetic similitude in the transumptive language of the end. The only day that is capable of fully synchronizing the progress of the poet with that of the visible church is the last day, which can only be approached, not rendered. In raising that point I am disagreeing not only generally with "similitude" readings of Herbert that allow likeness between concrete figures and transcendent meanings, and between poems and sacraments, but mildly and more specifically with John Bienz's view of the relationship between Herbert's eschatology and the holy moments of the calendar. In the latter version of metaphors as analogies, Herbert's concern with time, like John Cosin's more ritualistic effort to make worship compatible with the prayer book, does not conflict with liturgical worship but "functions as an extension of eschatological themes beyond the forms of public worship to reveal that the Day of the Lord is not finally to be equated with Easter or Sunday or any Holy Day— instead, it is potentially any day or hour" (14). So it may be, but what does "is" mean here, that baffling verb of existential assertion and equation? What kind of predication can link incident to *this* pattern or human perspective to divine omniscience? If one stresses "potentially" enough and does not forget the conflicts between nation and church, sinner and spiritual paradigm, some such statement is arguable. But God's immanence is in fact intermittent at best to even the most sanguine reader of the militant church's historical record.

To Herbert divine visitations are variable and unpredictable, and the absences are frequent and mysterious. The only rite in *The Church* that comes in close proximity to end things is communion, and it arrives in the special office of enacted divine "love," a general term that signifies the affective attraction of parts to whole, or in "Love 3," of the whole to a given part. Baptism has a more limited power; Easter, Whitsunday, and other calendar days come and go, and the poet may or may not rise during their privileged hours of sway. Sitting and eating has both a gestural and a psychological finality that enables the poet who catches it in his mimetic net to write *Finis* to the volume after a closing devotional commemoration. But as I will suggest in more detail later, Herbert's feast of words, his would-be service as a poet, is not exactly equivalent to a church supper or arrival at heaven's threshold. It is after all he who writes the poem and gives love its courtship technique, and what he writes is a past-tense narrative or simulated recollection that establishes a paradigm, not a permanent state. And the question of the relation of writing to rite persists up to the closing words. Before I go into that, however, we can profit from considering two other holy days, Lent and Christmas, both less prominent in Herbert than Easter and perhaps less important to him than baptism, but nonetheless days that survive his purge of the calendar.

Nativity and Lent

Herbert's "Christmas" begins with the odd insertion of a first-person narrative into the nativity, again, as in "Easter," as though the distance could be collapsed:

> All after pleasures as I rid one day,
>   My horse and I, both tir'd, bodie and minde,
>   With full crie of affections, quite astray,
> I took up the next inne I could finde.

In constructing this allegory of a search for a place of rest, Herbert juggles parallels between the journey of wise men to Bethlehem, runaway emotions in the "full cry of affections," and the horseman's pursuit of game. The conditions are set by the phrase "after pleasures," which eliminates some of the pursuits that might compete with the nativity. Like the speaker of "Trinitie Sunday," who could be the voice of the human race, this one is generalized as the product of long absence from the "dearest Lord." Requiring a refuge, he develops parallels in one of the more casual levels of story telling—his getting far from home and the seeming coincidence of the deer turning up as the "dear" Lord. Pivoting on that pun, he follows an anecdotal style with a deepening of the fable:

> There when I came, whom found I but my deare,
>   My dearest Lord, expecting till the grief
>   Of pleasures brought me to him, readie there
> To be all passengers most sweet relief?

. Conflating English and Italian sonnet forms, the speaker redirects his feelings after two quatrains and draws nearer the biblical account, which mixes anxiety with eagerness. Both are marked with "behold" and an emphasis on the confirmed annunciation. Without any further impulse to chase dog-pack affections, the speaker focuses on what gives access to glad tidings. A lord who chooses the companionship of beasts will surely not shy away from inhabiting a human soul, but he must inhabit the body as well, and it will become a "rack." As he is to bodies in rising from the grave, so meaning is to its narrative vehicle, a light contracted into the manger, which can be transcended once it has served its turn. For all its confessional preamble and its negotiated turn from the "full crie of affections, quite astray" to the archetypal Christmas story, the shift in the speaker is abrupt. He proceeds into the framing story without establishing the limits of his prior knowledge or reasons for the change beyond the discovery of the Lord already waiting. He goes unreproached for having pursued affections so exclusively in an exceptionally easy joining of stories of quite different magnitudes. The innkeeper who welcomes travelers is a comfortable figure, and such lines as "A willing shiner, that shall shine as gladly, / As frost-nipt sunnes look sadly" do not suggest that this speaker will produce the hymn he thinks the occasion warrants.

Like the hours of worship in the daily cycle of the matins, the seasons of faith and holy days ordinarily raise in Herbert a more acute awareness of the difficulty of approach. Both church rites and calendar occasions bring home the paradox that his message to Ferrar suggests: only surrender brings freedom; total surrender, total freedom. But like "Christmas," "Lent" brings the sinner to the holiday somewhat less guiltily, perhaps because mortification helps pay for participation:

> Welcome dear feast of Lent: who loves not thee,
> He loves not Temperance, or Authoritie,
>   But is compos'd of passion.
> The Scriptures bid us *fast*; the Church sayes, *now*:
> Give to thy Mother, what thou wouldst allow
>   To ev'ry Corporation.

The need to discipline desire, a central subject of "The Church Porch" as well, concedes a didactic function to poetry, which handles Lent more easily than it does Easter. Such a holiday can attract a poem explicitly in the service of devotional observance and implicitly argue against schism. Scripture says fast; the church designates when and how; the poem lends advice and encouragement. Compared to the country parson, who has much more to say on diet and the purposes of Lent, it takes a middle way between ritualized cleansing and preacherly instruction. Its emphasis falls on a broader definition of obedience than mere abstinence would suggest. The speaker's hope in fact is that even an imperfect imitation of Christ's self-denial will bring an encounter with him:

> Who goeth in the way which Christ hath gone,
> Is much more sure to meet with him, then one
> That travelleth by-wayes:
> Perhaps my God, though he be farre before,
> May turn, and take me by the hand, and more
> May strengthen my decayes.

In fitting wayfaring to the antitype, the speaker hopes to shrink the intervening time and glimpse the wilderness walker. But the effect is to station the viator outside the church, in the territory of the prepared spirit going recollectively into the wilderness. The meaning of "by-wayes" here is one's own episodic path. To get close to Christ through spiritual discipline may cause him to turn in his desert walk and approach and thus gather the individual story into his. But the wistful "perhaps" speaks more of his absence on other days than of Lenten discipline and a closing of the distance. The Lord may or may not turn back; the certainty is that as a divine/human he once took a wilderness path, and one way to discipline the appetitive self in these byways and thus to gain entry into the Christian pattern is to repeat the self-denial. But the temporal distance is great, and the absent God is now "farre before."

The Poetic "Church" and the Invisible Church

Herbert's *Church* clears from the calendar much of what Roman and Anglican devotional practice put there. Setting aside Christmas and matins, he settles basically into a stripped-down cycle of alienation (Lent), suspended waiting (Good Friday), rejoicing (Easter), and pentecostal visitation. The Anglican practice was to apply sermons not only to proclaimed celebrations (Ash Wednesday, Lent, Easter, Christmas) but to special days that linked church and magistrate (the fifth of November, coronations, funerals, the opening of Parliament—the chief occasions of Donne's and Lancelot Andrewes's sermons). Despite this limiting of links between sacred periodicity and secular events, Herbert finds natural enough some of the contemporary connections among church, university, and court. He remarks in "The Church Militant" that both empire and the arts "usher" gospel. He leaves it at that but implies that social stability and adornment give the church a shape, as the university gives it a forum. The church's (and the university's) observation of holy days supports the assumption that the social setting need not inhibit religious sincerity. Even so, the "ushering" state has little bearing on the speakers' intervals of tribulation or their outcome, whereas the church has a great deal, even if the decisive moments of many poems stand apart from it. In fact, the very internalizing of devotional observance can have the effect of strengthening the church's grip, since no corner of individual conscience or public activity goes unexamined. The poet probes as deeply as he can and brings the entire researched self to the holy days and rituals, as *The Temple* works through spiritual conflict toward submission simultaneously to Christ as master and to the church as an instrument of spiritual administration.

Personal surrender to the master is compatible with that administration for Herbert, but it is not always self-evident how a dramatic or narrative poetry that features the struggle serves either marked occasions or sacraments. If "Love 3" enacts a typical progress toward self-definition and simultaneously marks stages toward communion, it does so as a poem. To work as such it does not require an actual communion or even church membership to support it. Something similar might be said of translated and disseminated psalms, even those originally written to accompany processions in the Temple. If they served that purpose exclusively, they could be recited only in that context and not "read" in the sense of interpreted. But they are not so limited: they have a life as literature that survives the destruction of temples and persists in works of art.

One modern opinion of Scripture itself, as John Goldingay remarks (citing Austen Farrer), finds it "dynamic, intuitive, holistic, plurivocal, open-ended" and not "disciplined, reflective, conceptual, analytic, measured"; it lacks both a theology and a philosophy (Goldingay 177). On these grounds, it can exist as literature without churches, as indeed Milton found that the entire fable could, once a certain class of readers had been "church-outed by prelates." Two avenues toward that view were open to Herbert, radical resistance to church hierarchy of any kind—a way we know he did not take—and a return to a prophetic or "poetic" restoration of the spiritual life of the testaments. He did not consciously take the second alternative either, but it is possible for someone to slip into it who uses poetry, as "The Quidditie" says, as an instrument "which while I use / I am most with thee, and *most take all.*" If that is arguably the case with the final narrative of *The Church*, as the usual reading of "Love 3" when studied in isolation suggests, what of the spiritual course that leads to it? The basic question is whether Herbert's representation of conflict goes through or around the church's version of holy days and sacraments and directly to its presumed divine presence, or through the Bible's mediation alone, or through both that and the church's sacramentalizing of key episodes of the text. What authority does the church have in poetics? The chain of command in *The Temple* according to one model would look like this:

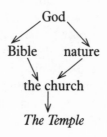

But according to another, like this:

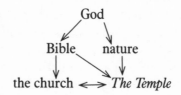

In the second model, the poems are not ornaments for the church's Easter, Whitsunday, Sundays in general, church pageantry, Christmas, Lent, or communion, as Christopher Harvey's imitation of Herbert makes them seem, and the corpus of the poems as a whole is not merely an image of the church. It is in a sense its own "church," a metaphoric one. That *The Temple* depends on the visible church is significant in either model, but the divine-human covenant enacted in "Love 3" and forecast frequently in *The Church* would obviously be freer of ritual forms and ecclesiastical hierarchy if we used the second model. I find it the better one on the grounds that much that the Bible contains but the visible church omits can be reinscribed in the personal odysseys of Herbert's idealized speakers. Moreover, the book of nature, which has virtually no role in the visible church, does have an emblematic, although not a dominant, role in the poems. Bot the source text and Herbert's include more social and political life, if very little outright secular life, than the church as such (if we ignore the pressure it applies to kings and parliaments, which is none of Herbert's concern). The church and *The Church* have different ways of approaching holy days, although both are rooted in the original biblical types and antitype.

Given these possibilities, we might ask again, what precisely is the poet's "church"? A mystical body that replaces the historical Messiah? A spirit that descends primarily but not exclusively in the reading of the sacred text? If the latter, what does it have to do with national ecclesiologies? Or is it a historical body with a numbered membership, a priesthood in apostolic succession supported by Christian magistrates? If the latter, how can each of several different such bodies all be "the" church, and how could Herbert's work be read profitably by readers who are not in the specific church he means? Insofar as the church *is* such a body, what is the relation of its members' sacred to their secular lives, and of the church to the state? Or is the church perhaps an *idea*, more or less embodied in different nations and in diverse lives? Is *The Temple*'s version of it a true representation, no more or less privileged than other narrative and iconological representations? Or finally, is *The Temple*'s "church" an affair of levels, partly historical (church militant) and partly anagogic (church mystical and triumphant)? If so, how does Herbert's representation of it compare to institutional versions, and how are the various levels related one to another?

If compelling answers to these and similar questions had been available in the 1620s when Herbert was juggling the competing demands of nature, science, the university, the court, the ministry, poetry, and Anglicanism, there would obviously have been less turmoil then, and there would be less now among Herbert's critics. As it is, extracting a definition of the church from Herbert's writings is difficult, particularly from his didactic and polemical poems that are specifically directed to the British church and church militant. Nor could we expect Herbert, not having been expelled by prelates, to consider an entirely independent poetic ministry of the word. What any complex religious writer becomes in part is a re-presenter of a sacred script that does not absolutely require either his poems or a great deal of commentary. A lyricist who succeeds in representing plausible spiritual conflicts discovers nonsacramental routes to the covenant of love, routes not the product of a catechizing ministry or identical with formulaic devotion.

"The Altar" and the Book

Herbert's altar also supplements and substitutes for—it does not merely represent—Anglican and biblical versions of the place and manner of sacrifice. When we turn from the end of *The Church* to the entry's observance of the passion, we find the heart as altar and must begin to distinguish among several levels and realms—location in the precincts of a more or less definable and visible English church, the undertaking of verbal artifices, representation of a typically hardened but contrite heart, and a partly implicit set of antecedents, which include both the Hebrew and the Christian bibles as well as other bodies of poetry. Knowing that an actual church altar is *not* a heart, we can see that "The Altar" is a "bookish" metonym, a substitution for the church's version of the sacrifice as well as a first-person imitation of it. What it substitutes literally is a printed shape for stones and "I" for the normal communal body. In that regard, one government metaphoric type for *The Church is* precisely metonymy, which is something different than a part (one member's poems) representing the whole (the entire visible church and all its history).

But metonymic substitution pure and simple is insufficient to describe "The Altar" because it does not account for differences between a struggling, tentative sacrifice and a set ritual in a defined institution. Despite the considerable scholarship and readerly ingenuity that have been brought to "The Altar" in recent years, we have still not really come to terms with either the dramatized spirit or the inherent playfulness of the word shape that Herbert juxtaposes with the tradition. It is no accident that he controls the reading of Christ's sacrifice with an altar made not of wood or unhewn stone or even of the flesh-and-blood poet's heart but first and foremost of syllables piled one beside and upon another. Herbert calls attention to the oddity as well as the service of words.

If we do not begin with that perhaps too-obvious (but sometimes forgotten) fact, we are not likely to make our way profitably through the intricacies of altar scholarship, even with the help of such able editors and commentators as F. E. Hutchinson, Rosemond Tuve, Chana Bloch, Joseph Summers, Stanley Fish, Thomas Stroup, Roger Lockyer, John Wall, and Albert Labriola. For instance, the pattern of expiation and sanctification that Labriola finds jointly in biblical typology and the poem ("The Rock" 61) is unquestionably there, but something unsettling is added to it by a poem so obviously manufactured and so prominently set in place. Herbert the man or Herbert the priest could have offered expiation without writing such a poem. Putting the contrite heart in a word shape threatens to make it less contrite, if only because the joy of building is too near the forbidden hewing of stones, one of the historical pollutions. All patterns begin with a hard heart and all of them look to someone's sacrifice as a means to soften it, but in the preemptive sacrifice of Christ Herbert inherits a complication that none of the Hebrew sacrifices have. He then adds to that the translation of the place of sacrifice from a public church to a private book—not only to these particular stacked words, capable of analysis, self-dissection, and wit, but to a book that someone decided to name *The Temple*.

The serious tone notwithstanding, this substitution of a verbal altar and personal sacrifice for a regular church fixture is playful. The words bring with them not only the visual device but the juxtaposition of various altars. Erecting the poem is an act of ingenuity, or what Dryden and the eighteenth century tended to regard as Herbert's gimmickry, thrusting up the shape of an "I" as a signature for the work. Herbert seems not particularly contrite about that aspect of his first fruits, which he makes the carrier of his heart. And if one *can* make such an offering, what happens to ordained procedures for cultic appeasement and collective appeals to a wrathful Father who accepts the sacrifice even of his own Son? Have the centralizing reforms of Josiah reached their ultimate defeat in this transfer of religion to the private study where poems are written and individual hearts summed up? Or does the poem's oblique reference to the typological tradition, the source book, and the cultural record of previous altars bring private meditation into conformity to a pattern, even as the publishing of the poem makes a kind of collective offering of it? But would the latter not then redefine the nature of the corporate body by basing its model specifically in a fictional speaker, as opposed to a real contrite man, since this heart is after all a construction, a poem? The speaker is inseparable from his identity as a maker of word shapes. And the reader also becomes a quite different party from a church initiate entering a real institution.

The relationship of the poem to any actual altar becomes all the more problematic by its close association with one particular church and its liturgy, as Thomas Stroup argues. *The Temple* is thus not only set up within a tradition but set against certain aspects of it and thereby becomes in part polemic. The idea of a sacrifice is riddled with the disputes that both anthropological and historical approaches have attempted to untangle (for instance in Edmund Leach and Douglas Davies [in Lang 136–50, 151–62] and in the earlier higher criticism [see Wellhausen 83–120]). In both testaments, whoever controls the place of sacrifice and the right to administer offerings controls the church, the people, and the way their history will be written. With the sacrifice goes the priesthood, and with the priesthood the right of church taxation and legislation, access to records, and the authorial capacity to commit history and prophecy to writing. The altar is the hub of the culture, at least as written in accounts of church history. The secular periphery is connected to it by law and custom. Where church history is taken to be the heart of social history, other institutional controls follow from the control of sacrifice: the placing of trust in a caste to perform the sacrifice, the bonding of participants as a community, and the linkage of priests to monarchs. The Hebrew practices are several and often in contention, as Aaron contests Moses, and the northern kingdom contests Jerusalem. Acceptable sacrifices are sometimes propitiatory signs to a jealous YHWH whose ire is aroused over sacrifices to foreign gods, but they can also be personal donatives in expression of sincere gratitude (Weinfeld, *Deuteronomy* 212). The penalties for losing the contest over where and when to offer sacrifice can be severe, both at the time and in posterity. The right to make sacrificial offerings is a way to sort out legitimate priests from self-appointed ones, as challengers to Moses and Aaron discover. In Herbert's church as well, only an ordained priesthood administers communion. And as Bacon's confession indicates, the descent is by direct line from the apostles. Such an institution is a full partner in social governance.

The new-covenant sacrifice of the Son both intensifies and suspends the practice of burnt offerings. In Milton's view the Law and its sacrifices can discover but not remove sin:

> Save by those shadowy expiations weak,
> The blood of Bulls and Goats, they may conclude
> Some blood more precious must be paid for Man,
> Just for unjust, that in such righteousness
> To them by Faith imputed, they may find
> Justification toward God, and peace
> Of Conscience, which the Law of Ceremonies

Cannot appease, nor Man the moral part
Perform.

(Paradise Lost 12.290–99)

By depriving the pious of their hoped-for king, that new sacrifice makes them
pay for their guilt psychologically. But it is not the willing sacrifice of those
who bring first fruits to a priesthood for its disposal; it is a sacrifice made by
unholy ones against the will of cultic followers, and a sacrifice of God himself.
"Properly" understood, in the transumptive mode of the new covenant
preempting the old, the new sacrifice is on behalf of a whole people. By
removing guilt and cultic possession of the sacrificial place, it unseats the old
priesthood, undermines its tithing privileges, and undoes its national location, at least temporarily. The eucharistic tasting of the sacrificial body
ritualizes that offering and may renationalize it by local differences in the
rite. Whether sacrificial offerings are regular or irregular, whether eucharists
are symbolic, transubstantiated, virtual, Lutheran, Roman Catholic, or Anglican, their purposes are primarily participatory.

But more pertinent to "The Altar" than the doctrinal choices of Herbert's
visible church is the difference it makes for readers entering Herbert's temple
to find not an old, new, Roman, Lutheran, or Anglican altar but a sacrifice
of the poet's own heart and the concluding realization that only a personal
link between that sacrifice and Christ's can sanctify this altar. The state
apparatus and church hierarchy are for the moment not vital parts of the
devotion. Yet neither does anything the speaker manages on his own have any
validity except the creation of a vocative presence and an addressee who can
enter the sacrificial place, the worded heart. If the addressee does so,
presumably we are no longer in the presence of an ordinary metonymy but
once again rising toward transumption: a heap of words taken over by *the*
word does not remain the same pile. Every part of it would undergo the
equivalent to transubstantiation or symbolic reassignment. This is more likely
to happen, the speaker says, if he chances to hold his peace, which presumably means something like grow quiet and wait. Where the noisy followers of
Jesus are prevented from proclaiming "peace in heaven, and glory in the
highest," Jesus tells the pharisees (Luke 19:38–40) that the very stones will
cry out "peace!" so powerful is the message of deliverance. Quiet creates a
vacuum into which the Spirit may rush, taking voice from whatever it seizes
upon.

Given this significant difference between the reader's entering the vocative
presence of poetry and entering an actual church, does Herbert prepare for

still other divergences from church ceremony? Can the poet also construct substitutes of his own for Easter or Christmas? Does the "communion" too differ? The bestowal of grace that "Love 3" dramatizes disallows the heart of "The Altar" and its effort to sacrifice itself. Love reverses the payment and takes over the sacrifice, which is not the one originally intended and yet is hinted at by the conclusion of "The Altar." Does that suggest serious errancy in the substitute verbal altar, or merely confirm what its last lines suggest, that to mean anything the poet's sacrifice must become the Savior's? Even if the latter, is "Love 3" then not another kind of verbal replacement of a church rite? As a drama of self-surrender, it may find a distant equivalent but not exact duplication in the "mystical repast" that makes a communion of the sacrifice. It puts its submission into recapitulative form and arrives at a subjected will not through group ritual but through a fictional dialogue, which is to say that together with "The Altar," it frames a tale of conflicts with artifice, after a series of uncanonized narrative lead-ins to the poet's participation.

The word "mystical" in "Superliminare," which points all the way through *The Church* to "I did sit and eat," suggests another side to that concluding poetic dialogue. If any total representation of love were possible, the repast would not be mystical; as it is, more than one kind of approximation may be allowable, one of them institutionalized and another verbal. Perhaps we are not meant to say which of several such representations best accommodates the mystery and might conclude that it is just as possible for it to appear in *The Church* as in the British church, even as both YHWH and the pentecostal spirit appear in various localities indoors and out, on mountain tops and in valleys, at wellsides and roadsides, in private and in large and small gatherings, some of them the subject of "Decay." Or as "Peace" says in expanding on "peace" in "The Altar," a dispersal that is truly spiritual is not a decentering but a constant recentering wherever gospel plants its wheat and individuals make bread of it. The only sacrifice that matters has already been made, and it is through the discovery of divine love rather than through contrite hearts that one participates in it.

One implicit claim of a book with such an ambitious title as *The Church*, however, is that the wording of poems may legitimately bring forward that spiritual "feast." If the covers of the book are its architecture, if words inscribe a "superliminare" warning, if still more words are its altars and windows, then the final words may enact the approach of divine love just now being impressed upon the reluctant sinner. As to publication, it is difficult to infer anything from it except that however Ferrar may have read the book (and perhaps named it), he too saw no disabling conflict between one form of devotion and another. A poetic altar and a poetic eucharist are perhaps no more autonomous finally than a sermon that expounds and recreates Scripture, but neither can they be exactly equated to anything preceding them. They are current attempts to reinscribe a scheme in a new setting that brings a simulated personal record into intimate contact with it. They restage Herbert's own spiritual combat, we are led to believe, yet settle it in paradigmatic ways that convert his masks and personas into Everyone, as the personal heart/altar, taken over by the sacrifice, becomes the heart of the participatory reader.

The Visible Church

If only so much can be said of the mystical church, a great deal can be and has been written about the historical church and about *The Temple*'s accommodation of it (see Anselment; Johnson 200–206; Stewart, *George Herbert* 112–16; Dickson 122; Carnes; Fish, *Living Temple* 143–48; Miller 117–42; and Hanley). Except in "The Church Militant," Herbert's attention is devoted primarily to Great Britain and the British church, which he defends against schism and uses as the institutional foundation of ritual and calendar poems. He rarely looks abroad even as far as Germany or Geneva. When in "Church-rents and schisms" he does glance at Asia, Europe, and Africa, he returns to find "debates and fretting jealousies" undermining the British portion of what should after all be the *universal* church. If we except his early satire of Andrew Melville, "Church-rents" is Herbert's most disturbed poem on the matter of institutional stability:

> Brave rose, (alas!) where art thou? in the chair
> Where thou didst lately so triumph and shine
> A worm doth sit, whose many feet and hair
> Are the more foul, the more thou wert divine.
> This, this hath done it, this did bite the root
> And Bottome of the leaves: which when the winde
> Did once perceive, it blew them under foot,
> Where rude unhallow'd steps do crush and grinde
>   Their beauteous glories. Onely shreds of thee,
>   And those all bitten, in thy chair I see.

With symbolism worthy of John of Patmos or William Blake, Herbert draws near enough to see the details of the desecration and point an accusing finger, "This, this hath done it, this did bite." Schism is unleashed in a very animated garden of personifications, a very intentional worm, and a perceiving and quite active harvesting wind. Mysterious steps trample the petals and finish their ruin. Although it would be difficult to specify parties to this ruin, the once-powerful church allows neighbors to rush in.

In "The British Church" Herbert praises not merely the accoutrements of the church but its exclusive rightness, which makes the recalcitrant errors of Asia and Africa (not to mention Scotland) the more inexplicable. In that respect, "The British Church" reverses the appeal in "Home" for God to reveal himself, and indeed as I suggested earlier no two juxtaposed poems in *The Church* collide more openly (unless we take the discovery of the church to be an answer of sorts to "O show thy self to me," and if so an odd answer). In "Home," "long differings," while God "dost ever, ever stay," wound the speaker "to the quick":

> So many yeares baptiz'd, and not appeare?
> As if thy love could fail or change.
> O show thy self to me,
> Or take me up to thee!

The seasons and the holidays contain nothing of value:

> Nothing but drought and dearth, but bush and brake,
> Which way so-e're I look, I see.
> Some may dream merrily, but when they wake,
> They dresse themselves and come to thee.
> O show thy, & c.

"The British Church" responds, "I Joy, deare Mother, when I view / Thy perfect lineaments and hue." The juxtaposition of a strongly felt, first-person appeal and an institution may be less jarring in this instance than it would in a demonstrable sequence, but like "Sion," which precedes it, "Home" takes no comfort in the temple. It makes an unfit receptacle unless God redeems it, and he has never done so permanently. Obviously in "Sion" by far the more important place is the heart; the temple's stones and brass are mere "heavie things, / Tombes for the dead, not temples fit for thee."

For the most part, *The Temple* is not overly preoccupied with the standing of an authoritative church, but more profitably with the spiritual education and sustaining recurrence of an institution entrusted to establish a mean between too little and too much in the re-presentation of God and reenactment of his historical moments. In "Sion" the former glory of the temple is long departed; God has removed his residence to the embattled heart. It is self-evident from the two destructions of the Temple and of the Jewish monarchy that the covenant for their protection was conditional; they both relied on human builders and administrators. Working against holidays and liturgical renewals in "The Church Militant" is an eventful sequence of calamities, typical of the history of such conditional affairs. Herbert expects evil to escalate and run free all the way to the last stages of the world. Readers who look past the visible church to the triumphant Church and who wish a collective conclusion for *The Temple* to match the individual one of "Love 3" have not always sufficiently stressed that. In "The Church Militant" the double westward journey of glory and sin is as emphatic as catastrophe often is in the Judaic prophets and historians, and indeed sin's "scattered jugglings" are compounded and united in recent churchmen. Throughout its history, the more powerful the Church has become, the more sin has thrived within it. If from Egypt religion gathered its petty deities and from Greece its claim to oracular infallibility, from Rome it took the use of church revenue and an alliance of secular and sacred power. In recent churchmen caught up in controversies, sin has been delighted to find that "a gown and pen" become "him wondrous well," as the very training grounds of priests and the devices of rhetoric turn against true devotion.

Lest we think that sin's westward conquest, for all that, will still be mastered in England, Herbert risks the often-quoted lines that caused Ferrar momentary difficulty when publishing *The Temple*:

> Religion stands on tip-toe in our land,
> Readie to passe to the *American* strand.
> (235–36)

Such lines are not really surprising in the context of the concern throughout the 1620s over recusant legislation, the much-debated Arminian alternative that was gaining power among Anglican clergy (see *Debates in the House of Commons in 1625*, Smuts 38, Lockyer 117–19, Russell 27, and Finlayson 84–97), and some radical dissent as well. A more general reason for religion's readiness to go elsewhere, beyond internal difficulties, is the height of malice, prodigious lusts, impudent sinning, witchcraft, and distrust that the entire "calender of sinnes" illustrates. With the word "calender" (244), Herbert probes a sore spot with the Dissenters, the ones who stand poised for flight. In the sun-darkness figure, obviously not the enlightenment figure here that it is in "The Sonne," he concedes the inevitability of sin's intrusion throughout the course of its historical run. Because even the Son cannot renew the faith permanently, the metaphor precludes millennial resurgence. As Kenneth Hovey observes in charting a mixture of linear progress and cycles in the Church, "Each state has a complete cycle of Religion. Religion dawns on it, attains its height in it, and then declines and disappears from it, leaving it in darkness again" (" 'Wheel'd about' " 74). Not until the Son and sin have circled the globe and returned to the source will final judgment arrive. In that global circuit, which gives all peoples an exposure to the Gospels and a chance to choose, Herbert suggests the peril of ventures into evangelizing, which can become virtually indistinguishable from the diaspora's submission of universal history to local history. Proselytizing has accelerated in intensity from the beginning of Hebraic monotheism but without suppressing the rival gods.

Once the Crucifixion has removed the Messiah from limited national boundaries and the *parousia* has failed, the universal God must either conquer the world through saints or remove the promised kingdom altogether from earth: no merely cultic proprietorship or administration by Providence will suffice. Hence, whatever the mood of "The British Church," Herbert's church militant finds no permanent home and perhaps can have none; it has long ago gone into an irreversible scattering, dissemination being virtually the same as homelessness. The end can be foreseen only in a kind of metalepsis that overshadows even the Christian appropriation of the Jews and their manner of sacrifice; it skips past stages and causal development to an eruptive end. It is finally apocalypse and not church ritual that provides the temporal solution to disquiet, provided that it is an apocalypse that softens wrath with love. All the more reason, then, to distinguish between *The Temple*, whose perspective is ultimately global; the militant church, locatable in several times and places but none permanently; and sacrament-administering churches here and now. In that respect, the visible church could do worse than approach not only the Bible but this poetic supplement with an eye toward reestablishing links with its historical source and its ultimate end. It is not for *The Temple* to reduce itself to one institution; it is for both institutions and poems to approach as best they can the ideal militant church, which is the anticipation of church triumphant. Whatever the collective church manages in its historical course, the individual approach is best charted in negotiations with Love, which in applying to everyone in the same way creates a communal body one member at a time.

7
THE END OF THE FABLE

Since I am comming to that Holy roome,
    Where, with thy Quire of Saints for evermore,
I shall be made thy Musique; As I come
    I tune the Instrument here at the dore,
    And what I must doe then, thinke now before.
            —John Donne, "Hymne to God my God,
                                in my sicknesse"

Approaching

One way of gauging Herbert's distinctiveness is to mark his departure from
the poet who best prepares for him, namely Donne in holy sonnets and other
religious lyrics. I want to consider here not only that preparation but one of
his more telling departures from Donne, located at the juncture between
history and what in allegorical terms would be anagogy. That happens also
to be the juncture between the personal speaker and the general pattern of
justification and atonement, the moment toward which everything points, the
time of times for both poets. The multileveled allegory of both rabbinical and
Christian interpretation hints at the linguistic difficulty of the crossing, and

both poets, despite abridgments, make some use of it. Tropes and figures that span the entire fourfold system that Dante expounds acknowledge first the likeness of two kinds of literal historical placement, usually one of them Hebrew and the other Christian. The *littera gesta* or actual happenings in histories and stories contribute to the overall development of the tribes, the Exodus from Egypt, and the founding of the nation. At the second level such incidents as the crossing of the Red Sea and the establishing of Jerusalem are then assigned Christian equivalents in the manner of the Epistle to the Hebrews. Building upon that retraction from and doubling of the original events is a moral or tropological level *(quid agas)*, which is emphasized both in rabbinical and Christian exegesis. In the last stage neoplatonism provides an upward thrust that converts preceding representations into shadows of a higher reality. Thus anagogy *(quo tendas)* disengages itself from previous representations, involved as these have been in historical episodes and the particulars of character, place, and culture. At that point—where the soul rediscovers its divine imprint and surrenders its accumulated vanities— Herbert stations some of his most extraordinary verse and marks his divergence from Donne.

I have reserved the term *metalepsis* or transumption for the skipping of steps and *catachresis* for category changes in which nothing quite prepares for traumatic relocation. If we were to proceed straightway from the earthly to the heavenly Jerusalem without pausing at the visible church, we would have a metaleptic crossing but not catachresis, since the figure of Jerusalem-as-church is too traditional and familiar to seem at all radical. Catachresis supposes a jarring connection (although one of John Smith's examples of it is running water, which having no feet cannot really run). Herbert's "Ev'n God himself being pressed for my sake" in "The Bunch of Grapes," because of the graphic wine pressed from the body, registers with more violence. If we actually see the flow of blood, as it seems Herbert intends, the incongruity of the man/god as grape, and the compounding of Law: sour juice and new covenant: sweet wine leaves a logical hiatus. It does so even if one is saturated in medieval iconology, as Rosemond Tuve would have us become to read that figure properly. We may detect an advance toward an ultimate place by way of the historical event, but it is obviously not a smooth progression: the story in Numbers does not unfold in revelatory stages or increasingly transcendent language. Its literal second event (the Crucifixion) is one of helpless submission yet signifies the complete mastery of history.

It is Donne with "when thou hast done, thou has not done" (where John Donne is the *littera gesta* and "done" the story's goal), or "see a Sunne, by rising set," the church/spouse that is more pleasing when "open to most men," and such lines as "nor ever chast except you ravish mee" who best prepares for the shock tactics of that systematic abuse of language. Unlike Bacon's movement in "Confession of Faith" from temporal logic to the "glory of the saints"—when "all things shall continue for ever in that being and state which they shall receive" (*Works* 7.225)—Donne places unusual stress on the juncture between worlds. He approaches end things with more urgency than Herbert, perhaps, as Gene Veith speculates (*Reformation Spirituality* 118–19), because he fears that the grace that propels one across the gap may not be irresistible to a given individual. To test the transition, Donne several times occupies a precarious cliff edge of contrition and fear. Such places tend to bring back the anxieties of sudden theophanies in both testaments, disturbed by the discrepancy between divinity and human nature.

Herbert is less inclined to place speakers so near the extremity. Although "Church Monuments," for instance, is a distinct and impressive *memento mori* poem, it concentrates on the lessons the soul reads the body and not on the peril of the soul itself. "Death" ignores the judgment and replaces the short-range decay of the body with a glimpse of the Resurrection. The likeness of the gathered saints to a social group compresses the immediate world and the triumphant church into one of his more effective images. Dying becomes a peaceful sleep, and a comfortable category-crossing gains vividness from being recast as metaphor. Every evening's journey to the bedchamber prepares for an equally easy journey to the grave. A graceful transition into the afterlife is guaranteed by the Resurrection. "Dooms-day" does not overwhelm the world with apocalyptic fire, but begins in eager anticipation of the great day and grows anxious only about its delay, not its coming.

These and other poems look beyond Donne's "*death of corruption* and *putrefaction* and *vermiculation* and *incineration*" and his violent scattering of numberless infinities of souls and bodies overthrown by "warre, dearth, age, agues, tyrannies." Donne's dread of reckoning colors virtually everything he imagines by way of preparation—in Matthew 25.36–51 and 26.1–13; Mark 13.30 and 29–37, and 2 Peter, which is, as we read the most important of work to be done. He tells the audiences of his last sermons that "all our *periods* and *transitions* in this life . . . are so many passages *from death* to *death*" (*Selected Prose* 312). Elaborating on the apostles' word *peregrinamur*, he remarks that "wee are but in *a pilgrimage,* and wee are *absent from the Lord*; hee might have stayd *dead,* for this whole *world* is but an *universal churchyard*, but our *common grave*; and the life and motion that the greater persons have in it, is but the shaking of buried bodies in their graves by an *earth-quake*" (314). Although not uncommon ideas, Donne's are more insistent than most in their reduction of earth to representations of disintegration and signs of the apocalypse. Such signs have intermittently been inserted by divine miracle into the destruction of Sodom, the flood, the conquest and destruction of Jerusalem, and a thousand less-notable plagues and burnings—all of which can be read as prefigurations of judgment that Donne gives a vividness quite unlike Herbert's approach to the restored dead.

Where personal histories count for Donne, it is primarily in the tabulation of sins. Except for the sharply paradoxical and reiterative style of the saying, Donne comes somewhat nearer Herbert in that self-estimate, the uniform result of the upward turn being the condemnation of lower levels and universalizing of sin and guilt. "*Our birth dyes* in *infancy*, and our *infancy* dyes in *youth* and the rest dye in *age*. . . . Our *youth* is *worse* than our *infancy*, and our *age worse* than our *youth*. Our *youth* is *hungry and thirsty*, after those *sinnes*, which our *infancy knew not*; And our age is *sory* and *angry*, that it *cannot pursue* those *sinnes* which our *youth* did" (*Selected Prose* 314). Such is the prolonged earthquake between origin in the flesh and vermiculation. Whereas here we "*have no continuing citty*, nay no *cottage* that continues, nay no persons, no bodies that continue" (314), after end things, possession will be continuous and full.

From the opposite direction for both Herbert and Donne comes the pressure of the beginning, the first of the three times of eternity "if times they may be called" in Bacon's chart. Once the middle phase has been added and has connected beginning to end, each part recalls the others. The fiery end is already implicit in the beginning and is featured again in the flood as the type of universal destruction. Donne's point in the appeal to remember the deeper past is that reconstructing the role of Adam and Eve and the Christian assimilation of the Hebrew narrative is part of the preparation for the end, which must become the chief business of these latter days. Hence any summing up on the verge is likely to retreat to the source and begin overleaping the localized interim to incorporate the entire heritage in one panorama, which everything heralds: "This is then the faculty that is excited, the memory; and this is the time, now, now whilest ye have power of election: The object is, the Creator, *Remember the Creator*" (*Selected Prose* 160). The end, whether just at hand or still a little off, must always be treated as if it were impending. We cannot wait until the very angel comes "which shall say and swear, that time shall be no more" (154).

The interplay between the beginning, end, and the few salient, emblematic moments in between (that herald best) occupies several of Donne's holy sonnets, two hymns, "A Nocturnal upon S. Lucies Day," the Anniversaries, several devotions, and the two sermons, "Valediction at My Going to Germany" (18 April 1619) and "Deaths Duel" (1631). In the earlier sermon, Donne takes such a dramatic leave of London in anticipation of his own end that his return was anticlimactic. In casting about for a way to break free of the burned-out carcase of the world, "The First Anniversary" begins with a jeremiad rejecting the world and proceeds to the call of "The Second Anniversary," "Up, up, my drowsie soule, where thy new eare / Shall in the Angels song no discord heare" (lines 339–40). The poet becomes a harbinger who summons readers. Because modern times have no prophets or new sacred texts to perform that summoning, the poet must take it upon himself to bridge the realms in his work.

Realizing that *eschata* can be approached only once past a certain point, Donne on most occasions backs away from the edge, perhaps most notably in "At the Round Earth's Imagin'd Corners" (Sonnet 4), where he confesses an incompleteness in his preparation:

> But let them sleepe, Lord, and mee mourne a space,
> For, if above all these, my sinnes abound,
> 'Tis late to aske abundance of thy grace,
> When wee are there; here on this lowly ground,
> Teach mee how to repent; for that's as good
> As if thou'hadst seal'd my pardon, with thy blood.

The personal narrative is summed up in the uncertain balance of abundant grace and repentance. The logic is difficult to untangle, especially the "As if" of the final line. If the pardon were sealed unconditionally, the speaker's repentance would be unnecessary. As it is, his accumulation of sin may prove to be too great. Of all the gospel teachings, the most crucial are instructions in how to repent, which are quite different from the teachings featured in Herbert's silk twist. Whereas Herbert's typical last-minute reversals in "The Collar," "Redemption," "Artillerie," and "Affliction 1" bring the speaker to submission after a brief articling for better conditions, Donne's obsession is not with personal calling and service but with peril in the face of divine wrath.

Donne's habit of approaching the end through such figures carries into his letters to friends and his farewells to members of the visible church. Although

his gift of a family seal to Herbert may have been made several years before
he began his more theatrical farewells, it offers a glimpse of the personal link
between them and the intrusion of the *quo tendas* into it. A seal ordinarily
secures a message with a family emblem or motto. As John T. Shawcross
points out, in giving Herbert this particular seal (a recent one) Donne glances
forward to the white horse of Revelation (19.11–12) and the Judgment ("Plura
tibi accumulet, sanctus cognominis, Ille / Regia qui flavo Dona sigillat
Equo"):

> Under that little Seal great gifts I send,
> Works, and prayers, pawns, and fruits of a friend.
> And may that Saint which rides in our great Seal,
> To you, who bear his name, great bounties deal.
>   "To Mr. George Herbert, with one of my Seales"

In Shawcross's more literal translation, the last two lines read, "May He heap
more upon you, sainted of surname, / who seals his princely gifts with a
glittering steed." The reference to Revelation makes what would otherwise
be a small gesture into something portentous—appropriately, since the seal
is a cross and anchor that remembers what governs end things. In the
conjunction of friends is thus a model of the gathering that inspires Donne's
reunited church in his valedictory sermon and anticipation of the choir in
"Hymne to God my God." That Herbert takes it in something of that spirit
is suggested by his remark that the seal secures "Love's Common-weal." The
current commonweal of princes and church militant is an interim affair that
each leaves at an appointed time, expecting to resume it under better
conditions.

From another standpoint, however, a seal does not necessarily seal anything, any more than a trope can actually signify the ultimate closure. An
envelope can be reopened for further insertions when the writer (or someone
else) has new business. An even more-than-usual inconclusiveness breaks in
here, since the last lines may be by someone else. It is as if a third party had
belatedly entered the exchange—or several parties by the time we count
Walton's recording of the incident and Helen Gardner's unscrambling of the
conditions of the gift and the poems that may have accompanied it (Gardner
130–47). The Herbert who reopens nearly all the issues of *The Church* again
and again and who knows the recurrent tests of postponement on this
occasion suggests the futility of Donne's gesture:

How sweet a friend was he, who being griev'd
His letters were broke rudely up, believ'd
'Twas more secure in great Loves Common-weal
(Where nothing should be broke) to adde a Seal.
                                             (*The Works* 439)

In "believ'd" and "should be," he looks askance upon that desire for a secured exchange within the insecurities of our familiar realm.

The other ragged piece of unfinished business that sticks out of the envelope here is that anyone who lives in anticipation of submission to the master must be prepared to diminish personal ties. After so many false starts at submission, a spiritual callousness may begin to form. We suspect it has momentarily around Bunyan's heart, for instance, when in *Grace Abounding* he reproaches those who are cast down when they meet with mere outward losses, "as of Husband, Wife, Child, &c" and remarks, "Lord, thought I, what a doe is there about such little things as these" (27), a remark we might expect too from Christian, whose first step in *The Pilgrim's Progress* carries him away from family and friends. (*Grace Abounding* sometimes gives a different impression, however; see 82 and 98.) If sealing "apocalyptically" a letter to a personal friend moves both sender and receiver toward an invisible commonweal of love, it also subtracts whatever is merely personal from their relationship. One side of world devaluation is again the loss of anecdotal connection, which makes this exchange of Latin poems somewhat aloof as well as twisted in its concern with final departures and the relative security of the cross. Timing is also an issue, since one must prepare today and then again tomorrow, like Yeats writing last poems and then more last poems; and so the departure from friends happens psychologically more than once, until death proves obliging: it may come after a dramatic farewell sermon, or it may decide to wait.

Divergent paths to the end encourage stylistic differences and individual voices. With Donne and Herbert, even the common end—as a judgment that reckons with personal records—carries a marked signature. Donne's seal stamps on his mail a type of the apocalypse, yet accompanied by verse it does so in a special Donnean way. Herbert answers the gift and its versified accompaniment as a fraternal poet, by way of dialogue, and thereby adds his signature. Yet his reply to Donne's witty entangling of his life's story, the cross, and the apocalyptic steed is not specifically autobiographical, and that again marks a difference between them. Whereas Donne in "A Hymne to God the Father" sums up and cancels everything that goes under his name,

Herbert has less of an inventoried personal nature to undo on the occasions that prepare. Except in the surrender of affliction and employment poems, he goes more theoretically back and forth between the uniformity of the belief and the personal ordeal of surrender. The fable never quite irons out the differences or undoes the singular voiceprints of either poet. Paradoxically, their strongest efforts at self-cancellation establish them as remarkable personas.

Arriving

Herbert grows less and less personal in the concluding poems of *The Church*, his most sustained visit to the Donnean brink. The curiously allegorical and schematic nature of his dialogues with and retorts to death show a readiness to look for love's commonweal elsewhere. "A Dialogue-Antheme," to take one version of that anticipation, is spoken in the exulting but not the personally triumphant voice of Donne's "Death be not proud," by a typical Christian ready at any time and quite unconcerned for things left behind:

> *Christian. Death.*
> Chr. Alas, poore Death, where is thy glorie?
>   Where is thy famous force, thy ancient sting?
> Dea. *Alas poore mortall, void of storie,*
>   *Go spell and reade how I have kill'd thy King.*
> Chr. Poore Death! and who was hurt thereby?
>   Thy curse being laid on him, makes thee accurst.
> Dea. *Let losers talk: yet thou shalt die;*
>   *These arms shall crush thee.*
> Chr.   Spare not, do thy worst.
>   I shall be one day better then before:
>   Thou so much worse, that thou shalt be no more.

Death accuses Christian of not reading the entire gospel and forgetting that the Crucifixion recurs again and again in typological repetitions. Christian answers that anyone who reads a little further discovers that the dead do not stay dead. The lack of personal involvement gives the exchange the odd tone of one upmanship beginning with the mock "Alas" and its retort. As again in "Death" and "Love 3," sociability is ironically put to use to end sociability.

Serious as it is, the poem is also a word game and a jockeying for position to see which participant can claim to have "last" words. We are seemingly to imagine the debate as something like the exchange of taunts before an epic battle. Christian takes note initially that death has always been troped as such a military figure, possessed of a mighty arm and a sting, so goes the ancient wisdom. Death makes the exchange even more literary by insisting on Christian's belatedness: no one can escape the age-old stories that emblematize the conventional wisdom. Both speakers proceed straightway to the critical juncture of the opening Easter sequence and the storied point at which "Redemption" concludes. Death may not be anything in itself, but it can be summed up in what it does, and both parties agree that what it does is put a stinging end to life as we see it, as it has to the life of the "king." But their respective stories stop at different places, which is the point of "Death" and the rest of the concluding series. Death can assemble a good deal of evidence, no less than the endings of all mortal stories; what it cannot do is believe in the parables and Revelation.

The escape of conventional wisdom and its reserve of grisly tropes has a joyous side in all Herbert's poems of the end, which remind us that one aspect of metalepsis is the cancellation of just such tropes along with the happier ones. The forward vision of Donne and Herbert extends a little past doomsday, and unlike prophets who herald the millennium, both think of it as their Augustinian colleagues do. They do not expect a reformed world where political and social orders count. In "Death," Herbert combines a similarly taunting address to death with a sense of abrupt break and another hint of the anthem that accompanies it:

> For we do now behold thee gay and glad,
>   As at dooms-day;
> When souls shall wear their new aray,
> And all thy bones with beautie shall be clad.

The vision is not that of a vengeful church triumphant, anymore than the intimacy of "Dooms-day" is. Herbert does not orchestrate a *dies irae* to go with the *requiescat*; instead, he closes with confidence and, compared to Donne, with a notable lack of last-minute anxiety. It is now that we behold death gladly, whether *we* are gay and glad or *death* is. The aesthetic claim for the image is telling, because it implies a further justification of poetic troping:

seeing death as a good citizen, grim-seeming for a few years but then comely, the poet establishes the visionary imagination as the foundation of present composure. In the mind's eye alone he beholds that comely figure, not on the evidence of flesh "being turn'd to dust, and bones to sticks."

The placidity of "Death" implicitly disarms the reckoning, as "Judgement" does explicitly. In the latter poem, Herbert's equanimity is the product not of an imagined gathering in new array or of accumulated merit but of a fully discounted sin and cleared personal record. Replacing with the sacrifice whatever the record holds, the Christian goes virtually imageless to the reckoning. The testament is guaranteed to work as a shield, at the very moment divine wrath is about to impose the logical end of the human chronicle. Wrath never concludes its dreadful business in Donne either, but the prospect of its doing so is awesome enough to make a strong anticipatory link between the summed-up life and commensurate reward or punishment. Those who plan to parade their records in Herbert's "Judgement" may be in for an unpleasant surprise, but the speaker does not threaten them directly. His own tactic is in keeping with his skepticism about works elsewhere. For Donne in "Hymne to God my God" and in the repentant sinner foreseeing doomsday, judgment imposes a logical completion of the earthly phase and a transition to a heavenly one that follows from it; Herbert moves the crucial accounting back to the sacrifice and uses it as his only passport.

That has the effect of making the ending even more decisive and of rendering basically disconnected everything human between Adam and the reception into heaven. The sacrifice could have come any time, since nothing in the unfolding middle demands that it arrive exactly when it does. Neither Michael's version of it in *Paradise Lost* nor Bacon's in his confession argues for either its placement or for the timing of the final judgment that it prepares for. For Milton it represents the second phase of the defeat of Satan's works following (at some distance) Christ's victory in the wilderness. Having dragged the prince of air in chains through all his realm, Christ leaves him confounded, and resumes his seat "at God's right hand, exalted high / Above all names in Heav'n" (12.454–58). He can then bring about the world's dissolution and judge "th' unfaithful dead." His final act gives closure to the directions bad men and good have already taken. The narrative difficulty lies not in the accounting and the break between life as lived and afterlife but simply in the length of time the world goes on "under her own weight groaning, till the day / Appear of respiration to the just" (12.537–40). Milton's choice of "respiration" in place of the "refreshing" of the Authorized Version (Acts 3.19) is telling because it connects the aspiration of things

"God before had shewed by the mouth of his prophets," the inspiriting of life in Adam at the beginning, and the reinspiriting of the end. Thus beginning, evangelizing middle, and ending come to focus in the judgment.

Donne is more explicitly defensive about timing, modeling his concept of it on Peter chastising the impatient. In a sermon on Acts preached to the "Honourable Company of the Virginia Plantation, 13 Nov. 1622" he remarks:

> Beloved, use godly means, and give God his leisure. You cannot beget a son, and tell the mother, I will have this son born within five months; nor, when he is born, say, you will have him past danger of wardship within five years. You cannot sow your corn today, and say it shall be above ground tomorrow, and in my barn next week. How soon the best husbandman, sowed the best seed in the best ground? God cast the promise of a Messiah, as the seed of all, in paradise, *in semine mulieris*; the seed of the woman shall bruise the serpent's head; and yet this plant was four thousand years after before it appeared; this Messiah four thousand years before he came. God showed the ground where that should grow, two thousand years after the promise; in Abraham's family; *in semine tuo*, in thy seed all nations shall be blessed. God hedged in this ground almost one thousand years after that; in Micheas' time, *et tu Bethlem*, thou Bethlem shalt be the place; and God watered that, and weeded that, refreshed that dry expectation, with a succession of prophets, and it was so long before this expectation of nations, this Messiah came. (*Four Sermons* 16–19)

The elaboration could go on indefinitely, but the answer is obvious immediately: patience is required both in expectations of paradise and in plantation founding.

By removing at the threshold of judgment the review of the middle period, thereby deleting personal achievements and disconnecting the world's life span from any conclusion derivable from it, Herbert compounds the problems of waiting. Nothing preceding the thrusting forward of the testaments matters except the establishment in history of the new covenant. The discontinuity between history and the end is somewhat concealed in "Death" and "Dooms-day" by the familiarity Herbert gives them. If dying and a pillow of dust are the same as sleeping and a pillow of down, the transition seems routine. Even the awakening at doomsday is like arising to greet any day:

> Come away,
>   Make no delay.
> Summon all the dust to rise,
> Till it stirre, and rubbe the eyes;
> While this member jogs the other,
> Each one whispring, *Live you brother?*

The transition from sleep to eternal life is governed by the psychology and the idiom of companions in a dormitory or a workhouse preparing to go forth. Or so it would be except that in place of "wake you" comes the quite different "live you." Nothing from within the midst dictates the timing or the nature of the end; and as the appeal proceeds, the immanent moment itself draws off. The last two stanzas come to a panorama remindful of the specular nature of Revelation but without Revelation's aloofness. Herbert's appeal is for God to stop the disintegration that necessarily comes with extended time:

> Come Away,
>   Thy flock doth stray.
> Some to windes their bodie lend,
> And in them may drown a friend:
> Some in noisome vapours grow
> To a plague and publick wo.

In this vision of dusty formlessness, the "membership" of the bodily church reaches its ultimate diaspora. All things bodily are broken into randomly flying particles and vapors. Having no say in the matter, man is "out of order hurl'd / Parcel'd out to all the world." The vision is still global, but for the time being it produces no replacement for total dissolution. To lyricize doomsday is to realize once again the tribulation—even the panic—of the moment. The outcome is now as close as it gets except for "Love 3," yet the Lord delays and the fear of abandonment encroaches. It is as though having troped the great awakening as a very small one, Herbert is struck by the powerlessness of humankind, which comes up to the moment and finds an indefinite span still remaining. Nothing appears to be of any use except the one bargaining point: the saved will hymn with voices joined in praise. It is odd to find this acute anxiety between the ritual calm of dying and the deflection of judgment, but reasons for it are not far to seek in the discontinuity between middle and end that "Judgement" uses to guarantee the safe passage of the sinner. Doomsday brings to a crisis what has been the recurrent testing of all special calendar days by the limited perspectives of speakers not yet gathered into a final sainthood. To be so gathered they must break with whatever it is they have become in their segments of the historical story.

The function of scripture and of the poem "Heaven" is to find a bridge other than the continuation of the sinful self. In Herbert's shortened arrangement, Heaven immediately follows "Judgement" and hell is omitted. I have considered the dynamics of human and heavenly voicing in "Heaven" elsewhere (*Pastoral* 133–35), but it is pertinent here to note the linking capacity that Herbert finds for it, in part as the dramatizing of what "Judgement" describes as the intercession of the testaments. The entire, seemingly impossible matter of connection without a moral logic—passing through works to reward—is here recast as the throwing out of human words and rebounding alterations of them. The result is a troping of secular poetry (a pastoral convention) and of dead or dying commonplaces and an ultimate transumption that passes from concrete image to nonspecular abstraction. The first echo establishes a personified power that undertakes the answering role in a kind of catechismic exchange. That correcting "I," the spirit of the scriptural leaves, fills in terms of the new lease that the speaker of "Redemption" has sought and completes the pattern of "H. Scriptures 2." Each answer contains a similitude and a cancellation in the manner of the Son/sun likeness and the dissimilarity of "Our Life is Hid," as words are issued, revised, and discarded by the answers.

This forceful cancellation enables Herbert to avoid the trap that P. S. Weibly (6–7) and Janis Lull (*The Poem in Time* 134–36) see in the use of almost the speaker's very words for the celestial responses. Heaven seizes upon the body of those words, but until the speaker himself is coached into anticipating better answers, it undoes the expectations housed in them. It thereby applies pressure to the speaker's biographical progress and its implied narcissism. In answer to the question "do we really ever get beyond a distorted version of our own voices" and to the possibility that "reading the Bible may not help readers to accommodate their egos to God's will, but only to assimilate the holy text to their own wills" (Lull), "Heaven" thus allows the reply that the best guarantees against self-concern are celestial corrections, seizing the dialectical initiative somewhat in the pattern of "Love 3." Human motives and vocal similarity must carry over or there could be no dialogue, but omniscience bears down on the questioner with a new perspective. Heaven's puns on the speaker's words carry from one semantic field to another barely in contact with it. The answers thus collaborate in the making of the poem, as "Deniall" and "A true Hymne" have hoped that some such divine voice might.

In the light, joy, and the leisure that lasts forever, the vocabulary that the celestial voice supplies is liberated from all but the barest traces of sense. The first of these terms deletes the cycles of the sun and the second the vacillations of emotion that attend historical ups and downs. The last fulfills the promise of "Peace" and of proleptic Sundays and reinscribes the individual beneficiary of leisure in the collective pattern of the ultimate leisure class, the saints. In making a ritualized game of it, the poem signals the triumph of a kind of lyric moment different from any that *The Church* has heretofore allowed. The antagonism of "Hope" and of the impatience poems is completely absent, and the anxieties of "Doomsday" are also left behind. Previous exchanges have been stationed at a measured distance from heaven; following death, doomsday, and judgment, Herbert can now approach nearer, and "Love 3" can proceed to open the door and invite the soul in. It is also true that such terms as light and joy describe heaven only minimally and that whatever Herbert's intent, the answering voice, to the reader, is as much the poet's doing as the questioning one. But neither voice is troubled, and every question, however mistaken in going forth, comes back in scriptural paraphrase. "Heaven" thus answers several of *The Church*'s questions about vocation and reward and manages a closure matched only by "Love 3" and the prayer-book coda.

Love and the Personal Record of Sin

"Love 3" is the poem featured in several approaches to Herbert, and obviously must be so as well in any exploration of the interplay of lyric and implied narrative. I have referred to it in several places, primarily in reading other poems as gestures toward it. I would now like to look backward from it, and of course directly at it as well, beginning with a general sense of how it has been situated in other approaches.

Chana Bloch finds in its language a wealth of scriptural echoes (99–102) that establish Herbert's dependence on the Bible—not a hard matter to prove but capable of yielding unexpected benefits and of specifying further the parallelism between the gathering of scriptural verses and the reading of *The Church*. It is a final demonstration of what "Judgement" means by the New Testament as a shield and what "Heaven" means by holy leaves and bliss. Establishing the intertexuality of "Love 3" is thus a way to get at the overall interwoven structure of *The Church*. Diana Benet makes apt use of its implications for service, vocation, and imitation of divine charity and thinks of it partly as a comment on the employment poems (*Secretary* 188–90)—one that allows a climactic wrapping up. So conceived, it comments on the cancellation of sin that disarms divine wrath in "Judgement" and the initiative that the celestial voice seizes from the questioner of "Heaven." Stanley Fish makes it an example of catechism at work, cutting short both questions and answers (*Living Temple* 132), which underscores its dramatic technique and a closure that puts an end to questioning. Rosemond Tuve's devotional Herbert, rather than escaping affliction by passivity or self-annihilation in it, sits and eats as a participant in the chief event of joy. It becomes thereby virtually a delivery of celestial bliss ("George Herbert and *Caritas*" 318), as it is also to Joseph Summers, for whom it offers a satisfying glimpse of the soul's reception into heaven. It is not merely a rite of the earthly church (*George Herbert* 89), a type of recurrent meeting of the human and the divine, but the ending of the story.

Less concerned with its completion of patterns than with its integrity as a lyric, Arnold Stein finds "Love 3" a prime example of Herbert's disciplined control of secular/sacred differences and similarities (194). That concentration on its relatively self-contained effects reminds us that even in isolation it can be a remarkable dramatic lyric, and that too is one of its legitimate uses, albeit not one that Herbert could have anticipated. To Richard Strier (*Love Known* 174) it is a demonstration of the steps by which self-denial becomes self-assertion and thus a companion poem to "The Holdfast," except that it emphasizes the more positive side of Genevan theology. Addressing its doctrine more basically, Anne Williams makes it a poem of and about accommodation. Indeed "Heaven" and several other poems could be said to be so, since the problem of finding a language that can reach from omniscience to mortal understanding is almost universal. In dramatizing that problem, Love's coaxing forth of the reluctant soul recapitulates a progressive revelation of divinity, which was once climaxed in history in the Incarnation and is reconstructed in parable form here. So read, the poem becomes an "embodiment of the multiple implications of a single term" (Williams 19). As I suggested, however, the problem of accommodation is involved in nearly all religious poetry, and divine/human relations are a prime subject of scripture and theology as well, not to mention the chief business of the church. What remains to be seen in this case is the effect of a language that carries so much social bargaining and sexual innuendo. Style and tone need to be more prominent in our assessment than Williams makes them, as does the strain on any metaphoric system when it is adopted to such a purpose.

Despite their obvious differences, good use can be made of these quite different approaches to "Love 3." They identify several functions that Herbert gives the poem in seeking to overcome the lack of connection between temporal and eternal life and the disappointments both of the absent god and the futility of human effort that *The Church* has chronicled. The poem reinscribes scattered scriptures in a final directive to bliss and substitutes communion for the initial altar. It is an Everyone parable to finish the implications of "Redemption," a solution to the problem of rewarded service, and much more. Herbert has prepared us in any number of poems to call its appealing figure "love." The abstraction of the title allows features of love to be collected from around *The Church* and compressed into the "one who bore the blame," which again signals the key event of the historical story and thus foretells its end. The church too is compressed into a ritual communion, changed to a banquet at which one sits rather than kneels (Williams 18). In short, a good deal of society, the church, and history converges in this model enactment. What does not make it through to the end is the self-concern that throughout *The Church* has been entangled in excessive egoism. Self-sacrifice separates Herbert not only from Donne but also from subsequent developments in lyric that Herbert in many ways foreshadows. Some of the demands of the self could be satisfied by a change of career, speakers have felt earlier, if one's domain widened to include the ways of learning, honor, and pleasure. The ego is constructed out of lesser triumphs in such fields of action. But something like "Yet I Love thee" or "Let me not love thee if I love thee not" has always blocked the way from the church to the academy or the court. The narratives that set the alternatives and attempt to renegotiate new leases give way to the master parable that Love constructs of the encounter. Counter motions are here reduced to the hesitant gestures of a not-fully-convinced sinner and his detouring motives. His reservations are basically those of anyone who is not yet fully present at the sacrifice and atonement.

Both the union of sinner and love and this reluctance have Donne as a forerunner in parabolic lyrics and small dramas, although Herbert's is again quite different. In "Goodfriday, 1613. Riding Westward," "Hymne to God my God, in my sicknesse," and "A Hymne to God the Father," Donne attempts to salvage both the poet's personality and his vocation. This is especially true of "A Hymne" with its litany of sins to be forgiven. The puns on "done" bring the full proper name and all its sins to a threshold similar to Herbert's threshold:

> Wilt thou forgive that sinne where I begunne,
>   Which is my sin, though it were done before?
> Wilt thou forgive those sinnes through which I runne,
>   And doe them still: though still I doe deplore?
>   When thou has done, thou hast not done,
>   For, I have more.

For Donne, the ego cannot fail to claim its sins because it has reveled in them and built them into a sense of self that comes from an active life of transgressions. Yet if sins were the *entire* self, they could not be renounced without total self-destruction. The difficulty is that even the currently expostulating Donne cannot totally eradicate them, and so they must be claimed and forgiven by God. The chief sin is that of fear (fear of perishing "on the shore"), and it can be quieted only by God's oath that the "Sunne / Shall shine as it shines now, and heretofore." Adding that to the accounting is to have Donne himself, sins and all.

Herbert does not proffer a detailed biography or an accumulated individual story in "Love 3," or for that matter in "Judgement" or "Heaven"; the approach to union with the divine goes by way of the general mending that makes each sinner not just forgivable but already forgiven. In "Goodfriday, 1613" Donne approaches such forgiveness cautiously, postponing the actual union with God until a small, pre-apocalyptic fire can be applied to him personally and his image can thereby be adjusted:

> O Saviour, as thou hang'st upon the tree;
> I turne my backe to thee, but to receive
> Corrections, till thy mercies bid thee leave.
> O thinke mee worth thine anger, punish mee,
> Burne off my rusts, and my deformity,
> Restore thine Image, so much, by thy grace,
> That thou may'st know mee, and I'll turne my face.

If in Donne's secular love poems the lovers possess a mutual world ("each hath one and is one"), he goes to the opposite extreme here in speaking as one who does not dare to present himself as he is. In effect, his soul too draws back guilty of dust and sin, but it is a soul distracted by the specific "westward" business of the speaker. The "I" who would be made known in the personal face cannot finally be that business-minded self, yet to begin with the reclaimed image of the creator would be to possess no personal history or *littera gesta*. It would be equivalent to removing "Donne" from the hymn, skipping Old Testament preparation, and going directly to the final moments of the greater story. But for Donne, the narratives of self and of history must go the lengthy way of adamic waste: no human way can go directly eastward. Memory's turning back to gaze on the divine image brings only a distant and reserved participation, which has been so far—at the moment of writing—a matter of meditation only. Tension thus persists between the Christocentric model with its emblems and metaphors (sun, cross, Father, Son) and this westward dispersal of energies that defines one's personal career. Self-making is defined as wayward truancy, and conformity as the divine image.

Donne's reviews of the personal record are not always this anxious, which is a reason not to assume that every speaker in Donne, any more than in Herbert, represents a personal conviction. His calm is surprisingly Herbert-esque in "Hymne to God my God, in my sicknesse," yet even here the autobiographical elements are far more prominent than in Herbert's encounters at the threshold. Tuning the instrument at the door prepares for the poet's blending into the heavenly choir—obviously a more pleasant form of preparation than burning off deformity and closer to the preparation that Herbert imagines. Donne keys anticipation to the soul's jubilee, glimpses the holy company, and balances the two states carefully—the permanent one to come and the current movement toward it. As a tuning at the door, meditation is a way not only to estimate and make plans but to gather enthusiasm out of the circumstances of one's very personal dying. Death is the cost, hence the urgency of "*must* do" and "think *now*," as the mind balances the present it knows against the future that it can only anticipate.

As I suggested, Herbert's tuning at heaven's door in "Love 3" renders unnecessary any particularized accounting, although judgment still hovers in the vicinity in "let my shame / Go where it doth deserve." Where Donne in "Hymn to God the Father" plays upon his own name and counts more and more sins for a score-keeping God, Herbert's invited guest is hypothetical; the "I" and the "mine" are grammatical devices to set the case. The fact that personal history makes him unworthy has no bearing finally on his eligibility, merely upon his concept of it. The touch-and-go relations of sonneteers to Cupid and to the beloved Herbert transforms into profound self-doubt:

> Love bade me welcome: yet my soul drew back,
>   Guiltie of dust and sinne.
> But quick-ey'd Love, observing me grow slack
>   From my first entrance in,
> Drew nearer to me, sweetly questioning,
>   If I lack'd any thing.

Besides filling out a pattern of hesitancies similar to Donne's, the speaker's reluctance gathers up other grounds for timidity from the realm of secular protocol. The grounds range from Wyatt's lovers in treacherous courtly situations to Jonson prudently offering reasons for not writing of love. In a single, brief gesture of withdrawal, Herbert thus crosses Christian realism with a considerable legacy on the decorum of courtship. The latter I'll return to in a moment; the former is inherent in history since Adam, based as it is on the universality of sin. It initiates the follow-up tactics of Love's sweet questioning and answering that constitute the body of the poem. That part of the encounter brings forward the often-intimate relations of YHWH to Adam's descendants, who in speaking with God in closeted situations are coaxed out of their fear (and sometimes their resentment) by a solicitous friend. Although that deity can also turn angry, *this* one is, of course, the New Testament variant, who comes after the atonement. But the personal touch of the Yahwist texts remains, embodied in the gesture and the psychology of the fearful speaker, bred into the very genes of an often-chastised humanity. In its New Testament phase, this divine voice also maintains the desire to conduct and teach that "The Pearl" discovers in the parables. It thus goes not only back to YHWH in Eden but forward to the post-apocalyptic calm of the final reception.

In both its courtly manner and its recapitulation of scriptural encounters, "Love 3" draws on Herbert's carefully constructed context by finishing echoing patterns, particularly of poems that have gone through less certain negotiations engineered by their speakers. Such poems have planted the potentially concluding effects of love amid situations not yet ready for them. The stages by which "dust and sin" are now canceled are reduced to a model few, which no longer have use for the patience, faith, and hope that have provided earlier wisdom statements. Thanks to the dramatic economy and its plain, socially laden idiom, "Love 3" makes of these echoes something other than a self-contained and detached ritual. As an imaginative fiction thus entangled in a web of cross-references, it underscores *The Church*'s unique standing as something different from a psalter or elaborate defense of doctrine. It is not precisely a scriptural commentary either and makes such antecedents as the gift of manna in the wilderness very distant foreshadowings at best.

As part of its location in literary history, it not only keeps some distance from the language of the psalter but comments on other love literature. In curing the impotence of the reluctant lover, the opposite of a roused and frustrated sonneteer, for instance, it reverses the usual patterns of courtship. The speaker's shame is less specific and more encompassing than that of the conventional lyricist, where love's glance makes its first entry into the vulnerable heart through the eye. (In Wyatt's poem "The Long Love" shame springs from the lover's "bold pretence" in coming forward, and once the lady reacts, it forces a retreat to the concealed heart, one of the traditional secretive places that shame "doth deserve.") The eye here first betrays a guilty "look" and then serves as the instrument of forgiveness. Where Herbert's unscolded speaker would go if he were in fact allowed to withdraw is open to speculation, but anyone who joins the communion must abandon the harbored heart, vanity's hideaway throughout *The Church*. As the expression of love, the god who serves himself as a "favor" (from the same Greek root that yields "charisma," a divinely conferred gift or power, and "eucharist," a divine feast) for the first time among his many appearances in *The Church* appears to withhold nothing. Strier appropriately cites "Dialogue" as a parallel that bears upon Love's motives in that unreserved gift (80–82). The speaker there as well "can see no merit, / Leading to this favour" or find a reason for its being offered. "Love 3" puts the poet under no obligation to respond in kind and indeed stops every response, which is a preliminary to the unconditional gift. In that respect, it provides an answer to several complaints, particularly in "Affliction 1." The vocational concern must be put away, although it persists until "My deare, then I will serve," the dying echo of a chorus of protests from around *The Church*.

The bearing of the poem on postponement and the relation of *The Church* to the church is implicit in this: for the moment at least, it cancels the anxiety of waiting and replaces the would-be servant with the received soul. We can now see more positively why Herbert sacrifices the lesser satisfactions of science, society, and pleasure in collecting everything into basically two eschatological points of rest foreshadowed by "Yet I love thee": the story's end, which redefines the historical and natural world, and sacramental reenactments of divine presence. To reach those ends, the soul of Everyone must accept the sacrifice. The chief task of that acceptance is to overcome not sin—since sin cannot be defeated by anyone—but doubt of the sacrifice's efficacy. "Love 3" is a demonstration of how the soul is to do that after its many holding actions. Herbert brings forward competing ambitions only to set them aside; he stifles the complaints of the affliction poems by the generosity of the host; and he has the soul find complete peace and freedom from conflict in the act of submission. The worldly knowledge of the more sophisticated and accomplished personas Love transforms into social adeptness, used to better ends than it normally is.

As Arnold Stein suggests in finding a concealed pun on the "perfect host" and as Michael Schoenfeldt argues at greater length, the etiquette of the transaction contrasts sacramental to social terms, and I want to turn to that aspect of Herbert's accommodation as another culmination of *The Church*'s language of "abuse." The radical crossing of idioms mixes literalism with anagogy, not as levels in a tiered allegory but as similitudes in contact with everyday experience. The collapsing of levels has the effect of reinstating under special conditions some of the lost civil life that Herbert's commitment to the church has sacrificed in poems such as "Redemption" and "The Quip." Ordinarily, love is not love unless it is also social and sexual. But Herbert can now answer the "lullings and relishes" and "propositions of hot bloud and brains" with a "quick-ey'd Love" that takes command of desire's devices. As Schoenfeldt suggests, "The power of the poem . . . lies in its ability to manifest its strenuous piety through the complex politics of Renaissance hierarchical relationships" ("Standing" 116). Whether specifically political or generally social, Herbert's language is implicitly hierarchical, and in its usual settings such language is an instrument of a quite different kind of negotiation that he can exploit for its ironies.

Manners show in the hesitant approach, the soul's equivalent to impropriety that makes it feel as though dust and sin were as mud on the shoes. In buttressing the case for the poem's social idiom, Schoenfeldt also draws upon manuals of conduct (125), which were developed to handle discrepancies in power that a deferential manner could both acknowledge and defuse. Such sensitivity to protocol we normally associate more with Spenser, Sidney, Shakespeare, Donne, and Jonson than with Herbert, but "Love 3" shows that he too has a keen perception of how one is "honored," particularly by the prince of princes. The implicit question—it is more nearly explicit in "The Pearl" and elsewhere—is why expend one's spirit in patronage situations when divine love is so solicitous? If omniscience makes Baconian enterprise suspect in the ways of learning, true love does the same for the ways of honor and pleasure.

The speaker's impotence compounds the sexual side of that preempted language of courtship, and indeed sexuality and courtly protocol are often figures for each other in the secular lyric that Herbert is reflecting. Gendered courtship is enough like hierarchical courtship that the poet can use the image of man pursing woman to suggest the courtier pursuing patronage. In "The Pearl" the expenditure of spirit in courtly striving closely parallels the pursuits of the flesh. The ways of pleasure extract a heavy cost in spirit, and the ways of honor are thoroughly compromised by "quick returns of courtesie and wit," thanks to which

> glorie swells the heart, and moldeth it
> To all expressions both of hand and eye,
> Which on the world a true-love-knot may tie,
> And bear the bundle, wheresoe're it goes.

In "Love 3" Herbert goes a step further. Love must coax out of the soul and egoism that lurks even in self-denial and in retrospect may be found in the supreme confidence of the master of all scenes in "The Pearl," despite his gestures of humility. Herbert capitalizes on the nuances of plain-style quips throughout *The Church* for ends not inherently theirs. His personas debate with God and with themselves in a language permeated with subservience. Extracted from *The Church,* that idiom of status and place would make up a detailed set of measurements for injury and slight, proposed advancements, and ego salvaged from the imagined indignities of subordination. "Love 3" can now shed new light on those sessions of imperfect self-monitoring and their edging toward better contracts. All the business left unfinished by "Your suit is granted" can be summed up in the speaker's discovery at last of the reply, which is actually not so much a reply as an act of participatory gratitude properly set up by the purging of doubts and hesitations.

The byways of egoism nonetheless remain a stubborn part of the soul's progress. Without the idiom of rival pursuits, there would be no way to talk about an otherwise unthinkable divine/human relation, which has only biblical precedents and no exact match in secular lyric genres. Negotiating poems such as "Heaven" and "Love 3" build their echoing likenesses amid vast differences, as those between the issuing words and the celestial replacements in "Heaven." The value of any likeness must be granted if the enterprise of writing or calling forth is not to collapse altogether; but catachresis remains the figure of the moment and decorum is unquestionably stretched, both by the initial slack entry and what comes back, as in the

terms of the command "You must sit down, sayes Love, and taste my meat."
This particular recasting is especially ironic in its twisting of a banquet term.
Into the one startling word "meat" Herbert compresses the language-abuse
tactics of many poems, the bond and finance levels of "Redemption," for
instance, the miserliness of "The Holdfast," and the confusion of blood and
wine in "The Bunch of Grapes." If Christian hermeneutic is to justify its
sacrifice of a historical Jerusalem to a heavenly city—if the anagogical level is
to replace tropological and literal levels—it must be on the basis of some
similitude. "Meat" places the challenge squarely where the poet finds the
best upward translation, in a literalizing of incarnation. That *kenosis* or
reduction of divine knowledge and power has made possible the realization
of divine love, as it now enables the personal intimacy of received grace. The
human and the divine—not to mention the social and the sexual—join in
meat.

Herbert the poet and Herbert the priest are more nearly parallel at this
particular moment than they often are in *The Church*, which like the
sacramental church collapses historical distance into model enactment. "The
Altar" has foreseen that abridgment of distance, but as I suggested it also
holds out hope for a participatory sacrifice on the part of the poet and his
reformed heart. In between has come an exploration of the many detours of
the psyche, lamenting and rejoicing in alternate moments, twisting and
squirming to hurry God's permanent reception of the soul. If "Love 3" does
not fully answer the problems of an era that must wait until the apocalypse
for Christ's delayed return, and if it does not take up the problems of dissent
or a besieged church, it nonetheless achieves a significant closure of the
simulated personal conflict. It can leave the rest to "The Church Militant."
By implication it retracts the tentatively offered first fruits of "The Dedication"—or reinforces the retraction already planted there in "Yet not mine
neither: for from thee they came, / And must return." The recognition is
now decisive in the speaker's capitulation that only one party can serve "The
churches mysticall repast," which is the property not really of priest or poet
at all but of the spirit of the mystical church.

Conclusions

In summing up sacrifices and computing the rate and price of the pearl,
Herbert offers nothing like what Isaiah-like prophets see from their positions

at a magistrate's side, nothing like the public voice of Milton. "The Church Militant" expects no great betterment through concerted action—through either the word or the sword—although the struggle for a holy empire goes on around the globe. Allan Megill's devaluing of such theological forerunners in the post-Kantian "collapse of historicism" in *Prophets of Extremity* (xiii) is less than compelling in this respect but represents a general tendency to underestimate the crises of other eras and institutions, especially when those institutions seem on the surface as placid as the church of Richard Hooker and George Herbert. Prophets from the beginning were never less than extreme, and when they are reintroduced they increase anxiety over such things as droughts, pestilence, and war by compounding them with divine punishment. They are never invoked to explain business as usual or to encourage halfway measures or to counsel prudence. As Herbert's spiritual conflicts suggest, a crisis is possible whenever anyone matches prophetic promise against experience. By thinning out things indifferent, seventeenth-century eschatology in a great number of theologians and poets attempted to pressure events into becoming divine signs. These and modern totalists have more in common than either group has with its contemporary pragmatists and materialists—as my account of the fundamental differences between Bacon and Herbert has been designed in part to suggest.

Herbert's more notable personas assess the difficulty of subduing human nature in its ambitious self-making and of waiting for the end that substitutes for secular goals. He is not only Donne's heir in that but the predecessor of plain-style poets such as Thomas Hardy and Emily Dickinson with her "hymnody of the attic" (Hollander 233). The literary history that we have been coached to see in repercussive stages from Milton onward could as well include him as spokesman for this worldview, which remains under scrutiny among those who seek alternatives to it all along the track from Dryden to the romantics and postromantics. Admittedly, he is much more limited in range than Milton. His concern with social ills is infrequent and subordinated to the overriding preoccupation with personal sin. He lived much of his life in London and its vicinity and yet observed nothing of it in poetry or prose (as Jonson and Donne did). But he follows labyrinthine turns of mind with great sensitivity and selects genres that allow insight into the recesses of the ego. His craft in doing so, and in locating all moments of note within one *mythos*, gives him special status as the most popular and most emulated poet of the seventeenth century. It would justify our putting him more often beside modern prophets of extremity such as Yeats, Eliot, Stevens, and other postromantics who do not allude directly to him but can be seen working within the heritage he cross-examines so thoroughly and eloquently. Stevens's lifelong search for a substitute supreme fiction acknowledges the attraction of a global story and the modern poet's need to posit one. Like Herbert and like the biblical countering of epic measures that Harold Fisch charts, he frequently deploys collapsing and belittling figures against the stretching grandeur of that supreme fiction. Not even the most integrated of volumes such as Yeats's *Tower* and Stevens's *Transport to Summer* and *Auroras of Autumn* can point toward a generally acknowledged end as Donne and Herbert can, but a logical first step in realizing what they *can* do is to explore what that lack of closure means. In a historicism without genesis and apocalypse, what are the principles of self-making, what are the principles of beginning, duration, and ending that define narrative limits? What are the relations of plain-style realism to sublimity? Our realizing more fully the organizing principles of *The Temple* and its recurrent struggle with stylistic levels and adjustments of limited and omniscient perspectives is a heuristic prelude to our realizing more fully the implications of the alternatives that poems such as *The Prelude* and books such as *The Tower* propose.

It is at least arguable, then, that Herbert—together of course with Donne, Vaughan, Milton, and others—is continuous with the subsequent development of the lyric's inner landscape. In distinguishing Herbert from biblical psalmists, Fisch goes a step further, setting him in the company of Wordsworth and apart from psalmists who are never as far as he is from family, tribe, and people: "The 'I' of the Psalms stands at a great distance from the autonomous ego that figures so largely in European poetry of the nineteenth century and earlier. George Herbert in the seventeenth century took a deep imprint from the dialogic poetry of the Psalter—more so it sometimes seems than any other Western poet of his time or since. . . . Nevertheless, Herbert presents himself to us as a *person*: we see him as a priest going about his duties, we see him as a poet sitting at his desk" blotting what he has begun (Fisch 113). Such a poet is closer to Puritan diarists than one might suspect from Herbert's sacramental and ceremonial side. Although Herbert would himself quite properly deny any such connection, it is nonetheless true that he is "autobiographical in a way that the psalmists never are" (Fisch 113). His "hymnody of the rectory" (Hollander 233) and colloquial precision tap into an emotional and spiritual plausibility that enlivens all his allusions to and borrowings from the two bibles and the lyric tradition.

As Fisch recognizes, this self-scrutiny is in part owed to "the conviction that the individual soul is the supreme locus of the religious life. There and there alone the signs of Grace and Justification are to be sought." Because of this solitude within the solidarity of the church, it is but a step to "the lonely leech-gatherer of Wordsworth's poetry. That all-important solitude is what gives the lyric voice its pathos, its special resonance and power" (113). The personas of *The Church* seldom speak to anyone other than the divine "friend" except in scenes of temptation and rejection when the merry world comes by clinking its coins. When they speak with special resonance and power, it is to some aspect of divinity or about wrenching departures from everything the secular ego cherishes. In the development of the complex personality of the poet, apart from the formulaic social formulas that in courtly poetry place him in the company of patrons, lovers, and enemies, Herbert thus plays a significant role. In the cancellation of individuality in the last poems of *The Church*—investigating the dangers of romanticized individual feeling that Rosemond Tuve finds him warning us against—he is without peer even in Donne.

If finding an idiom for that many-sided exploration of ego is perhaps his best gift to the lyric, however, it is accompanied by a parabolic lifting of self into types. These types may rise first out of psychology, but they end among scriptural commonplaces. The intricate mapping of the inner world is thus only half the point; the other half is the narrative context, and it is this context that modern lyric extremists seek to replace with some other gathering and connecting principle—Yeats with his vast cycles and gyres, Stevens with his concept of perpetual motion played out in recurrent tropes and fictions. In this regard, nothing could ring truer than the reluctance of the embarrassed sinner of "Love 3" and the kindly coaxing of the host. Whether we project that encouter all the way to the gates of heaven or leave it in the study of the fiction-maker (as Fisch seems inclined to do), its tracing of the inner shape of desire—of the soul afraid of its own forwardness and ashamed of its past—it composes a lyric drama of surprising dimension.

My sense of it has been that what Herbert requires of our criticism is an assessment of self-imposed limits amid scientific, intellectual, and religious alternatives that the seventeenth century was only beginning to explore. As a poet he has but intermittent concern for the governing apparatus of institutions, even of the church. As a member of Parliament, he knew something of the operations of the Virginia Company and the French and English pillaging of the colonies ("*The Church Militant*" 247–52). Yet none of this caused him to question the basic collaboration between bishops and kings or the fundamental connection of all phenomena to the unfolding panorama that he encapsulates in poems such as "Easter-wings" and "The World." For him Jerusalem is less a combined temple and capital city than it is for many; the

Lord of power and vengeance who dominates Hebrew political thought scarcely figures in his poetry, as such a Lord did more and more in contemporary concepts of the Christian prince. When he refers to the "Lord of power," it is to register personal reactions to an active providence and to counterbalance him with the "Lord of love." The final word of course goes to the latter side of deity as the best guide to the mending soul.

While recognizing that sensitivity to the unreliable heart is in large part what distinguishes him as a poet, we note his exclusion not only of materials from the more historically embedded Bible but from Donne, Sidney, and Jonson. Some of his choices constitute handicaps to any attempt to propose a Herbert with strong interests outside the church. But he is recurrently aware of what his dominant commitment means and draws upon the linguistic resources of the social and scientific arenas to define it. His narrowing of interests to divinity is not a handicap to our identifying the personal imprint he leaves on the materials he gathers. His intensity and concentration are owed to the focus that comes of acknowledged and carefully weighed exclusions.

Beyond this, his retreat from the natural world and from the social interests of his predecessors and contemporaries makes a timely historical statement. It separates the language of secular titles in a prevailing poetry of patronage from the preeminent claim of the one Lord. If Milton dismantles and reconstructs analogies between the social and secular hierarchies more energetically, Herbert works effectively at them also. His denial of secular obligations comes with an urge for an end that cancels any service the soul might use to earn its way. It is unusual for either Anglicans or separatists to move so exclusively into the sacred book and individual heart, yet as I suggested at the outset, we should not imagine Herbert's removal being decisively accomplished; it is a subject of recurrent struggle, enacted as one of perhaps two of the most problematic strategies in his construction of a special arena for poetry, the other being the binding of church, Bible, and book of poems to the sacrifice. Poetry occupies a distinct realm self-consciously perceptive of the jagged edge between aesthetic, historical, and divine matters. It has secular roots as well as biblical ones, but it subordinates nature, society, and historical types to the mystical church and the antitype who emerges finally as love. It exercises a prerogative to point beyond history to the anagogic level of that figure's "kingdom."

Such metaphoric maneuvering is complicated by the fact that, as Kenneth Burke remarks, "human speech can have no positive terms for the supernatural order, all expressions for this order necessarily being borrowed from our terms for [three other] orders: the natural, the social, and the linguistic" ("On Covery" 225). This is the reason that "divinity has been traditionally equated with just about everything in the way of imagery" (226), from royalty to shepherdom, from seedtime to harvest. So entangled are politics, the language of courtship, religion, nationalism, and contemporary confusions of king, bishop, and Providence that it is impossible to talk of one without implicating the others. Herbert's main models for exploiting that confusion— Spenser, Sidney, Shakespeare, Greville, Donne, and Jonson—operate nearer the borders of social, natural, and religious symbolism. Bacon and Milton try to decide what to make of an active humanistic burden, Milton by assigning the poet missions within a volatile society; Herbert has mainly to arrange the heart's receptiveness to Love's invitation and to manage an indefinite historical span by turning the energy of worldly pursuits against itself.

BIBLIOGRAPHY

Abbreviations

ELH	*English Literary History*
ELN	*English Language Notes*
ELR	*English Literary Renaissance*
GHJ	*George Herbert Journal*
HLQ	*Huntington Library Quarterly*
JEGP	*Journal of English and Germanic Philology*
JWCI	*Journal of the Warburg and Courtauld Institutes*
MLN	*Modern Language Notes*
SEL	*Studies in English Literature*
SP	*Studies in Philology*
TLS	*Times Literary Supplement* (London)
UTQ	*University of Toronto Quarterly*

Ainsworth, Henry. *An Apologie of Defense of Brownists.* 1604. Amsterdam: Theatrum Orbis Terrarum Press, 1970.
———. *A True Confession of the Faith.* 1596. Amsterdam: Theatrum Orbis Terrarum Press, 1969.
Alexander, Paul J. *The Byzantine Apocalyptic Tradition.* Ed. Dorth deF. Abrahmse. Berkeley and Los Angeles: University of California Press, 1985.
Alison, Richard. *A Confutation of Brownism.* 1590. Amsterdam: Theatrum Orbis Terrarum Press, 1968.
Alstead, Heinrich. *The Beloved City or, The Saints Reign on Earth a Thousand Years.* William Burton, 1643.
Alter, Robert. *The Art of Biblical Narrative.* New York: Basic Books, 1981.
———. *The Art of Biblical Poetry.* New York: Basic Books, 1985.
Alter, Robert, and Frank Kermode, eds. *The Literary Guide to the Bible.* Cambridge: Harvard University Press, 1987.
Anselment, Raymond A. " 'The Church Militant': George Herbert and the Metamorphoses of Christian History." *HLQ* 41 (1978): 299–316.
Asals, Heather A. R. *Equivocal Predication: George Herbert's Way to God.* Toronto: University of Toronto Press, 1981.
Augustine. *On Christian Doctrine.* Trans. D. W. Robertson, Jr. Indianapolis: Bobbs-Merrill, 1988.

Bacon, Francis. *The Advancement of Learning*. Ed. G. W. Kitchin. London: Dent, 1915.
——. *The New Organ*. Ed. Fulton H. Anderson. Indianapolis: Bobbs-Merrill, 1960.
——. *A Selection of His Works*. Ed. Sidney Warhaft. Indianapolis: Bobbs-Merrill, 1978.
——. *The Works*. 1857–59. Ed. James Spedding, R. L. Ellis, and Douglas D. Heath. 7 vols. London, 1883.
Balke, William. *Calvin and the Anabaptist Radicals*. Trans. William J. Heynen. Grand Rapids, Mich.: William B. Eerdmans, 1981.
Ball, Bryan W. *A Great Expectation: Eschatological Thought in English Protestantism to 1660*. Leiden, The Netherlands: E. J. Brill, 1975.
Bangs, Carl. *Arminius: A Study in the Dutch Reformation*. 1971. Grand Rapids, Mich.: Francis Asbury Press, 1985.
Barlow, William. *The Conference at Hampton Court*. 1604. Amsterdam: Theatrum Orbis Terrarum Press, 1975.
Barnes, Robin Bruce. *Prophecy and Gnosis: Apocalypticism in the Wake of the Lutheran Reformation*. Stanford: Stanford University Press, 1988.
Barrow, Henry, and John Greenwood. *The Writings, 1591–1593*. Ed. Leland H. Carlson. London: George Allen & Unwin, 1970.
Bauckham, Richard. *Tudor Apocalypse: Sixteenth-Century Apocalypticism, Millenarianism and the English Reformation*. Oxford: Sutton Courtenay Press, 1978.
Baughe, Thomas. *The Summons to Judgement*. London, 1614.
Baxter, Richard. *The Autobiography, being the Reliquiae Baxterianae*. London: Dent, 1931.
Bell, Ilona. "Herbert and Harvey: In the Shadow of the Temple." In *Like Season'd Timber*, ed. Edmund Miller and Robert DiYanni, 255–80. New York: Peter Lang, 1987.
——. "Setting Foot into Divinity." In *Essential Articles for the Study of George Herbert's Poetry*, ed. John R. Roberts, 63–83. Hamden, Conn.: Archon Books, 1979.
Benet, Diana. "Herbert's Experience of Politics and Patronage in 1624." *GHJ* 10 (1986/87): 33–45.
——. *Secretary of Praise: The Poetic Vocation of George Herbert*. Columbia: University of Missouri Press, 1984.
Berggren, Douglas. "From Myth to Metaphor." *Monist* 50 (1966): 530–52.
Bernard, Richard. *The Key of Knowledge for the Opening of the Secret Mysteries of Johns Mysticall Revelation*. London, 1617.
Bienz, John. "Herbert's 'Daily Labour': An Eschatological Pattern in 'The Church.' " *GHJ* 12 (1988):1–16.
Bloch, Chana. *Spelling the Word: George Herbert and the Bible*. Berkeley and Los Angeles: University of California Press, 1985.
Bloom, Harold. " 'Before Moses Was, I Am': The Original and the Belated Testament." *Notebooks in Cultural Analysis* 1 (1984): 3–14.
——, ed. *Exodus*. New York: Chelsea House, 1987.
Booty, John E. "George Herbert's *The Temple* and *The Book of Common Prayer*." *Mosaic* 12 (1979): 75–90.
Bowers, Fredson. "Herbert's Sequential Imagery: 'The Temper.' " *Modern Philology* 59 (1962): 202–13.
Brandon, S.G.F. *Jesus and the Zealots: A Study of the Political Factor in Primitive Christianity*. Manchester: Manchester University Press, 1967.

Brightman, Thomas. *A Revelation of the Apocalyps of S. John.* Amsterdam, 1611.
Broughton, Hugh. *A Revelation of the Holy Apocalypse.* 1610.
Browne, Raymond E., ed. *The Jerome Biblical Commentary.* Englewood Cliffs, N.J.: Prentice-Hall, 1968.
Browne, Robert, and Robert Harrison. *The Writings.* Ed. Alpert Peel and Leland H. Carlson. London: George Allen & Unwin, 1953.
Brueggeman, Walter. *Hopeful Imagination: Prophetic Voices in Exile.* Philadelphia: Fortress Press, 1986.
———. *The Message of the Psalms: A Theological Commentary.* Minneapolis: Augsburg Publishing House, 1984.
Bruns, Gerald L. "Canon and Power in the Hebrew Scriptures." *Critical Inquiry* 10 (1984): 462–80.
———. "Midrash and Allegory." In *The Literary Guide to the Bible,* ed. Robert Alter and Frank Kermode, 625–46. Cambridge: Harvard University Press, 1987.
Budick, Sanford, and Geoffrey Hartman, eds. *Midrash and Literature.* New Haven: Yale University Press, 1986.
Bultmann, Rudolf. *The History of the Synoptic Tradition.* Trans. John Marsh. New York: Harper & Row, 1968.
Bunyan, John. *Grace Abounding to the Chief of Sinners.* Ed. Roger Sharrock. Clarendon: Oxford University Press, 1962.
———. *Pilgrim's Progress.* Ed. N. H. Keeble. New York: Oxford University Press, 1984.
Burgess, Walter H. *John Smith, the Se-Baptist: Thomas Helwys and the First Baptist Church in England.* London: James Clarke, 1911.
Burke, Kenneth. *Language as Symbolic Action.* Berkeley and Los Angeles: University of California Press, 1966.
———. "On Covery, Re- and Dis-." *Accent* 13 (1953): 218–26.
———. *The Rhetoric of Religion.* Boston: Beacon, 1961.
Burton, Henry. *The Seven Vials.* London, 1628.
Caldwell, Patricia. *The Puritan Conversion Narrative.* Cambridge: Cambridge University Press, 1983.
Calvin, John. *Calvin's Commentaries: The Acts of the Apostles.* Trans. John W. Fraser. Vol. 2. Grand Rapids, Mich.: William B. Eerdmans, 1966.
———. *Institutes of the Christian Religion.* Ed. John T. McNeil. Philadelphia: Westminster Press, 1960.
Capp, Bernard. "Godly Rule and English Millenarianism." *Past and Present* 52 (1971): 106–17.
Carmichael, Calum M. *Law and Narrative in the Bible.* Ithaca: Cornell University Press, 1985.
Carnes, Valarie. "The Unity of George Herbert's *The Temple*: A Reconsideration." *ELH* 35 (1968): 505–26.
Cartwright, Thomas. *A Christian Letter of Certaine English Protestants.* 1599. Amsterdam: Theatrum Orbis Terrarum Press, 1969.
Charles, Amy M. *A Life of George Herbert.* Ithaca: Cornell University Press, 1977.
Christianson, Paul. *Reformers and Babylon: English Apocalyptic Visions from the Reformation to the Eve of the Civil War.* Toronto: University of Toronto Press, 1978.
Clark, Ira. *Christ Revealed: The History of the Neotypological Lyric in the English Renaissance.* Gainesville: University of Florida Press, 1982.
Cogley, Richard W. "Seventeenth-Century English Millenarianism." *Religion* 17 (1987): 379–96.

Cohn, Norman. *The Pursuit of the Millennium*. Fairlawn, N.J.: Essential Books, 1957.
Cohn, Robert. *The Shape of Sacred Space: Four Biblical Studies*. Chico, Calif.: Scholars Press, 1981.
Collins, John J. *The Apocalyptic Imagination: An Introduction to the Jewish Matrix of Christianity*. New York: Crossroad, 1984.
Collinson, Patrick. *The Religion of Protestants: The Church in English Society 1559–1625*. Clarendon: Oxford University Press, 1982.
Cook, Elizabeth. *Seeing Through Words: The Scope of Late Renaissance Poetry*. New Haven: Yale University Press, 1986.
Coolidge, John S. *The Pauline Renaissance in England: Puritanism and the Bible*. Clarendon: Oxford University Press, 1970.
Cosin, John. *A Collection of Private Devotions*. 1627. Ed. P. G. Stanwood. London: Oxford University Press, 1967.
Cowper, William. *Pathmos; or, A Commentary on the Revelation of S. John*. London, 1619.
Crashaw, Richard. *Steps to the Temple*. In *The Poems*, ed. L. C. Martin. Clarendon: Oxford University Press, 1927.
Cross, Frank Moore. "The Epic Tradition of Early Israel." In *The Poet and the Historian*, Richard Elliott Friedman, 13–40. Chico, Calif.: Scholars Press, 1983.
Damrosch, Leopold. *God's Plot and Man's Stories: Studies in the Fictional Imagination from Milton to Fielding*. Chicago: University of Chicago Press, 1985.
Daniel, Stephen H. "Myth and the Grammar of Discovery in Francis Bacon." *Philosophy and Rhetoric* 15 (1982): 219–37.
Davies, Godfrey. "Arminian versus Puritan in England, ca. 1620–1640." *Huntington Library Bulletin* 5 (1934): 157–79.
Davies, Horton. *Like Angels from a Cloud: The English Metaphysical Preachers 1588–1645*. San Marino, Calif.: Huntington Library Press, 1986.
———. *Worship and Theology in England from Andrewes to Baxter and Fox, 1603–1690*. Princeton: Princeton University Press, 1975.
Davies, J. G. *The Early Christian Church*. New York: Holt, Rinehart & Winston, 1965.
Davis, J. C. *Utopia and the Ideal Society: A Study of English Utopian Writing 1516–1700*, Cambridge: Cambridge University Press, 1981.
Debates in the House of Commons in 1625. Ed. Samuel Rawson Gardiner. London: Camden Society, 1873.
Debus, Allen G. *Man and Nature in the Renaissance*. Cambridge: Cambridge University Press, 1978.
Dent, Arthur. *The Opening of Heaven Gates, or the Ready Way to Everlasting Life*. London, 1610.
———. *The Plaine Mans Path-way to Heaven*. 1601. Amsterdam: Theatrum Orbis Terrarum Press, 1974.
Di Cesare, Mario A. "God's Silence: On Herbert's 'Deniall.' " *GHJ* (1986/87): 85–102.
Dickson, Donald R. *The Fountain of Living Waters: The Typology of the Waters of Life in Herbert, Vaughan, and Traherne*. Columbia: University of Missouri Press, 1987.
Donne, John. *The Complete Poetry*. Ed. John T. Shawcross. Garden City, N.J.: 1967.
———. *The Divine Poems*. Ed. Helen Gardner. Clarendon: Oxford University Press, 1952.

——. *Four Sermons upon Special Occasions*. Ed. Thomas Jones. London, 1624.

——. *Selected Prose*. Ed. Neil Rhodes. New York: Viking Penguin, 1987.

——. *The Sermons*. Ed. George R. Potter and Evelyn M. Simpson. Berkeley and Los Angeles: University of California Press, 1962.

Draxe, Thomas. *An Alarum to the Last Judgment*. London, 1615.

Dyson, A. E., and Julian Lovelock. "Herbert's 'Redemption,' " In *Masterful Images: English Poetry from Metaphysicals to Romantics*, 29–35. London: Macmillan, 1976.

Eiselen, Frederick Carl, ed. *The Abingdon Bible Commentary*. New York: Doubleday, 1929.

Elsky, Martin. "George Herbert's Pattern Poems and the Materiality of Languages: A New Approach to Renaissance Hieroglyphics." *ELH* 50 (1983): 245–60.

——. "History, Liturgy, and Point of View in Protestant Meditative Poetry." *SP* 77 (1980): 67–83.

——. "The Sacramental Frame of George Herbert's 'The Church' and the Shape of Spiritual Autobiography." *JEGP* 83 (1984): 313–29.

Empson, William. *Seven Types of Ambiguity*. New York: Meridian Books, 1957.

Endicott (Paterson), Annabel. "The Structure of Herbert's *Temple*." *UTQ* 34 (1965): 226–37.

Ferguson, Arthur B. *Clio Unbound: Perception of the Social and Cultural Past in Renaissance England*. Durham, N.C.: Duke University Press, 1979.

Finch, Sir Henry. *The Worlds Great Restauration, or the Calling of the Jewes*. London, 1621.

Finlayson, Michael G. *Historians, Puritanism, and the English Revolution*. Toronto: University of Toronto Press, 1983.

Firth, Katharine R. *The Apocalyptic Tradition in Reformation Britain, 1530–1645*. Oxford: Oxford University Press, 1979.

Fisch, Harold. *Poetry with a Purpose: Biblical Poetics and Interpretation*. Bloomington: Indiana University Press, 1988.

Fish, Stanley. "Letting Go: The Dialectic of Self in Herbert's Poetry." In *Self-Consuming Artifacts*, 156–223. Berkeley and Los Angeles: University of California Press, 1972.

——. *The Living Temple: George Herbert and Catechizing*. Berkeley and Los Angeles: University of California Press, 1978.

Ford, Brewster. "George Herbert and Liturgies of Time and Space." *South Atlantic Review* 49 (1984): 19–29.

Freeman, Rosemary. *English Emblem Books*. London: Chatto & Windus, 1948.

Freer, Coburn. *Music for a King*. Baltimore: Johns Hopkins University Press, 1972.

Frei, Hans W. *The Eclipse of Biblical Narrative: A Study in Eighteenth and Nineteenth Century Hermeneutics*. New Haven: Yale University Press, 1974.

Friedman, Richard Elliott. *The Exile and Biblical Narrative*. Chico, Calif.: Scholars Press, 1981.

——. *Who Wrote the Bible?* New York: Summit Books, 1987.

Frye, Northrop. "Approaching the Lyric." In *Lyric Poetry: Beyond New Criticism*, Chaviva Hosek and Patricia Parker, 31–37. Ithaca: Cornell University Press, 1985.

——. *The Great Code: The Bible and Literature*. New York: Harcourt Brace Jovanovich, 1983.

Fuller, Thomas. *The Church-History of Britain*. London, 1655.

Gardiner, Samuel R. *History of England from the Accession of James I to the Outbreak of the Civil War, 1603–1642*. 10 vols. Vol. 4, 1621–1623. London: Longmans, Green, 1883.

Gardner, Helen, ed. Appendix G to *John Donne, The Divine Poems*, 130–47. Clarendon: Oxford University Press, 1952.

George, Charles H., and Katherine George. *The Protestant Mind of the English Reformation*. Princeton: Princeton University Press, 1961.

George, Timothy. *John Robinson and the English Separatist Tradition*. Macon, Ga.: Mercer University Press, 1982.

Gerrish, B. A. *Grace and Reason: A Study in the Theology of Luther*. London: Oxford University Press, 1962.

Geveren, Sheltoo. *Of the End of This Worlde, and Second Coming of Christ*. London, 1589.

Gifford, George. *Sermons upon the Whole Book of Revelation*. London, 1596.

Gilman, Ernest B. "The Pauline Perspectives in Donne, Herbert, and Greville." In *The Curious Perspective*, 167–302. New Haven: Yale University Press, 1978.

Goldberg, Jonathan. "Herbert's 'Decay' and the Articulation of History." *Southern Review* 18 (1985): 1–21.

Goldberg, Michael. *Jews and Christians: Getting Our Stories Straight*. Nashville: Abingdon Press, 1985.

Goldingay, John. *Theological Diversity and the Authority of the Old Testament*. Grand Rapids, Mich.: William B. Eerdmans, 1987.

Goodman, Godfrey. *The Fall of Man, or the Corruption of Nature*. London, 1616.

Gottlieb, Sidney. "Herbert's Case of 'Conscience': Public or Private Poem?" *SEL* 25 (1985): 109–26.

———. "The Social and Political Backgrounds of George Herbert's Poetry." In *"The Muses Common-weale,"* ed. Claude J. Summers and Ted-Larry Pebworth, 107–18. Columbia: University of Missouri Press, 1988.

Grenfield, Nathaniel. *A Great Day*. London, 1615.

Greville, Fulke. *Poems and Dramas*. Ed. Geoffrey Bullock. 2 vols. New York: Oxford University Press, 1945.

Guibbory, Achsah. *The Nap of Time: Seventeenth-Century English Literature and the Ideas of Pattern in History*. Chicago: University of Illinois Press, 1986.

Gunkel, Hermann. *The Legends of Genesis*. Trans. W. H. Carruth. New York: Schocken Books, 1970.

Hakewill, George. *An Apologie of the Power and Providence of God in the Government of the World*. Oxford, 1627.

Hanley, Sara W. "Temples in *The Temple*: George Herbert's Study of the Church." *SEL* 8 (1968): 121–35.

Hanson, Paul D. *The Dawn of Apocalyptic*. Philadelphia: Fortress Press, 1975.

Harman, Barbara Leah. *Costly Monuments: Representations of the Self in George Herbert's Poetry*. Cambridge: Harvard University Press, 1982.

———. "Herbert, Coleridge and the Vexed Mark of Narration." *MLN* 93 (1978): 888–911.

Harnack, Andrew. "Both Protestant and Catholic: George Herbert and 'To All Angels and Saints.' " *GHJ* 11 (1987): 23–40.

Harvey, Christopher. *The Complete Poems*. Ed. Alexander B. Grosart. London, 1874. New York: AMS reprint, 1983.

Hastings, Robert. " 'Easter Wings' as a Model of Herbert's Method." *Thoth* 4 (1963): 15–23.

Headley, John M. *Luther's View of Church History*. New Haven: Yale University Press, 1963.

Helwys, Thomas. *Objections Answered.* 1615. Amsterdam: Theatrum Orbis Terrarum Press, 1973.

Herbert, George. *The Bodleian Manuscript of George Herbert's Poems: A Facsimile of Tanner 307.* Introduction by Amy M. Charles and Mario A. Di Cesari. Delmar, N. Y.: Scholars' Facsimiles, 1984.

————. *Complete Works in Verse and Prose.* 1874. Ed. Alexander B. Grosart. 3 vols. New York: AMS Press, 1983.

————. *The Williams Manuscript.* Ed. Amy M. Charles. New York: Scholars' Facsimiles, 1977.

————. *The Works.* Ed. F. E. Hutchinson. Clarendon: Oxford University Press, 1941.

Hill, Christopher. *The Collected Essays.* 3 vols. Amherst: University of Massachusetts Press, 1985–86.

————. *Intellectual Origins of the English Revolution.* Clarendon: Oxford University Press, 1980.

————. *Society and Puritanism in Pre-Revolutionary England.* London: Secker & Warburg, 1964.

————. *The World Turned Upside Down: Radical Ideas during the English Revolution.* New York: Viking Press, 1972.

Hirst, Derek. "Parliament, Law and War in the 1620s." *Historical Journal* 23 (1980): 455–461.

Holifield, E. Brooks. *The Covenant Sealed: The Development of Puritan Sacramental Theology in Old and New England, 1570–1720.* New Haven: Yale University Press, 1974.

Hollander, John. *Vision and Resonance.* 1975. New Haven: Yale University Press, 1985.

Hooker, Richard. *Of the Laws of Ecclesiastical Polity.* London: Dent, 1907.

Hovey, Kenneth Alan. "Church History in 'The Church.' " *GHJ* 6 (1982): 1–14.

————. " 'Diuinitie, and Poesie, Met': The Baconian Context of George Herbert's Divinity." *ELN* 22 (1985): 30–39.

————. "Holy War and Civil Peace: George Herbert's Jacobean Politics." *Explorations in Renaissance Culture* 11 (1985): 112–19.

————. " 'Wheel'd About . . . into *Amen*': 'The Church Militant' on Its Own Terms." *GHJ* 10 (1986/87): 71–84.

Hull, John. *Saint Peters Prophesie of These Last Daies.* London, 1610.

Huntley, Frank L. "George Herbert and the Image of Violent Containment." *GHJ* 8 (1984): 17–27.

James I. *The Workes of the Most High and Mightie Prince, James: A Paraphrase upon the Revelation of the Apostle S. John.* London, 1616.

Jobling, David. *The Sense of Biblical Narrative: Structural Analyses in the Hebrew Bible.* 2 vols. Sheffield: JSOT Press, 1986.

Johnson, Lee Ann. "The Relationship of 'The Church Militant' to *The Temple*." *SP* 68 (1971): 200–206.

Jones, Nicholas R. "Text and Contexts: Two Languages in George Herbert's Poetry." *SP* 79 (1982): 162–76.

Josipovici, Gabriel. "The Epistle to the Hebrews and the Catholic Epistles." In *The Literary Guide to the Bible,* ed. Robert Alter and Frank Kermode, 503–21. Cambridge: Harvard University Press, 1987.

Katz, David S. *Philo-Semitism and the Readmission of the Jews to England 1603–1655.* Clarendon: Oxford University Press, 1982.

Keeble, N. H. *The Literary Culture of Nonconformity in Later Seventeenth-Century England.* Leicester: Leicester University Press, 1987.

Kellison, Matthew. *A Survey of the New Religion*. 1605. London: Scolar Press, 1977.

Kinnamon, Noel. "Notes on the Psalms in Herbert's *The Temple*." *GHJ* 4 (1981): 10–29.

Kittay, Eva Feder. *Metaphor: Its Cognitive Force and Linguistic Structure*. Oxford: Clarendon Press, 1987.

Klause, John L. "George Herbert, *Kenosis*, and the Whole Truth." In *Allegory, Myth, and Symbol*, ed. Morton Bloomfield, 209–25. Cambridge: Harvard University Press, 1981.

Knevet, Ralph. *A Gallery to the Temple*. Ed. Guilano Pellegrini. Pisa: Libreria Goliardica, 1954.

Kronenfeld, Judy Z. "Probing the Relations between Poetry and Ideology: Herbert's 'The Windows.' " *John Donne Journal* 2 (1983): 55–80.

Kugel, James L. *The Idea of Biblical Poetry: Parallelism and Its History*. New Haven: Yale University Press, 1981.

Labriola, Albert C. "The Rock and the Hard Place: Biblical Typology and Herbert's 'The Altar.' " *GHJ* 10 (1986/87): 61–70.

Lamont, William M. *Godly Rule: Politics and Religion, 1603–1660*. London: Macmillan, 1969.

———. "Puritanism as History and Historiography: Some Further Thoughts." *Past and Present* 44 (1969): 133–46.

———. *Richard Baxter and the Millennium*. London: Croom Helm, 1979.

Lang, Bernard, ed. *Anthropological Approaches to the Old Testament*. Philadelphia: Fortress Press, 1975.

Lanham, Richard A. *A Handlist of Rhetorical Terms*. Berkeley and Los Angeles: University of California Press, 1968.

Latourette, Kenneth Scott. *A History of Christianity*. New York: Harper & Brothers, 1953.

Leach, Edmund. "The Logic of Sacrifice." Ed. Bernard Lang. *Anthropological Approaches to the Old Testament*. Philadelphia: Fortress Press, 1985.

Leiter, Louis H. "George Herbert's Anagram." *College English* 26 (1965): 543–44.

Lerner, Laurence. "The Bunch of Grapes." In *An Introduction to English Poetry*, 52–61. London: Edward Arnold, 1975.

Lewalski, Barbara Kiefer. *Protestant Poetics and the Seventeenth-Century Religious Lyric*. Princeton: Princeton University Press, 1979.

Littell, Franklin Hamlin. *The Anabaptist View of the Church*. Boston: Starr King Press, 1958.

Lockyer, Roger. *The Early Stuarts: A Political History of England 1603–1642*. London: Longman, 1989.

Lods, Adolphe. *The Prophets and the Rise of Judaism*. London: Routledge & Kegan Paul, 1937.

Low, Anthony. *Love's Architecture: Devotional Modes in Seventeenth-Century English Poetry*. New York: New York University Press, 1978.

Lull, Janis. "George Herbert's Revisions in 'The Church' and the Carnality of 'Love' (III)." *GHJ* 9 (1985): 1–16.

———. *The Poem in Time: Reading George Herbert's Revisions of The Church*. Newark: University of Delaware Press, 1990.

Luther, Martin. *A Commentary on St. Paul's Epistle to the Galatians*. English translation, 1575. London: James Clark, 1953.

Lynch, Kathleen. "*The Temple*: 'Three Parts Vied and Multiplied.' " *SEL* 29 (1989): 138–55.

Maarsingh, B. *Numbers: A Practical Commentary.* Trans. John Vriend. Grand Rapids, Mich.: William B. Eerdmans, 1987.

McCanles, Michael. "The Dialectical Structure of Metaphysical Lyric: Donne, Herbert, Marvell." In *Dialectical Criticism and Renaissance Literature,* 54–117. Berkeley and Los Angeles: University of California Press, 1975.

McConnell, Frank, ed. *The Bible and the Narrative Tradition.* New York: Oxford University Press, 1986.

McKeon, Michael. *The Origins of the English Novel, 1600–1740.* Baltimore: Johns Hopkins University Press, 1987.

McLaughlin, Elizabeth, and Gail Thomas. "Communion in *The Temple.*" *SEL* 15 (1975): 111–24.

Malcolmson, Cristina. "George Herbert's *Country Parson* and the Character of Social Identity." *SP* 85 (1988): 245–66.

Manley, Frank. "Toward a Definition of Plain Style in the Poetry of George Herbert." In *Poetic Traditions of the English Renaissance,* ed. Maynard Mack and George deForest Lord, 203–17. New Haven: Yale University Press, 1982.

Manning, Brian, ed. *Politics, Religion and the English Civil War.* London: Edward Arnold, 1973.

Marcus, Leah. "George Herbert and the Anglican Plain Style." In *"Too Rich to Clothe the Sunne": Essays on George Herbert,* ed. Claude J. Summers and Ted-Larry Pebworth, 179–194. Pittsburgh: University of Pittsburgh Press, 1978.

Martz, Louis L. *The Poetry of Meditation.* New Haven: Yale University Press, 1954.

Marvell, Andrew. *Marvell's Poems and Letters.* Ed. H. M. Margoliuth. Clarendon: Oxford University Press, 1952.

Mason, Thomas. *A Revelation of the Revelation.* London, 1619.

Matar, N. I. "The Idea of the Restoration of the Jews in English Protestant Thought, 1661–1701." *Harvard Theological Review* 78 (1985): 115–48.

Mazzaro, Jerome. "Donne and Herbert: Stepping through the Mask." In *Like Season'd Timber,* ed. Edmund Miller and Robert DiYanni, 241–54. New York: Peter Lang, 1987.

Mazzeo, Joseph Anthony. *Renaissance and Revolution.* New York: Pantheon Books, 1965.

Mede, Joseph. *The Key of Revelation.* London, 1643.

Megill, Allan. *Prophets of Extremity.* Berkeley and Los Angeles: University of California Press, 1987.

Merkel, Ingrid, and Allen G. Debus, eds. *Hermeticism and the Renaissance.* Washington, D.C.: Folger Shakespeare Library, 1988.

Merrill, Thomas. *Christian Criticism: A Study of Literary God-Talk.* Amsterdam: Rodopi N.V., 1976.

———. "George Herbert's 'Significant Stuttering.' " *GHJ* 11 (1988): 1–18.

Miller, Edmund. *Drudgerie Divine: The Rhetoric of God and Man in George Herbert.* Salzburg: Institute für Anglistik und Amerikanistik, 1979.

Miller, Edmund, and Robert DiYanni, eds. *Like Season'd Timber: New Essays on George Herbert.* New York: Peter Lang, 1987.

Mills, Jerry Leath. "Recent Studies in Herbert." *ELR* 6 (1976): 105–18.

Montagu, Richard. *Appello Caesarem: a Just Appeale from Two Unjust Informers.* 1625. Amsterdam: Theatrum Orbis Terrarum Press, 1972.

de Montenay, Georgette. *Emblemes ou devises christiennes.* 1571. Menston: Scolar Press, 1973.

Moreland, Kim. "The Rooted Flower and the Flower That Glides: An Interpretation of Herbert's 'The Flower.' " *GHJ* 6 (1983): 37–45.

Morillo, Marion. "Herbert's Chairs: Notes to *The Temple.*" *ELN* 11 (1974): 271–75.

Morrison, Peter. "Taking the *H* out of Shame: The Blemished Mirror in La Tour's *Magdalen* and Herbert's 'Easter-Wings.' " *New Orleans Review* 11 (1984): 54–68.

Moulin, Peter. *The Anatomy of Arminianisme.* 1620. Theatrum Orbis Terrarum Press, 1976.

Mulligan, Lotte. "Puritans and English Science: A Critique of Webster." *Isis* 71 (1980): 456–69.

Napeir [Napier], John. *A Plaine Discovery of the Whole Revelation of Saint John.* Edinburgh, 1593.

Napier, Davie. *Song of the Vineyard: A Guide through the Old Testament.* Philadelphia: Fortress Press, 1981.

Neill, Stephen. *The Interpretation of the New Testament, 1861–1961.* London: Oxford University Press, 1964.

Nestrick, William. "George Herbert: The Giver and the Gift." *Ploughshares* 2 (1975): 187–205.

Nicolai, Philipp. *Chronologia Sacra.* Trans. David Forbes. Edinburgh, 1630.

Noth, Martin. *A History of Pentateuchal Traditions.* Trans. Bernhard W. Anderson. Englewood Cliffs, N.J.: Prentice-Hall, 1972.

Novarr, David. *The Making of Walton's Lives.* Ithaca: Cornell University Press, 1958.

Nuttall, A. D. *Overheard by God: Fiction and Prayer in Herbert, Milton, Dante, and St. John.* London: Methuen, 1980.

Olson, Dennis T. *The Death of the Old and the Birth of the New: The Framework of the Book of Numbers and the Pentateuch.* Chico, Calif.: Scholars Press, 1985.

Ormsby-Lennon, Hugh. "Rosicrucian Linguistics: Twilight of a Renaissance Tradition." In *Hermeticism and the Renaissance,* ed. Ingrid Merkel and Allen G. Debus, 311–41. Washington, D.C.: Folger Shakespeare Library, 1988.

Ottenhoff, John H. "Herbert's Sonnets." *GHJ* 2 (1979): 1–14.

Pahlka, William H. *Saint Augustine's Meter and George Herbert's Will.* Kent, Oh.: Kent State University Press, 1987.

Parry, Graham. *Seventeenth-Century Poetry: The Social Context.* London: Hutchinson, 1985.

Pasarella, Lee. "The Meaning of the Tent in George Herbert's 'Anagram.' " *ELN* 21 (1983): 10–13.

Patrides, C. A., ed. *The English Poems of George Herbert.* London: Dent, 1975.

———, ed. *George Herbert: The Critical Heritage.* London: Routledge & Kegan Paul, 1983.

van Pelt, Robert Jan. "The Utopian Exit of the Hermetic Temple; or a Curious Transition in the Tradition of the Cosmic Sanctuary." In *Hermeticism and the Renaissance,* ed. Ingrid Merkel and Allen G. Debus, 400–23. Washington, D.C.: Folger Shakespeare Library, 1988.

Perkins, William. *A Golden Chaine, or the Description of Theologie, Containing the Order of the Causes of Salvation and Damnation.* Cambridge, 1597.

———. *The Whole Treatise of the Cases of Conscience.* 1606. Theatrum Orbis Terrarum Press, Amsterdam: 1972.

———. *The Works.* Ed. Ian Breward. Appleford, U.K.: Sutton Courtenay Press, 1970.

Polzin, Robert, and Eugene Rothman, eds. *The Biblical Mosaic.* Philadelphia: Fortress Press, 1982.

———. *Moses and the Deuteronomist.* Vol 1. New York: Seabury Press, 1980.

Post, Jonathan F. S. "Reforming *The Temple*: Recent Criticism of George Herbert." *John Donne Journal* 3 (1984): 221–47.

Preus, J. Samuel. "Religion and Bacon's New Learning: From Legitimation to Object." In *Continuity and Discontinuity in Church History*, ed. F. Forrester Church and Timothy George, 267–84. Leiden, The Netherlands: E. J. Brill, 1979.

von Rad, Gerhard. *Deuteronomy: A Commentary*. Philadelphia: Westminister Press, 1966.

Reimarus, Hermann Samuel. *The Goal of Jesus and His Disciples*. Trans. George Wesley. Leiden, The Netherlands: E. J. Brill, 1970.

———. *Reimarus: Fragments*. Ed. Charles H. Talbert. Philadelphia: Fortress Press, 1970.

Ricoeur, Paul. *The Rule of Metaphor*. Trans. Robert Czerny. Toronto: University of Toronto Press, 1977.

Roberts, John R., ed. *Essential Articles for the Study of George Herbert's Poetry*. Hamden, Conn.: Archon Books, 1979.

———. *George Herbert: An Annotated Bibliography of Modern Criticism, 1905–1984*. Columbia: University of Missouri Press, 1988.

Robinson, John. *A Justification of Separation from the Church of England*. Amsterdam, 1610.

Rodriguez, Alfonso. *A Short and Sure Way to Heaven*. 1630. London: Scolar Press, 1975.

Rogers, William. "Gestures toward a Literary History and Lyric." In *The Three Genres and Interpretations of Lyric*, 176–270. Princeton: Princeton University Press, 1983.

Rosenberg, Joel. *King and Kin: Political Allegory in the Hebrew Bible*. Bloomington: Indiana University Press, 1986.

———. "Meaning, Morals, and Mysteries: Literary Approaches to Torah." *Response* 9 (1975): 67–94.

Ross, Malcolm Mackenzie. *Poetry and Dogma*. New Brunswick, N.J.: Rutgers University Press, 1954.

Rowley, H. H. *The Relevance of Apocalyptic: A Study of Jewish and Christian Apocalypses from Daniel to the Revelation*. New York: Association Press, 1944.

Rubey, Daniel. "The Poet and the Church Community: Herbert's Affliction Poems and the Structure of *The Temple*." *SEL* 20 (1980): 105–24.

Russell, Conrad. *Parliament and English Politics, 1621–29*. Clarendon: Oxford University Press, 1979.

Schleiner, Louise. *The Living Lyre in English Verse from Elizabeth through the Restoration*. Columbia: University of Missouri Press, 1984.

Schmithals, Walter. *The Apocalyptic Movement*. Trans. John E. Steely. New York: Abingdon Press, 1975.

Schoenfeldt, Michael C. "Standing on Ceremony: The Comedy of Manners in Herbert's 'Love (III).' " In *"Bright Shootes of Everlastingnesse,"* ed. Claude J. Summers and Ted-Larry Pebworth, 116–33. Columbia: University of Missouri Press, 1987.

———. " 'Subject to Ev'ry Mounters Bended Knee'; Herbert and Authority." *The Historical Renaissance*, ed. Heather Dubrow and Richard Strier, 242–69. Chicago: University of Chicago Press, 1988.

———. "Submission and Assertion: The 'Double Victim' of Herbert's 'Dedication.' " *John Donne Journal* 2 (1983): 39–49.

Scholem, Gershom. *The Messianic Idea in Judaism and Other Essays on Jewish Spirituality*. New York: Schocken Books, 1971.

Schweitzer, Albert. *The Quest of the Historical Jesus: A Critical Study of Its Progress from Reimarus to Wrede*. 1906. New York: Macmillan, 1960.

Seelig, Sharon Cadman. *The Shadow of Eternity: Belief and Structure in Herbert, Vaughan, and Traherne*. Lexington: University of Kentucky Press, 1981.

Select Hymns Taken out of Mr. Herbert's Temple. 1797. Los Angeles: William Andrews Clark Memorial Library, 1962.

Selincourt, Basil de. "George Herbert." In *George Herbert: The Critical Heritage*, ed. C. A. Patrides, 343–47. *TLS*, March 1933.

Selincourt, Ernest de. "George Herbert." *Hibbert Journal* 39 (1941): 389–97.

Sessions, William A. "Bacon and Herbert and an Image of Chalk." In *"Too Rich to Clothe the Sunne,"* ed. Claude J. Summers and Ted-Larry Pebworth, 165–78. Pittsburgh: Pittsburgh University Press, 1978.

Sharpe, Kevin. *Criticism and Compliment: The Politics of Literature in the England of Charles I*. London: Cambridge University Press, 1987.

Shaw, Robert. *The Call of God: The Theme of Vocation in the Poetry of Donne and Herbert*. Cambridge, Mass.: Cowley Publications, 1981.

Sherwood, Terry G. *Herbert's Prayerful Art*. Toronto: University of Toronto Press, 1989.

Shields, David S. "Herbert and Colonial American Poetry: Then Shall Religion to America Flee." In *Like Season'd Timber*, ed. Edmund Miller and Robert DiYanni, 281–96. New York: Peter Lang, 1987.

Shullenberger, William. *"Ars Praedicandi* in George Herbert's Poetry." In *"Bright Shootes of Everlastingnesse,"* ed. Claude J. Summers and Ted-Larry Pebworth, 96–115. Columbia: University of Missouri Press, 1987.

Simon, Elliott M. "Bacon's *New Atlantis*: The Kingdom of God and Man." *Christianity and Literature* 1 (1988): 43–61.

Slights, Camille Wells. *The Casuistical Tradition in Shakespeare, Donne, Herbert, and Milton*. Princeton: Princeton University Press, 1981.

Smith, John. *The Mystery of Rhetoric Unveiled*. 1657. Menston: Scolar Press, 1969.

Smith, Nigel, ed. *A Collection of Ranter Writings from the Seventeenth Century*. London: Junction Books, 1983.

Smith, Morton. *Palestinian Parties and Politics That Shaped the Old Testament*. New York: Columbia University Press, 1971.

Smuts, R. Malcolm. *Court Culture and the Origins of a Royalist Tradition in Early Stuart England*. Philadelphia: University of Pennsylvania Press, 1987.

Smyth, John. *The Works*. Ed. W. T. Whitley. 2 vols. Cambridge: Cambridge University Press, 1915.

Some, Robert. *A Godly Treatise*. 1588. Amsterdam: Theatrum Orbis Terrarum Press, 1974.

Stambler, Elizabeth. "The Unity of Herbert's 'Temple.' " *Cross Currents* 10 (1960): 251–66.

Stanwood, P. G. "Time and Liturgy in Herbert's Poetry." *GHJ* 5 (1981–82): 19–30.

Steadman, John M. *Nature into Myth*. Pittsburgh: Duquesne University Press, 1979.

Stein, Arnold. *George Herbert's Lyrics*. Baltimore: Johns Hopkins University Press, 1968.

Sternberg, Meir. *The Poetics of Biblical Narrative: Ideological Literature and the Drama of Reading*. Bloomington: Indiana University Press, 1985.

Stewart, Stanley. *George Herbert*. Boston: G. K. Hall, 1986.

——. "Time and the Temple." *SEL* 6 (1966): 97–110. Reprinted in *Essential Articles*, ed. John R. Roberts, 363–73. Hamden, Conn.: Archon Books, 1979.

Stocker, Magarita. *Apocalyptic Marvell: The Second Coming in Seventeenth Century Poetry*. Sussex: Harvester Press, 1986.

Strauss, David Friedrich. *In Defense of My Life of Jesus against the Hegelians*. Trans. M. C. Massey. Hamden, Conn.: Archon Books, 1983.

——. *The Life of Jesus, Critically Examined*. 1860. Trans. Marian Evans. 2 vols. New York: Calvin Blanchard, 1970.

Strier, Richard. "George Herbert and the World." *Journal of Medieval and Renaissance Studies* 11 (1981): 211–36.

——. "Getting off the Map: Response to 'George Herbert's Theology: Nearer Rome or Geneva?' " *GHJ* 11 (1987): 41–48.

——. *Love Known: Theology and Experience in George Herbert's Poetry*. Chicago: University of Chicago Press, 1983.

Stroup, Thomas B. " 'A Reasonable, Holy, and Living Sacrifice': Herbert's 'The Altar.' " *Essays in Literature* 2 (1975): 149–63.

Stull, William L. "Sacred Sonnets in Three Styles." *SP* 79 (1982): 78–99.

Summers, Claude J. "The Bride of the Apocalypse and the Quest for True Religion: Donne, Herbert, and Spenser." In *"Bright Shootes of Everlastingnesse": The Seventeenth-Century Religious Lyric*, ed. Claude J. Summers and Ted-Larry Pebworth, 72–95. Columbia: University of Missouri Press, 1987.

Summers, Claude J., and Ted-Larry Pebworth. "Herbert, Vaughan, and Public Concerns in Private Modes." *GHJ* 3 (1979/80): 1–21.

——. "The Politics of *The Temple*: 'The British Church' and 'The Familie.' " *GHJ* 8 (1984): 1–15.

——, eds. *"Too Rich to Clothe the Sunne": Essays on George Herbert*. Pittsburgh: University of Pittsburgh Press, 1978.

Summers, Joseph. "From 'Joseph's Coat' to 'A true Hymne.' " *GHJ* 2 (1978): 1–12.

——. *George Herbert: His Religion and Art*. London: Chatto & Windus, 1954.

Swaim, Kathleen M. "Herbert's 'Paradise.' " *GHJ* 8 (1985): 19–32.

Taylor, Mark. *The Soul in Paraphrase: George Herbert's Poetics*. The Hague: Mouton, 1974.

Taylor, Thomas. *Christ Revealed*. 1635. Delmar, N. Y.: Scholars' Facsimiles and Reprints, 1979.

Todd, Richard. *The Opacity of Signs: Acts of Interpretation in George Herbert's The Temple*. Columbia: University of Missouri Press, 1986.

Toland, John. *Christianity Not Mysterious*. Stuttgart–Bad Cannstatt: Friedrich Frommann Verlag, 1964.

Toliver, Harold. *Lyric Provinces in the English Renaissance*. Columbus: Ohio State University Press, 1985.

——. *Pastoral Forms and Attitudes*. Berkeley and Los Angeles: University of California Press, 1971.

Toon, Peter. *Puritans, the Millennium, and the Future of Israel: Puritan Eschatology 1600–1660*. London: James Clarke, 1970.

Tuve, Rosemond. "George Herbert and *Caritas*." *JWCI* 22 (1959): 303–31.

——. *A Reading of George Herbert*. London: Faber & Faber, 1953.

——. " 'Sacred Parody' of Love Poetry, and Herbert." *Studies in the Renaissance* 8 (1961): 249–90. Reprinted in *Essays*. Princeton: Princeton University Press, 1970.

Tuveson, Ernest Less. *Millennium and Utopia*. New York: Harper & Row, 1964.

Tyacke, Nicholas. *AntiCalvinists: The Rise of English Arminianism c. 1590–1640.* London: Oxford University Press, 1987.

Urbach, Ephraim E. *The Sages: Their Concepts and Beliefs.* Trans. Israel Abraham. Jerusalem: Magnes Press, 1975.

Vaughan, Henry. *The Works.* Ed. L. C. Martin. Clarendon: Oxford University Press, 1957.

Vawter, Bruce. *On Genesis: A New Reading.* New York: Doubleday, 1977.

Veith, Gene Edward, Jr. *Reformation Spirituality: The Religion of George Herbert.* Lewisburg, Pa.: Bucknell University Press, 1985.

————. "The Religious Wars in George Herbert Criticism: Reinterpreting Seventeenth-Century Anglicanism" *GHJ* 11 (1988): 19–36.

Vendler, Helen. *George Herbert.* Cambridge: Harvard University Press, 1975.

Vickers, Brian. *Essential Articles for the Study of Francis Bacon.* Hamden, Conn.: Archon Books, 1968.

————, ed. *Occult and Scientific Mentalities in the Renaissance.* Cambridge: Cambridge University Press, 1984.

————. "On the Function of Analogy in the Occult." In *Hermeticism and the Renaissance,* ed. Ingrid Merkel and Allen G. Debus, 265–92. Washington, D.C.: Folger Shakespeare Library, 1988.

Wagar, W. Warren. *Terminal Visions: The Literature of Last Things.* Bloomington: Indiana University Press, 1982.

Walker, John David. "The Architectonics of George Herbert's *The Temple.*" *ELH* (1962): 289–305.

Wall, John. *Transformations of the Word: Spenser, Herbert, Vaughan.* Athens: University of Georgia Press, 1988.

Walton, Izaak. *The Lives of John Donne, Sir Henry Wotton, Richard Hooker, George Herbert & Robert Sanderson.* London: Oxford University Press, 1956.

Walzer, Michael. *The Revolution of the Saints.* New York: Atheneum, 1970.

Wardropper, Bruce W. "The Religious Conversion of Profane Poetry." In *Studies in the Continental Background of Renaissance English Literature,* ed. Dale Randall and George Williams, 203–21. Durham, N.C.: Duke University Press, 1977.

Webster, Charles. *From Paracelsus to Newton: Magic and the Making of Modern Science.* Cambridge: Cambridge University Press, 1982.

————. *The Great Instauration.* London: Duckworth, 1975.

Weibly, P. S. "George Herbert's 'Heaven': The Eloquence of Silence." *GHJ* 4 (1981): 1–9.

Weinberger, G. J. "George Herbert's 'The Church Militant.' " *Connecticut Review* 4 (1971): 49–57.

Weinfeld, Mosche. *Deuteronomy and the Deuteronomic School.* Clarendon: Oxford University Press, 1972.

————. "Zion and Jerusalem as Religious and Political Capital: Ideology and Utopia." In *The Poet and the Historian,* ed. Richard Elliott Friedman, 75–116. Chico, Calif.: Scholars Press, 1983.

Wellhausen, Julius. *Prolegomena to the History of Ancient Israel.* New York: Meridian Books, 1957.

Wengen-Shute, Rosemary Margaret Van. *George Herbert and the Liturgy of the Church of England.* Oegstgeest, The Netherlands: Drukkerij de Kempenaer, 1981.

Westerweel, Bart. *Patterns and Patterning: A Study of Four Poems by George Herbert.* Amsterdam: Rodopi, N.V., 1984.

White, B. R. *The English Separatist Tradition from Marian Martyrs to the Pilgrim Fathers.* London: Oxford University Press, 1971.

White, Helen C. *The Metaphysical Poets*. 1936. New York: Collier, 1962.

Wilkinson, John. *An Exposition of the Thirteenth Chapter of the Revelation*. 1619.

Williams, Anne. "Gracious Accommodations: Herbert's 'Love III.' " *Modern Philology* 82 (1984):13–22.

Wither, George. *Britain's Remembrancer*. 2 vols. Manchester, 1880.

Witney, Charles. "Bacon and Herbert as Moderns." In *Like Season'd Timber*, ed. Edmund Miller and Robert DiYanni, 231–40. New York: Peter Lang, 1987.

———. *Francis Bacon and Modernity*. New Haven: Yale University Press, 1986.

Wood, Chauncey. "George and Henry Herbert on Redemption." *HLQ* 46 (1983): 298–309.

———. "A Reading of Herbert's 'Coloss.3.3.' " *GHJ* 2 (1979): 15–24.

Yearwood, Stephenie. "The Rhetoric of Form in *The Temple*." *SEL* 23 (1983): 131–44.

Zagorin, Perez. *Culture and Politics: From Puritanism to the Enlightenment*. Berkeley and Los Angeles: University of California Press, 1980.

Ziegelmaier, Gregory. "Liturgical Symbol and Reality in the Poetry of George Herbert." *American Benedictine Review* 18 (1967): 344–53.

INDEX